Cape Cod

Patricia Harris and David Lyon
Photography by Kindra Clineff

COMPASS AMERICAN GUIDES
An imprint of Fodor's Travel Publications

Compass American Guides: Cape Cod

Editor: Craig Seligman
Designer: Siobhan O'Hare
Compass Editorial Director: Daniel Mangin
Compass Creative Director: Fabrizio La Rocca
Compass Senior Editor: Kristin Moehlmann
Production Editor: Linda Schmidt
Photo Editor and Archival Researcher: Melanie Marin
Map Design: Mark Stroud, Moon Street Cartography

ISBN 1–4000–1310–0
ISSN 1543–1584

The details in this book are based on information supplied to us at press time, but changes
occur all the time, and the publisher cannot accept responsibility for facts that become outdated
or for inadvertent errors or omissions.

This book is available for special discounts for bulk purchases for sales promotions or premiums. Special
editions, including personalized covers, excerpts of existing books, and corporate imprints, can be created
in large quantities for special needs. For more information, write to Special Markets/Premium Sales, 1745
Broadway, MD 6-2, New York, New York 10019, or e-mail specialmarkets@randomhouse.com.

Cover photo by Kindra Clineff

Compass American Guides, 1745 Broadway, New York NY 10019
PRINTED IN CHINA
10 9 8 7 6 5 4 3 2 1

To HDT, who (as usual) got there first

C O N T E N T S

Literary Extracts

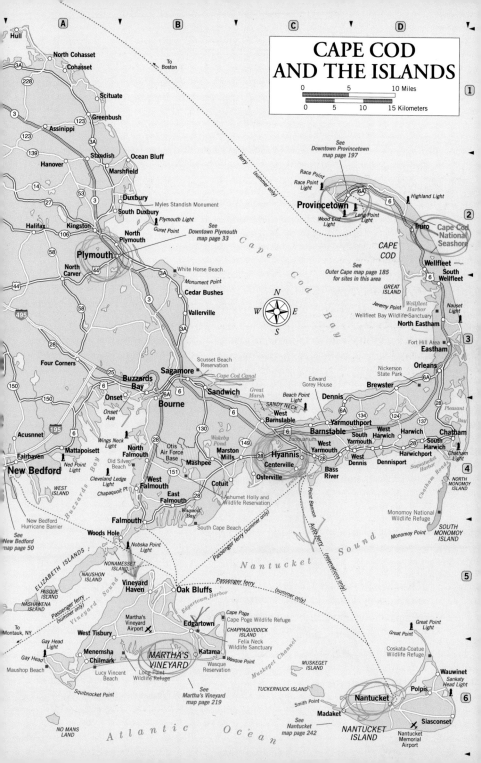

CAPE COD AND THE ISLANDS

0   5   10 Miles

0   5   10   15 Kilometers

Hull

North Cohasset
Cohasset

Scituate

Greenbush
Assinippi

Standish
Ocean Bluff
Marshfield

Hanover

Duxbury
Myles Standish Monument
South Duxbury
Plymouth Light
Guret Point

Halifax
Kingston
North Plymouth

Plymouth

North Carver

White Horse Beach

Monument Point
Cedar Bushes

Vallerville

Four Corners

Buzzards Bay
Sagamore
Scusset Beach Reservation
Cape Cod Canal

Onset
Onset Ave
Bourne
Sandwich
Great Marsh

Acusnet
Wings Neck Light
North Falmouth
Otis Air Force Base
Marston Mills
Wakeby Pond

Fairhaven
Mattapoisett
Ned Point Light
Old Silver Beach
Cleveland Ledge Light
Chapaquoit Pt

New Bedford
WEST ISLAND

West Falmouth
East Falmouth
Mashpee
Cotuit
Ashumet Holly and Wildlife Reservation
Waquoit Bay

New Bedford Hurricane Barrier
See New Bedford map page 50

Falmouth
South Cape Beach

Woods Hole
Nobska Point Light
Passenger ferry (summer only)

ELIZABETH ISLANDS
NONAMESSET ISLAND
NAUSHON ISLAND
FASQUE ISLAND
NASHAWENA ISLAND
To Montauk, NY

Vineyard Haven
Oak Bluffs
Passenger ferry
(summer only)

Martha's Vineyard Airport
Edgartown
Cape Poge
Cape Poge Wildlife Refuge
CHAPPAQUIDDICK ISLAND
Felix Neck Wildlife Sanctuary

West Tisbury
Katama
Wasque Point

Menemsha
Chilmark
MARTHA'S VINEYARD
Lucy Vincent Beach
Long Point Wildlife Refuge
Wasque Reservation

Gay Head Light
Gay Head
Maushop Beach
Squibnocket Point

See Martha's Vineyard map page 219

NO MANS LAND

To Boston

ferry (summer only)

See Downtown Provincetown map page 197

Race Point
Race Point Light

Provincetown
Wood End Light
Long Point Light

Highland Light

Truro
Cape Cod National Seashore

CAPE COD

Wellfleet
South Wellfleet

See Outer Cape map page 185 for sites in this area

GREAT ISLAND

Jeremy Point
Wellfleet Harbor
Wellfleet Bay Wildlife Sanctuary
Nauset Light
North Eastham

Fort Hill Area
Eastham

Nickerson State Park
Orleans

Edward Gorey House
Brewster

Dennis
Beach Point Light
SANDY NECK
West Barnstable
Yarmouthport
South Yarmouth
West Harwich
Harwich
Chatham
Barnstable
Zooquarium
West Yarmouth
West Dennis
Harwichport
South Harwich
Chatham Light

West Dennis
Dennisport

Hyannis
Centerville
Osterville
Bass River

See Downtown Plymouth map page 33

White Horse Beach

Cape Cod Bay

N
W   E
S

Saquatucket Harbor
Chatham Light
NORTH MONOMOY ISLAND

Monomoy National Wildlife Refuge
Monomoy Point
SOUTH MONOMOY ISLAND

Pleasant Bay

Nantucket Sound

Auto ferry (reservations only)

Point Barnon Road

Muskeget Channel

Edgartown Harbor

MUSKEGET ISLAND
TUCKERNUCK ISLAND
Smith Point

Great Point Light
Great Point

Coskata-Coatue Wildlife Refuge

Wauwinet
Sankaty Head Light

Polpis

Nantucket
Madaket
Siasconset
Nantucket Memorial Airport
NANTUCKET ISLAND

See Nantucket map page 242

Atlantic Ocean

INTRODUCTION

We have one critical piece of advice for anyone visiting Cape Cod: as in life, always seek the higher ground. The nubby tops of glacial drumlins, the precipitous and crumbling edges of seaside bluffs, and even the crests of high dunes serve as crow's-nest overlooks. From these perches, water stretches to the left, to the right, before you, and behind you. And with that vision, you will understand the essential fact of Cape Cod: the land, with its mutable shore, is no more than a temporary interruption of the sea.

Glaciers carved Cape Cod, but the ocean remakes it every day and night, as tides and currents nip away a little here, deposit a little there—sculpting, painting, padding like a potter unsatisfied with a lump of clay. The actions are visible in the broad light. Waves gnaw at the base of the Highlands cliffs along the National Seashore. Wind and wave have cut open the face of Aquinnah on Martha's Vineyard to reveal a hundred million years of planetary history. The tide washes in—ever so slowly—on Brewster's Cape Cod Bay shore, leaving behind a thin film of new sand as it recedes. You walk the beach a mile to the ocean's edge and clams squirt their protests from flats beneath your toes. You clatter over the boardwalk through Nauset Beach's thirty-foot dunes, great heaps of sand the ocean has kicked up as casually as a child building a sand castle.

Water washes all around you on Cape Cod. You wade into the gentle waves at Scusset Beach and fall into the waltzing rhythm of a crawl—dip-stroke-breathe, dip-stroke-breathe—along the breadth of the beach. Or you fight your way into the surf at Chapoquoit until you are out beyond the bar, where the big swells rise like waking whales, and you turn back to paddle swiftly until a wave rises and carries you on its back, flinging you toward shore in the hissing rush of its crest. Or perhaps you step from the recesses of dark pines to the still, deep waters of a glacial kettle pond, chill as the winter it remembers in its depths, fresh as a new day. On the shallow, protected waters of Nauset Marsh or Nantucket harbor, you slide into the skin of your kayak, snap on the skirt, and raise your paddle to glide like a duck, moving in near-silence along that interstice of land and water in which it's nearly impossible to tell where one ends and the other begins.

(opposite) A perfect day at Mayflower Beach. (following pages) Harvesting oysters.

The sea is ever present in the air. It makes the weather. It creates the blanket of blue-white fog that grips the water and the land, smothering even the sound of the channel bell buoys and the lonesome hoots of foghorns as the fishermen come into the harbor, slowly, lest they run afoul of one another. When Boston swelters in July, Cape Cod and the islands are ten degrees cooler; when the mainland shivers in February's single digits, Provincetown is close to freezing, idyllic under the gentle flakes of lake-effect snow. The ocean slowly warms and slowly cools. The temperature gradient between water and land breeds wind—wind that fills the canvas of a sailor's sloop at Hyannis harbor, wind that sends a kite surfer skittering across the waves along Coast Guard Beach, wind that sweeps across the highland heath at Wellfleet, cropping the bearberry and scrub pine close to ground. And the sea brings rain, making gray sky, gray ocean, and gray land virtually indistinguishable.

Cape Cod, Martha's Vineyard, and Nantucket are lands at sea. The ocean has dictated their economy and history from the start. Along the old colonial road of the King's Highway, you will see the homes of sea captains and merchants who thought little of sailing halfway around the world in wooden ships with canvas sails if there was profit in it. You might glimpse the jury-rigged, ill-planked, tumbledown shacks planted on the sea of dunes amid the Province Lands, a reminder of the artists who struck a hard and lonely bargain with the hallucinogenic light. The sea and its bounty brought the immigrants—the English, the Italians, the Portuguese—to man the nets and lines of the Cape and island fishing fleets. You can walk those harbors where much of New England's catch still comes ashore. Watch bluefin tuna being unloaded from harpoon boats at Chatham harbor, or marvel at the tenuous life of the tiny dock and modest vessels at Menemsha on Martha's Vineyard, perhaps the last and sweetest and most iconic of the fishing villages.

The salt air will make you hungry, but the ocean will provide. Few morsels are so choice as a Wellfleet oyster, naked of all but the briny water it swam in. Feast on Chatham mussels steamed in wine, P'town swordfish grilled on charcoal, blue-eyed Nantucket scallops tossed with garlic, Harwich lobster dipped in butter. Catch your own bluefish and plaster the fillets with mustard for a seaside feast finer than one on any millionaire's yacht.

Cape Cod, Martha's Vineyard, and Nantucket are not the ocean. They are the exceptions, the little spits of land cast up a few thousand years ago and destined to vanish a few thousand hence. They are not the ocean—not yet. But they are close enough to taste it.

Dinghies await a rising tide at North Wharf in Nantucket Harbor.

MAKING CAPE COD

■ THE LAND

Every reluctant geology student should visit Cape Cod, where the mark of glacial ice is branded on the earth and the forces of wind and water constantly reshape the land in real time. The Cape's densest soils and highest points are little more than dust and grit that once were scraped off the granite hills of New England and dumped as sandy heaps along the melting face of a two-mile-thick slab of ice. Think of Cape Cod's sandy beaches, shady ponds, and brimming waters as geological payback for an awfully long winter.

Beginning between fifty thousand and seventy thousand years ago, the Laurentide ice sheet oozed south and east across New England from its birthplace near Hudson Bay. It finally stalled on the coastal plain, on a line that represents the present-day coordinates of Nantucket, Martha's Vineyard, and Long Island. And there the wall of ice stood, melting along its southern face while more ice and grit pushed down from the north. The heaps of sand and gravel that accumulated on the melting edge became the hills of the present-day islands. The glacier shrank back to another standstill along what are now Buzzards Bay, Falmouth, and the north coast of the Cape. By fifteen thousand years ago, the glacial sheet began its final retreat and left behind the soil and crushed rock that had been suspended in the ice.

A rudimentary Cape Cod was born as highlands on a coastal plain. The sea was five hundred feet lower at that point, and the high sand cliffs of the Cape Cod National Seashore were two miles inland, the back side of a sloping bank of sand and gravel that has since eroded away. Martha's Vineyard and Nantucket were connected to the mainland across the plain. Plants began growing on the land shortly after the ice released its grip. Pine, oak, and beech forests stabilized the highlands. Grasses and sedges pinned down the shifting sands, and a thin layer of soil began to spread across the sandbanks that underlie all of Cape Cod.

As the glaciers melted back toward their origins, their water filled the oceans, until the sea reached something close to its present level thirty-five hundred to four thousand years ago. The coastal plain was inundated, but Cape Cod and the

Chappaquiddick Island, off Martha's Vineyard.

islands remained above the sea, their shorelines a ragged approximation of their modern shapes. Over the ensuing centuries, wind and wave began to create the landscape of today.

The eroding action of storms and the riverlike currents that run along the shoreline have distributed the sand and silt more evenly, smoothing the contours of the 559-mile coast and creating long, sandy beaches. Where sandbars filled in, salt marshes began to grow behind them. Where the brunt of the waves and wind blew up sand in great heaps, persistent grasses and rugged little pitch pines colonized the crests, and the great rolling dunes of the Outer Cape took shape.

The processes that sculpted the Cape are hardly over. Stand above the beach at Nauset Light on the day after a storm and you can see the swirling sand heading south toward Monomoy and Nantucket Islands. Take a kayak up Scorton Creek from Barnstable and across the town line into Sandwich, and what seemed a river suddenly becomes a bog, only to open up again as a thin tidal arm of ocean. When a nor'easter howls, the Atlantic gnaws voraciously at the shore, and what was a peninsula the night before is an island at morning light. Inland New England may be the rock of ages—Cape Cod is made up of the evanescent shifting sands of time.

THE CAPE, SLICED AND DICED

For such a small piece of real estate, Cape Cod is often divided into several different areas, with boundaries that depend almost entirely on who is doing the dividing. Henry David Thoreau gave the classic description: "Cape Cod is the bared and bended arm of Massachusetts; the shoulder is at Buzzard's Bay, the elbow, or crazy-bone, at Cape Mallebarre [Chatham], the wrist at Truro, and the sandy fist at Provincetown." Of course, he didn't have to contend with the tortured divisions of real estate hucksters.

Ignoring Plymouth and Buzzards Bay and beginning at the Cape Cod Canal, modern definitions of Cape Cod tend to distinguish the **Upper Cape** (Bourne, Sandwich, Falmouth, Mashpee), the **Mid Cape** (Barnstable/Hyannis, Dennis, Yarmouth, Harwich, Brewster), the **Lower Cape** (Chatham, Orleans, Eastham), and the **Outer Cape** (Wellfleet, Truro, Provincetown). Just to confuse visitors, Cape Codders sometimes lump the Lower Cape and Outer Cape together, calling them by either name, and rental agents disingenuously list properties in Harwich and Brewster as "Lower Cape."

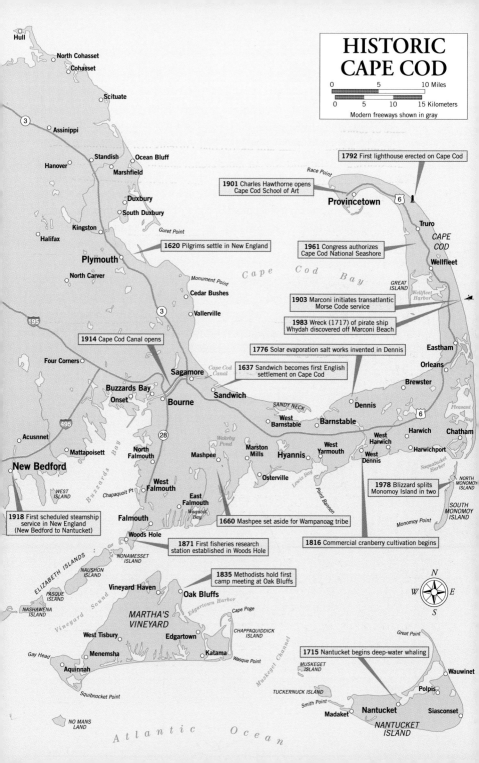

HISTORIC CAPE COD

0   5   10 Miles
0 5   10   15 Kilometers
Modern freeways shown in gray

Hull
North Cohasset
Cohasset
Scituate
Assinippi
3
Hanover
Standish
Ocean Bluff
Marshfield
Duxbury
South Duxbury
Kingston
Halifax
Plymouth
North Carver
Guret Point

1792 First lighthouse erected on Cape Cod

1901 Charles Hawthorne opens Cape Cod School of Art

Race Point

Provincetown
6

Truro

CAPE COD

Wellfleet

Cape   Cod   Bay

Monument Point
Cedar Bushes
Vallerville
3

1961 Congress authorizes Cape Cod National Seashore

GREAT ISLAND
Wellfleet Harbor

1903 Marconi initiates transatlantic Morse Code service

1983 Wreck (1717) of pirate ship Whydah discovered off Marconi Beach

1620 Pilgrims settle in New England

195

1914 Cape Cod Canal opens

Four Corners

Sagamore

Cape Cod Canal

1776 Solar evaporation salt works invented in Dennis

1637 Sandwich becomes first English settlement on Cape Cod

Eastham
Orleans
Brewster

Buzzards Bay
Onset
Bourne

Sandwich

SANDY NECK

Dennis

Pleasant Bay

495

Acusnnet
Mattapoisett
North Falmouth
28

West Barnstable
Barnstable
6
West Dennis
Harwich
Chatham
West Harwich
Harwichport

Wakeby Pond
Mashpee
Marston Mills
West Yarmouth
Hyannis

New Bedford

WEST ISLAND

Buzzards Bay
Chapaquoit Pt
West Falmouth
Osterville
Lewis Bay
Point Barmon
Saquatucket Harbor

NORTH MONOMOY ISLAND

1978 Blizzard splits Monomoy Island in two

SOUTH MONOMOY ISLAND

East Falmouth
Waquoit Bay

1918 First scheduled steamship service in New England (New Bedford to Nantucket)

Falmouth
Woods Hole

1660 Mashpee set aside for Wampanoag tribe

Monomoy Point

1816 Commercial cranberry cultivation begins

1871 First fisheries research station established in Woods Hole

NONAMESSET ISLAND

ELIZABETH ISLANDS
NAUSHON ISLAND
PASQUE ISLAND
NASHAWENA ISLAND

1835 Methodists hold first camp meeting at Oak Bluffs

Vineyard Haven
Oak Bluffs

Vineyard Sound

Edgartown Harbor

Cape Poge

N
W   E
S

MARTHA'S VINEYARD

CHAPPAQUIDDICK ISLAND

West Tisbury
Edgartown
Menemsha
Katama
Wasque Point

Gay Head
Aquinnah

Muskeget Channel

1715 Nantucket begins deep-water whaling

Great Point

Squibnocket Point

MUSKEGET ISLAND

TUCKERNUCK ISLAND

Wauwinet

Polpis

Smith Point
Madaket
Nantucket
Siasconset

NO MANS LAND

NANTUCKET ISLAND

Atlantic   Ocean

■ THE PEOPLE

The English explorer Bartholomew Gosnold literally put Cape Cod on the map in 1602 when he named the sandy hook of land for the fish so abundant in the surrounding waters. Portuguese, Breton, and Basque fishermen had known about the fishing grounds for a century or more, but, a typically close-mouthed bunch, they kept the find to themselves. Not Gosnold. He explored and mapped most of the region covered in this book, from Buzzards Bay to Plymouth harbor, stopping to meet with the inhabitants along the way. In 1614, John Smith (of Jamestown, Virginia, fame) explored Cape Cod Bay's shoreline and filled two ships with salt cod, which brought a tidy profit back in Europe. As much promoter as explorer, he published a glowing report, *Description of New England,* that encouraged a group of English "merchant adventurers"—early venture capitalists—to secure the rights to the region. Needing colonists, they agreed to back a band of religious refugees to settle the wilderness and send back fur and timber. This unlikely group of pioneers called themselves Separatists because they chose to sever their ties with the Church of England. History calls them Pilgrims.

After an arduous voyage, the *Mayflower* anchored in Provincetown harbor on Saturday, November 11, 1620. Believing themselves outside the district of their land grant, the Pilgrim leaders believed they were also outside the law. On the following day they drew up and signed rules for self-governance. The Mayflower Compact became the first in a succession of documents leading up to the U.S. Constitution. Men from the ship explored the coast, finding a freshwater spring. They also discovered that their new land was already inhabited.

Human beings had begun living on Cape Cod nine thousand to eleven thousand years ago, when Paleoindians occupied the ice-free coastal region. Little is known about them, because the rising sea has since inundated most of their dwelling sites. By twenty-five hundred years ago, Cape Codders had settled into summering at the beach and wintering at pond encampments in the protected woodlands. Corn crops and land management through fire both came to the region about a thousand years ago, perhaps with the Algonquian-speaking peoples who inhabited the area at the time of European contact. By circa 1600, an estimated hundred thousand Native Americans lived in sixty-seven villages stretching from present-day Provincetown to Plymouth and New Bedford. Except for the Nausets in Eastham and the Pamets in Truro, they belonged to the Wampanoag Confederacy, which covered Cape Cod north to Duxbury and west to

Narragansett Bay. But between 1616 and 1617, an unknown disease, probably of European origin, swept the New England coast. More than half the inhabitants of Cape Cod died, and entire villages were abandoned.

One such village was Pawtuxet, where the Pilgrims eagerly settled after rejecting sites across the bay in Provincetown, Wellfleet, and Eastham. The plague had rendered their neighbors more hospitable than they might have been a few years earlier. Massasoit, the most powerful sachem of the Wampanoag Confederacy, took note of his weakened people, weighed his strained relations with the bellicose Narragansetts on his western flank, and made peace with the newcomers—leaving the Pilgrims free to struggle with the wilderness rather than with their neighbors.

By 1627, Plymouth was firmly planted and swelling to capacity with new settlers. The English began to expand, first buying a parcel of land from the Wampanoags in Duxbury for seven coats, nine hatchets, eight hoes, twenty knives, four moose skins, and ten and one-half yards of cotton cloth.

Settlement of Cape Cod proceeded under the jurisdiction of the Plymouth Colony, which is why some Cape shops and historical references use the term "Old Colony." Many of the settlers were drawn, in fact, from neighboring Massachusetts Bay Colony (Boston, Salem, and points in between), but once they moved to Cape Cod they fell under the laws of Plymouth. Between 1639 and 1651, the four original towns of the Cape—Sandwich, Barnstable, Yarmouth, and Eastham—were purchased from local tribes and thinly settled by the English. These four spawned nine of the other ten towns on Cape Cod. (As public land not organized into a township until 1727, Provincetown was, as always, an exception.) By 1645, half the population had left Plymouth to settle on Cape Cod.

■ FARMERS & FISHERMEN

Early Cape Cod colonists were farmers by necessity. By all historical accounts, they did not know how to fish. Corn was their primary crop, and water-powered gristmills sprang up in every village where a stream fed into the harbor. On parts of the Cape where the wind never ceased, windmills ground the corn. But as the settlers denuded the forests and depleted the thin soils with intensive corn growing, the Cape could no longer support general agriculture. Only a few regions with deeper soils—parts of Falmouth and Barnstable, and West Tisbury on Martha's Vineyard—remained farmland. On Cape Cod today, agriculture is chiefly limited

(following pages) The catch comes in at Chatham Fish Pier.

Cape Cod Tart

No sight can rival the autumn cranberry harvest for sheer color: millions of red berries bobbing on the blue waters of flooded bogs. It's a commonplace sight in Plymouth County and on Cape Cod, and if you're lucky you'll be driving along a back road just as a grower plows through his bog with a paddle-wheel "egg beater" to batter the berries from their underwater vines.

Cranberries grow where little else will. They prefer flat, boggy, acid soil with sand on top and virtually impenetrable clay underneath—exactly the conditions in the glacial swamps of Cape Cod and the nearby mainland. Six hundred families tend the more than seventeen thousand acres of cranberry bogs that produce nearly half the national harvest.

The Wampanoags and Narragansetts ate fresh cranberries, combined them with cornmeal to make bread, and mashed them with fat and dried venison to make pemmican. A Pilgrim cookbook of 1663 records a cranberry sauce, but the astringent little fruit didn't catch on in a big way until cheap sugar became available from the West Indies in the nineteenth century. The first commercially grown cranberries were cultivated in Dennis in 1816; whaling ships took barrels aboard to prevent scurvy.

By 1888, cranberry cultivation had become so widespread that the Cape Cod Cranberry Growers Association was formed, and in 1930 the Ocean Spray Cooperative was founded. Between September and December each year, Ocean Spray (based in Lakeville, near Plymouth) sells about seventy million cans of jellied cranberry sauce, a product developed in 1912 that became available nationally in 1941.

to cranberry cultivation, an industry born in the bogs of Dennis in 1816. Indeed, Dennis and West Yarmouth remain two important cranberry-growing regions, along with the inland bogs south of Plymouth.

Most of the Cape was forced to take to the sea. The settlers learned from the Wampanoags to exploit the brooks and streams for the annual spawning runs of anadromous shad, sturgeon, and herring. The English shed their squeamishness about shellfish and began to harvest quahogs, littlenecks, and oysters. They also began to harvest the whales that beached themselves. Pods of pilot whales, called blackfish by the colonists, often strand themselves on Cape Cod—an environmental tragedy from the modern perspective, but a stroke of God's fortune from the viewpoint of the colonists, who stripped the animals of meat and tried out the fat for oil. By the late 1600s, "shore whalers" were venturing out in the shallow waters of Barnstable and Yarmouth harbors in small boats, driving several species of whales to shore. In 1715, records show that two hundred men were employed as shore whalers in Barnstable alone. In 1758, aboard newly designed Truro vessels, Cape Cod's whalers began to head to deep water; a generation later, the whalers of Wellfleet, Truro, Provincetown, Nantucket, Edgartown, and New Bedford were circling the globe for their quarry.

Cape Codders were also fishing, both close to home and hundreds of miles away on the North Atlantic banks. Fishermen began working the Grand Banks as early as 1730, often putting in to salt and dry their catch on the desolate beaches of Newfoundland, and then sailing to the West Indies to trade fish for rum and molasses, which they sold for cash back home. After the Revolution, Cape fishermen took smaller boats to ply the coast of Newfoundland and, until a treaty closed the area to them in 1818, the sheltered waters of the Bay of Chaleur, south of Québec's Gaspé Peninsula. These fish were cured on the sandy beaches of Cape Cod for sale in Boston. All across the Cape, windmills pumped seawater to evaporating pans to make sea salt. In 1830, some 440 saltworks dotted the Cape landscape, producing more than five hundred thousand bushels of salt annually to preserve codfish and mackerel.

The closure of Canadian waters in 1818 drove Cape fishermen to overcome their traditional aversion to the currents and riptides of Georges Bank, a fertile shallows much closer to home. By this time, Provincetown, Wellfleet, and Truro had joined the hunt, and as fishermen discovered how to trawl Georges Bank, the application of the purse seine (a net designed so that top and bottom can be closed simultaneously) to mackerel fishing made Cape harbors boom.

ODYSSEUS ON CAPE COD

A great proportion of the inhabitants of the Cape are always thus abroad about their teaming on some ocean highway or other, and the history of one of their ordinary trips would cast the Argonautic expedition into the shade. I have just heard of a Cape Cod captain who was expected home in the beginning of the winter from the West Indies, but was long since given up for lost, till his relations at length have heard with joy, that, after getting within forty miles of Cape Cod light, he was driven back by nine successive gales to Key West, between Florida and Cuba, and was once again shaping his course for home. Thus he spent his winter. In ancient times the adventures of these two or three men and boys would have been made the basis of a myth . . . .

—Henry David Thoreau, *Cape Cod*, 1865

By the end of the Civil War, the boom was beginning to go bust. Cheap mineral salt drove the saltworks out of business, and larger ships from Gloucester and New Bedford began to muscle the small Cape schooners out of the fish markets. Wellfleet turned from deep water to its tidal flats, maintaining a near-monopoly on the New England oyster trade through the nineteenth century. The glass industry at Sandwich fell in the face of more efficient companies in the Ohio Valley, and the soils were so depleted that when credit grew tight after the Civil War, some farmers abandoned their land. Cape Codders were ripe for another source of income, Tourism was about to be born.

■ **SUMMER PEOPLE**

The first travelers to Cape Cod came seeking sport and spirit. In the early nineteenth century, recreational hunters and anglers began flocking to the marshes, woodlands, and shores. Among them were the statesman and orator Daniel Webster, who often stayed in the Sandwich hostelry that now bears his name, and Deming Jarves, who was so impressed with Sandwich he returned to build a glassworks. Seekers of salvation began summering on the Cape when the first Methodist camp meeting convened in Wellfleet in 1819. Revival sessions became annual fixtures in Eastham, Yarmouth, and Craigville, as well as Oak Bluffs, on Martha's Vineyard.

Summer revelers head for the sand at Herring Cove Beach in Provincetown.

How Cape Cod *Really* Came to Be

When Cape Cod and the Islands are blanketed in fog, Wampanoags say that the giant Moshup must be smoking his pipe. Indeed, the legendary figure—so huge that he caught whales with his bare hands and roasted them over bonfires he built by tearing whole trees from the ground—is credited with shaping the contours of the land. The valleys and dunes of the Outer Cape, the stories claim, were born as the giant tossed and turned in restless sleep. Vineyard Sound, they say, was dug when he dragged his big toe on the way from the mainland. Martha's Vineyard and Nantucket were created when he dumped the sand from his moccasins. The Aquinnah Wampanoag of Martha's Vineyard, in a sly dig at the neighboring island, suggest Nantucket isn't sand at all—just the ash tamped from the bowl of Moshup's pipe.

Slowly but surely, passenger rail service from Boston pressed down the length of Cape Cod, reaching Sandwich in 1848; Henry David Thoreau was an early customer. By 1854 it extended to Hyannis and the ferry landings for Martha's Vineyard and Nantucket in present-day Hyannisport. By 1873, it reached the tip of Provincetown and ran down to Wood's Hole, making that village the prime port for travelers to Martha's Vineyard.

Predictably, the first summer people were the rich. But they were the modest rich, in pursuit of a more tranquil summer idyll than the ostentation of Newport, Cape May, and Sarasota. As Henry James put it in *The Bostonians,* "It was a place where people could lie on the ground and wear their old clothes." The rusticity of Cape Cod, enhanced by its Pilgrim history, became the region's primary attraction, and practical Cape Codders turned to creating a service economy.

One of the Cape's first planned resorts of small cottage lots was laid out in Falmouth Heights in the 1870s. Large resort hotels soon began to rise along the beaches. In the era of limited mobility, families often came to spend the season—July and August—at a single lodging, where they also took all their meals. As James O'Connell recounts in *Becoming Cape Cod,* by 1888 there were 118 hotels on Cape Cod, 25 on Nantucket, and 28 on Martha's Vineyard. The Chatham Bars Inn, which opened in 1914, was one of the last grand hotels to be built, and is also one of the last still performing its original function.

The automobile changed everything. By the early 1920s, Cape Cod had eleven hundred miles of paved road. The Victorian grand hotels began winking dark as more mobile and less wealthy travelers discovered the Cape and created a demand for campgrounds, cottage colonies, and motels. The cottage colony flourished on the Outer Cape along Route 6. Days Cottages in North Truro's Beach Point, one of the first such colonies, still stands as a Monopoly-house landmark that signals Provincetown on the horizon. The first motel opened in Hyannis in 1939, and Route 28 between Hyannis and Chatham remains the Cape's main motel gulch.

The shift to a summer-tourism economy brought a concomitant explosion in recreation and the arts. Hyannis and Cummaquid built the Cape's first golf courses in the 1890s, by which time organized competitive baseball was already firmly established. In 1901, Charles Hawthorne opened the Cape Cod School of Art in Provincetown, and American Impressionists became the first in a long line of artists to take inspiration from the Outer Cape's spare landscape and its vast and spreading light. By 1916 the Provincetown Players, including the playwright Eugene O'Neill, were forging a revolutionary American theater. In 1927, the Cape Playhouse opened in Dennis, firmly planting summer stock in the midst of vacationland. The Cape Cod Melody Tent opened in Hyannis in 1950, beginning an age of entertainment spectacle. By the early 1950s, tourism had taken hold as the chief industry of Cape Cod, and the state provided highways to assist the boom. The Mid-Cape Highway opened, piece by piece, from 1950 to 1959, and the four-lane Route 28 from the Bourne Bridge to Falmouth was finished in the late 1950s.

■ CONSERVATION

As tourists thronged onto Cape Cod and the year-round population began to rebound from the post–Civil War doldrums, new development began to threaten the very wildness and—Thoreau's word—desolation that made the place so attractive to begin with. Conservation came late to Cape Cod, but better late than never. In 1934, Roland Nickerson's nineteen-hundred-acre estate in Brewster, the largest contiguous woodland on the Cape, was donated to the state and became the first Massachusetts state park. In 1943, the Lowell Holly Reservation on Conaumet Neck between Mashpee and Wakeby Ponds was permanently dedicated for public use, and a year later the U.S. National Wildlife Refuge System created a nature preserve on Monomoy Island, famous hunting grounds of a century earlier. Monomoy was designated a National Wilderness Area in 1970. The conservation movement's capstone achievement, though, was a bill passed by Congress in 1961 establishing the Cape Cod National Seashore, "so that the inspiration of its surpassing beauty can be kept intact and handed down to future generations of Americans."

PLYMOUTH & ENVIRONS

The past is never far below the surface in Plymouth, the little community that proclaims itself "America's Home Town." Every Thanksgiving morning, fifty-one men, women, and children swathe themselves in the muted cloaks of 1621, huddle by the seashore (usually in biting cold, often in driving rain or snow), and, after suitable oratory, march uphill to church. Hundreds of onlookers follow this "Pilgrims' Progress," while on Cole's Hill a group of Native Americans mill around the statue of Massasoit, stamping their feet and blowing on their hands to stay warm. They watch the Pilgrims and wait their turn to declare a National Day of Mourning.

So much history, so much myth—Plymouth nearly sinks beneath the weight of it all. Those fifty-one marchers represent the Pilgrims who lived through the first winter. They came to this shore as seekers; they stayed as survivors. In a town where one resident in ten claims descent from a *Mayflower* passenger, the marchers symbolize a shared family history. This community of fifty-two thousand people, forty-one miles south of Boston and fifteen miles north of the Cape Cod Canal, represents the incarnation of an idea that would become a nation.

■ PLIMOTH PLANTATION   *map page 33, C-3*

On Route 3A, 2.5 miles south of downtown Plymouth, the open-air historical museum of Plimoth Plantation occupies a hundred-forty-acre tract that virtually clones the site of the original Pilgrim settlement. A partially cleared hillside stands above the tidal flats of the shore, with a small river running down the south side. Numerous brooks trickle from the hill, promising a dependable source of fresh water.

Three months and ten days after leaving Plymouth, England, the *Mayflower* anchored on Saturday, December 16, 1620, in the harbor that would become the new Plymouth. On the hillside above stood the fallow cornfields and cleared land of the Wampanoag village of Pawtuxet, abandoned after the epidemic of 1616 and 1617. Parties of men went ashore to cut, haul, and split wood to build shelter. Despite their best efforts, exactly half the colony died before spring, prompting the survivors to hold the March prayer service reenacted each Thanksgiving since 1921.

Plimoth Plantation: Goodwife Anable tends her garden.

Plimoth Plantation, where the calendar never advances past 1627.

With reinforcements and supplies from England, the frontier outpost looked far more viable by 1627, the year that Plimoth Plantation recycles in perpetuity. When you leave the modern orientation building, a sign announces, "Welcome to the 17th Century." Costumed interpreters assume the identities of actual settlers, their vocabulary and accents frozen in Elizabethan English and their minds seemingly ignorant of any post-1620s event or invention.

They relate the gossip of the community, expatiate on the proper way to cook a goose, and launch, with only the slightest provocation, into the arcane details of land ownership and debt repayment, 1627 style. But all the while they are planting, hoeing, weeding, washing clothes, splitting wood, tending fires, and performing all the hand-toughening, back-breaking labor of pioneer life. Go with the flow, and the reality of Pilgrim life seeps into your consciousness.

At the crest of the hill, the **Fort/Meetinghouse** stands as a bastion of preparedness—a lookout on the harbor, an emplacement for artillery, a pulpit from which to beseech the aid of Almighty God. One broad dirt street runs downhill, flanked on each side by modest houses. Small gardens flourish behind each dwelling, and wooden pales wall out the wilderness.

Even a figure such as Myles Standish—who looms large in history and myth as the colony's military commander and the spurned suitor of Priscilla Mullins—lived in a home so cold, dark, and lacking in privacy that one wonders how the Pilgrims were ever able to be fruitful and multiply. Steeply pitched thatch roofs top the mud-daubed, rough-hewn, weathered clapboard structures. Swinging wooden shutters cover the few windows, for the colonists had no glass.

Inside **Myles Standish's house** hangs a re-creation of his soldier's helmet and cuirass with metal breastplate. You can imagine him clad in the cumbersome armor leading an expedition through the swamplands in search of new waterways, looking like a mad conquistador on the wrong edge of the continent. His house is full of creature comforts compared to many: a curtained bed, a big table, and a carved chest and chairs from England. But the floor, like most, is dirt, and the fireplace is a tiny open hearth. (Standish found a wife among the passengers who arrived aboard the *Anne* in 1623, presumably making it easier to have John and Priscilla Mullins Alden as next-door neighbors.)

The Eel River Nature Walk leads from the pales of the 1627 Village to **Hobbamock's Homesite,** the museum's stab at representing Wampanoag life of the

BREAKING BREAD WITH MASSASOIT

Our harvest being gotten in, our Governour sent foure men on fowling, that so we might after a more speciall manner reioyce together, after we had gathered the fruit of our labors; they foure in one day killed as much fowle, as with a little helpe beside, served the Company almost a weeke, at which time amongst other Recreations, we exercised our Armes, many of the *Indians* coming amongst vs, and among the rest their greatest King *Massasoyt*, with some nintie men, whom for three dayes we entertained and feasted, and they went out and killed fiue Deere, which they brought to the Plantation and bestowed upon our Governour, and upon the Captaine, and others. And although it be not alwayes so plentifull, as it was at this time with vs, yet by the goodnes of God, we are so farre from want, that we often wish you partakers of our plenty.

—Edward Winslow, in a letter of December 11, 1621,
as printed in *A RELATION OR Iournal of the beginning and proceedings
of the English Plantation settled at Plimoth in NEW ENGLAND,
by certaine English Aduenturers both Merchants and others,* 1622

LOVE ON THE ROCKS

White Horse Beach, in the village of Manomet, six miles south of downtown Plymouth on Route 3A, takes its name from a documented shipwreck and an accompanying legend of thwarted love. On Christmas Day, 1778, the privateer *General Arnold* broke up in a gale off Plymouth harbor. Only 24 of the 170 crew members survived, including twenty-one-year-old Roland Doane, who was taken to the home of a Mr. Paine to recover from frostbite. Doane fell in love with Paine's daughter, Helen, and they married secretly, against her father's wishes. According to the tale, the couple planned for Doane to anchor his schooner offshore on the night of August 24, 1779, to pick up his new bride. That night, Helen fled her father's house on his white horse, rode into the surf, and perished.

same period. Beginning in 1621, Hobbamock lived with his family near the English settlers; he served as their liaison with other Algonquian speakers and as a guide to the trails and waterways of the region until his death, sometime before 1643.

The Homesite is frankly more generic than the 1627 Village, and the staff, despite its 1620s Wampanoag garb, forgoes role-playing in favor of modern speech and sensibility. The Homesite re-creates Wampanoag thatched dwellings that are more comfortable (and drier) than the colonists' houses. Throughout the season, interpreters demonstrate open-fire cookery, canoe-making, basketry, and pottery. What's missing is personal detail; the colonists were well described in letters and chronicles, but history stands mute on Hobbamock and his family. *Route 3A; 508-746-1622. Open Apr.–Nov.*

■ PLYMOUTH CENTER   *map page 33*

Fast-forward nearly four centuries to modern Plymouth, sprawling along its harbor with tiers of streets rising up the sloped shore to the rocky ridge above. Unlike Virginia's Jamestown, where the original settlement site was abandoned, Plymouth grew up around its colonial beginnings.

Significant fragments of Pilgrim life remain. Perhaps the most famous is **Plymouth Rock,** a granite boulder subjected to both veneration and ridicule over the centuries. Speaking to an 1881 meeting of the New England Society in Philadelphia, Mark Twain quipped, "The Pilgrims were a simple and ignorant race. They never had seen any good rocks before, or at least any that were not watched, and so they were excusable for hopping ashore in frantic delight and clapping an iron fence around this one." Sarcasm aside, Twain was perpetuating the long oral tradition that the *Mayflower* Pilgrims first stepped ashore at Plymouth Rock. No written record establishes the steppingstone to the New World, but true believers cling to the 1741 identification of the Rock by Thomas Faunce, then ninety-five. Faunce learned the tale from his father, who claimed to have heard it first-hand from a *Mayflower* passenger.

Thin historical evidence has never slowed efforts to hold up the Rock as a symbol. In the early days of the American Revolution, Plymouth patriots brought screw jacks and thirty yoke of oxen to move the Rock, but ended up splitting it in two. Undaunted, they hauled the seven-thousand-pound top portion to the Liberty Pole they had

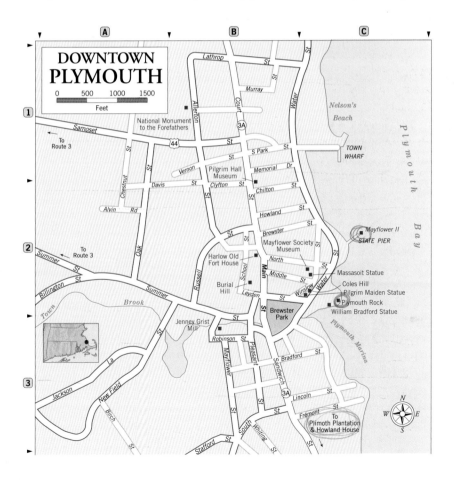

DOWNTOWN PLYMOUTH

0   500   1000   1500
Feet

To Route 3

Samoset

Lathrop St

Murray St

National Monument to the Forefathers

Nelson's Beach

44

Vernon

Pilgrim Hall Museum

S Park St

Memorial Dr

TOWN WHARF

Davis St

Clyfton St

Chilton St

Alvin Rd

Howland St

To Route 3

Summer St

Billington St

Brewster St

Mayflower Society Museum

Mayflower II STATE PIER

Harlow Old Fort House

North St

Massasoit Statue

Middle St

Coles Hill

Burial Hill

Leyden St

Pilgrim Maiden Statue

Plymouth Rock

William Bradford Statue

Brook

Town

Jenney Grist Mill

Brewster Park

Robinson St

Bradford St

Jackson

New Field

La

Birch

Mayflower

Sandwich

Pleasant

3A

Lincoln St

Fremont

To Plimoth Plantation & Howland House

South

Whiting St

Stafford St

Plymouth Bay

Plymouth Marina

N
W   E
S

A Greek Revival portico surrounds the reassembled Plymouth Rock.

planted by the courthouse. It was but the beginning of the stone's many mutilations and humiliations. Chips and fragments of the True Rock were displayed all over the country, Alexis de Tocqueville observed in 1831, like American holy relics.

The lower portion of the Rock was protected with an arched canopy and an iron fence beginning in 1867. By 1880, the top portion, which had been dragged all over Plymouth for more than a century, was rejoined to the base; the date 1620 was chiseled into the stone. In 1921, during Plymouth's tercentenary celebration, a massive Greek Revival portico was erected above the site, creating the peculiar shrine that persists today and making Plymouth Rock, in the words of the historian James Seelye, "at once a disillusionment and something of a mystery, a humble and diminished thing, yet stubbornly and solidly final."

The *Mayflower II,* a reproduction of a typical seventeenth-century bark, bobs beside State Pier within sight of Plymouth Rock. Artisans built the 106.5-foot-long vessel between 1955 and 1957 at Upham Shipyard, in England, with seventeenth-century materials: English oak, hand-sewn linen sails, hemp cordage, hand-forged nails, and Stockholm tar. When she set sail from Plymouth, England, on April 20, 1957, using seventeenth-century navigation practices but on a slightly more southerly route than her namesake took, the press gave the vessel about an even chance of completing the crossing. The *Mayflower II* finished the journey, but, despite the emphasis on

---

SCALING THE HEIGHTS

The earliest symbol to be associated with the Plymouth settlers is the famous, or perhaps infamous, chunk of granite known as Plymouth Rock. Most Americans know of it, and even a breed of chicken has been named after it. Lacking hard numbers, it is not possible to say it is the most popular attraction in modern Plymouth, but one has the intuitive sense that such is the case. An apocryphal story in Plymouth has it that two elderly ladies, walking along the waterfront, were overheard when one said to the other, "We must get to bed early tonight, because we have to climb Plymouth Rock in the morning."

—James Deetz and Patricia Scott Deetz, *The Times of Their Lives: Life, Love, and Death in Plymouth Colony,* 2000

---

authenticity, Capt. Alan Villiers ran afoul of historical accuracy by forbidding women on the ship—a blunder Plimoth Plantation has righted with its costumed interpreters, who talk about life during the crossing and the horrible first winter, when many Pilgrims lived aboard. Even with just a dozen visitors, the hold induces claustrophobia as you try to imagine the 102 passengers squatting on the floor or crowded into tiny "cabins"—often little larger than a baby's crib. The matter-of-fact tales of deprivation make the generosity of Christopher Jones, master of the first *Mayflower,* all the more remarkable. When the Pilgrims ran out of beer—an essential part of their diet—he shared a portion of the crew's stores to stave off starvation and disease. *State Pier; 508-746-1622. Open Apr.–Nov.*

From State Pier, **Capt. John Boats** (508-747-2400) operates a seasonal (late May–late September) ferry that crosses Cape Cod Bay to Provincetown, essentially reversing the trip the *Mayflower* made from its first New World anchorage to its final destination. Across the harbor, Town Wharf is home to Plymouth's small fleet of whale-watching and excursion vessels, as well as to inshore fishing and lobstering boats. **Woods Seafood Market & Restaurant** (508-746-0261) holds down a prominent spot at the base of the wharf, with a fresh fish market on one end and a glassed-in dining room and take-out fish shack on the other.

What might be deemed the Pilgrim trail continues south on Water Street to the **statue of William Bradford,** sculpted by Cyrus Dallin for the city's 1921 tercentenary but not installed until 1971. When governor John Carver died early in April

1621, Bradford, already one of the colony's leaders and its chronicler, became governor, a post he held or shared until 1656. His writings reveal a man of quick wit, humility, fairness, and civic virtue.

Facing Bradford across Water Street on the crest of Cole's Hill is a larger-than-life **statue of Massasoit,** sachem of the Pokanoket Wampanoags. He and Bradford hammered out a mutual defense treaty that lasted until Massasoit's death in 1661. Although North America's native peoples had earlier and certainly less positive encounters with European settlers, Massasoit's statue has become a symbol of Native American rights movements; it's here that the National Day of Mourning has been proclaimed each Thanksgiving since 1970.

Just feet away from Massasoit, a modest granite sarcophagus holds the moldered remains of some of the first Pilgrims. During what has come to be called the Starving Time of early 1621, the Pilgrims buried their dead at night on Cole's Hill and in the spring sowed corn to hide the graves, lest their Native American neighbors detect how weakened their numbers had become.

The original settlement lay just below Cole's Hill along the banks of **Town Brook,** the "sweet brook…under the hillside" that helped convince the Pilgrims to settle here. The first buildings were constructed along the north side of the brook, on what is now Leyden Street. Following the brook uphill, you leave behind the souvenir shops and ice cream parlors of the modern town. The landscaped grounds here are a popular spot for wedding photos. Bridal parties often gather in the shadow of the **Pilgrim Maiden** statue of 1924, dedicated to "those intrepid English women whose courage and fortitude brought a new nation into being."

The trail climbs along the south side of the brook to **Jenney Grist Mill.** A fish ladder below the dam allows herring to make their spring spawning run up Town Brook, as they have since time immemorial, and the mill pond and grounds surrounding this anachronistic edifice constitute a set piece of pastoral tranquility. Most sites associated with the Pilgrims are nonprofit museums, but the mill is a commercial operation, just as it was when John Jenney built Plymouth's first mill here in 1636. The phrase "nose to the grindstone" takes on fresh meaning during a Sunday afternoon corn-grinding demonstration. The corn is ground between a fixed bottom stone and a revolving top stone—each weighing twenty-five hundred pounds. The miller lowers the top stone closer and closer to produce a finer and finer meal (available for sale

Oarsmen from the Mayflower II *in seventeenth-century costume. (following pages) The Jenney Grist Mill, still grinding corn after nearly four centuries.*

in the shop). If the stones touch, friction sets the corn on fire; the miller can judge the clearance by putting his nose to the grindstone to sniff the corn. The original mill lasted more than two centuries before fire destroyed it in 1847—the current structure is a 1970 replica. It's open daily from spring through fall, and sporadically at other times; call for hours. *Off Summer Street; 508-747-4544.*

Nearby, the greatest schism in New England Protestantism is manifest in the two church buildings on Town Square, at the head of Leyden Street. The Pilgrim Separatists of Plymouth Colony and the Puritan reformers of the Massachusetts Bay Colony eventually merged their churches, calling their faith Congregationalism. But when Unitarianism swept through New England in the years shortly after the Revolution, many Congregational parishes embraced the religious revolution. The Plymouth congregation split in two. The Unitarian-Universalist **First Parish Church** (508-747-1606) kept the building on the site of the original Pilgrim house of worship. Stained-glass windows over the altar, including a depiction of the Signing of the Mayflower Compact, assert the Pilgrim connection with images of early Plymouth. A few feet away, dissenters who preferred the trinitarian Congregational theology built the **Church of the Pilgrimage** (508-746-3026), where the parishioners like to say that the First Parish "kept the church, but we kept the faith."

The Pilgrims' Progress Thanksgiving march winds between the churches to **Burial Hill,** behind First Parish. The site of the colony's first marked burials (the clandestine burials on Cole's Hill near the harbor remained unmarked for centuries), this lofty perch overlooks both the new and the old buildings of Plymouth and provides a clear view of Plymouth harbor. Not coincidentally, this is where Myles Standish sited the colony's first fort.

When the fort was dismantled in 1677, the Harlow family used the timbers to construct what is now known as the **Harlow Old Fort House.** The Plymouth Antiquarian Society has operated it since the 1920s, and with its wide floorboards, low ceilings, slanting floors, and balky iron front-door latch, the house feels almost antediluvian. Costumed interpreters guide visitors through the homestead and sometimes give demonstrations of hearth cooking. (Walking in when a pie is baking or a pork roast is turning slowly on a jack spit suggests that olden times had their rewards.) Since 1930 the house, which is open on Fridays in July and August, has hosted the popular Pilgrim Breakfast on the Fourth of July. *119 Sandwich Street; 508-746-0012.*

Slightly closer to town, the 1666 **Howland House** is furnished with antiques from the late seventeenth and early eighteenth centuries. Jabez Howland built this two-and-a-half-story structure with hip roof and central chimney. He was the son of *Mayflower* Pilgrims John and Elizabeth Tilley Howland, and when their farm burned in 1670, he invited them to move into the Sandwich Street house—the basis for its billing as "the last house left in Plymouth whose walls have heard the voices of the *Mayflower* Pilgrims." *33 Sandwich Street; 508-746-9590. Open late-May–mid-Oct.*

Traveling north, Sandwich Street becomes Main Street, then Court Street. The **All American Diner** is a quintessential small-town short-order restaurant where both Portuguese fishermen and descendants of the Pilgrims sip coffee and chow down on chef-owner Mark Santos' breakfast specials. The fishcakes—which the Diner supplies for the Pilgrim Breakfast—come New England style, with baked beans and corn bread. *60 Court Street; 508-747-4763.*

Practically across the street, there's a grandeur for the ages about **Pilgrim Hall Museum,** built in 1824 and refaced with a Doric portico for the tercentenary. One of New England's oldest local-history museums, Pilgrim Hall calls itself America's Museum of Pilgrim Possessions—but you could think of it as Plymouth's family attic. Among the items on display are the swords of Myles Standish, the pre–King James Bible owned by William Bradford, and the cradle of Peregrine White, the first English child born in Plymouth. The "great chairs" of William Bradford and William Brewster (elder of the church) are here, as is the portrait of Edward Winslow, the only image of a *Mayflower* Pilgrim painted from life. In their modest way, the anonymous quotidian artifacts—the last surviving Pilgrim hat, a tankard, a razor, broken pottery salvaged from excavations—rescue the Pilgrims from the pedestal of history by revealing them as flesh and blood. *75 Court Street; 508-746-1620. Open Feb.–Dec.*

Plymouth's most ambitious tribute to the Pilgrims—a thirty-six-foot neoclassical statue of Faith atop a forty-five-foot pedestal—marks the northward passage out of town. Inspired by the Bunker Hill Monument in Charlestown, the Pilgrim Society laid the cornerstone for the **National Monument to the Forefathers** in 1859. It was not finished until 1889, by which time the installation of the Statue of Liberty in New York had stolen its thunder. Plymouth consoles itself, however, with the knowledge that although the project was scaled back to half its planned size, it is nonetheless the largest free-standing granite monument in the world. *Allerton Street, one block north of Route 44.*

■ **DUXBURY** *map page 7, B-2*

Route 3A winds north along the shore through Kingston and into upscale Duxbury, which made its own contribution to the late-nineteenth-century craze for erecting monuments. Begun in 1872 and completed in 1898, the **Myles Standish Monument** rises like a lighthouse atop Captain's Hill in South Duxbury. The stone tower ascends 110 feet to an observation deck that supports a sixteen-foot-tall statue of Standish. (Such stature might have pleased the height-challenged Standish, whom Thomas Morton, the so-called Pagan Pilgrim, derisively dubbed Captaine Shrimpe.) He faces east, toward the ocean, clutching the colonial charter in one hand while his other rests, ever ready, on the hilt of his sword. From mid-May through mid-October, you can climb 125 stairs to the top of the pedestal for views of church spires all along the coast, several nineteenth-century lighthouses, sandy Duxbury Beach, the white-capped waters of Cape Cod Bay, and, to the northwest, the softly rounded Blue Hills. *Crescent Street; 508-866-2580.*

Standish was but one of the Plymouth settlers who took advantage of the 1627 land division in Duxbury. The Plymouth government allowed the new landowners to farm their properties but required them to return to Plymouth each winter, until a church was erected in Duxbury in 1632. The town was finally chartered in 1637 as the second community in the Plymouth Colony.

John and Priscilla Alden also moved to Duxbury, building two smaller houses before constructing, probably in 1653, the home now known as the **Alden House.** Alden had prospered—he had shipped on the *Mayflower* as a cooper, but by 1653 he had served as assistant governor and treasurer of the colony—and the original portion of the weathered clapboard house is large by seventeenth-century standards. He and Priscilla, the daughter of a shoemaker, raised ten children to adulthood, possibly losing one other in infancy. Their descendants include Presidents John Adams and John Quincy Adams, Henry Wadsworth Longfellow, the choreographer Martha Graham, and Vice President Dan Quayle. Although the house has been modified over the years, it has remained in the Alden family. The current owners, the nonprofit Alden Kindred, open the house for guided tours from mid-May through mid-October and try to keep a handle on the Alden descendants, estimated at some five million today. *Alden Street; 781-934-9092.*

The Harlow Old Fort House, where victuals are prepared the way they were in Pilgrim days.

N E W   B E D F O R D
& E N V I R O N S

The salt air of New Bedford harbor tastes of great cold links of iron chain. The whiff of diesel floats down the pier as a mechanic fires up an engine, revving it to send blue plumes out the exhaust stacks. He shuts it down again, curses in Portuguese, and cracks open another can of Marvel Mystery Oil. The tinny stink of machine grease overwhelms the residual fish smell coming from steel boats with names like *Dinah Jane, Santa Isabel, Invincible*. Just in to unload and reprovision, they leave again on runs down Buzzards Bay to drag for scallops, out onto the Nantucket shoals to haul for flounder, or farther out to ply the Stellwagen and Georges Banks for haddock and cod.

There was a time when great fires burned on the New Bedford wharves; cauldrons bubbled, and the air smelled of the pitch and tar used to caulk wooden ships against the elements. Those ships bore tall pine masts on live oak keels and carried canvas into the wind. The *Eliza,* the *Clarice,* the *Abigail,* the *Mercury,* and the *Roscoe* were whalers all, bound off on voyages of up to five years, a few dozen hard-bitten men before the mast as they hunted the oceans for the leviathans of the deep.

Like Herman Melville's Ishmael, New Bedford gets mean-eyed and restless if it stays too long ashore. Settled in 1640, the village set itself on a path to sea when Quakers from Nantucket, Martha's Vineyard, and Cape Cod arrived in the 1760s to take advantage of its sheltered harbor at the mouth of Buzzards Bay. Shipwrights soon lined the docks, and the deep-water port eclipsed Nantucket as the whaling capital in 1823. By 1850, New Bedford was sending more whaling vessels to sea than the rest of the world combined. When petroleum displaced whale oil, maritime New Bedford concentrated on fishing. In the 1920s, a New Bedford fisherman invented the otter trawl—a tubular net dragged along the ocean floor—and New Bedford's fleet expanded to rival those of Provincetown, Boston, and Gloucester. Today New Bedford has the largest fishing fleet on America's eastern seaboard. It usually ranks in the top ten ports in the country in pounds of fish landed, and it frequently boasts the most valuable annual catch of any American port.

Centuries on, New Bedford remains one of the country's premier fishing ports.

■ WATERFRONT *map page 50*

Whenever you order a plate of scallops, sole meunière, or roasted haddock in a New England restaurant, chances are good that the fish passed through New Bedford on the way to your plate. Indeed, the catch could have come off one of the boats tied up along the edges of **Fisherman's Wharf,** a trapezoidal expanse that juts into the harbor nearest the bridge to Fairhaven.

The farthest reach of the wharf, **Corner Point,** provides a sharp perspective on New Bedford's strategic position. The harbor is technically the mouth of the Acushnet River, but the tidal channel is deep enough to accommodate oceangoing freighters. The shipyards of Fairhaven, where fishing vessels go for repairs, stand on the opposite shore. Pope's Island in the middle of the river is home to the **New Bedford Marina,** which has about two hundred slips for pleasure craft. But recreational boating is an afterthought in New Bedford—maritime life revolves around the comings and goings of the fishermen. Whatever the season, trawlers with their huge spooled nets typically venture out for a week; the scallopers ply their metal dredges for two weeks or more. One of the last stops before leaving port is the large red-brick building on the north side of Fisherman's Wharf, where Crystal Ice company typically loads each boat with ten tons or more of ice to chill the catch.

A generation ago, boats returning to port made their first call at the **Wharfinger Building.** Built under the Works Project Administration from 1934 to 1935 to house the office of the wharfinger—the city official who collected wharfage fees— the building gained an addition in 1947 to house the New Bedford fish auction. These days New Bedford's catch, now exceeding a hundred million pounds a year, goes to market at a dedicated building south of the main waterfront, where digital cameras and online bidding speed the process. Today the Wharfinger Building houses the Waterfront Tourist Information Office, where tour and school groups gather before boarding the state's floating classroom. *Pier 3; 508-979-1745.*

That classroom is the schooner ***Ernestina,*** docked at the head of the adjacent State Pier. The *Ernestina* has one of the deepest résumés of any tall ship afloat. She was constructed in the Essex boatyards on the Massachusetts North Shore in 1894, and she fished the Grand Banks, stretching offshore from Nova Scotia and Newfoundland east nearly to Greenland, and along coastal Nova Scotia and Newfoundland. During two decades of Arctic exploration, she set the farthest-north record for a wooden ship. After World War II, the *Ernestina* ran cargo and immigrants between the Cape Verde Islands and the United States and served the Cape Verdean inter-island trade. Donated to the States as a gift from the Republic of Cape Verde, the *Ernestina* functions as a day-sail and dockside teaching vessel— appropriately enough, in a city with one of America's largest populations of Cape Verdean descent. *State Pier; 508-992-4900.*

Just behind the Wharfinger Building, a large former lobster boat, the ***Alert II*** (508-992-1432), ferries passengers to Cuttyhunk, the only one of the Elizabeth Islands open to the public. (The Forbes publishing family owns the rest of the chain, which trickles off the southwest corner of Cape Cod north of Martha's Vineyard, forming the southern boundary of Buzzards Bay.)

For a century and a half, **Steamship Pier** served as the terminal for the ferry to Martha's Vineyard and Nantucket. The first scheduled steamship service in New England was inaugurated on June 25, 1818, when the *Eagle* departed for Nantucket. Today, the only ferry to the large islands, going to Oak Bluffs on Martha's Vineyard, is the **M/V Schamonchi** (East Rodney French Boulevard; 508-997-1688), which departs from Billy Wood's Wharf, a few miles south of the main waterfront. The long finger of Steamship Pier now hosts in-shore fishing and some lobster boats, though the majority of lobstermen tie up at Leonard's Wharf, two piers to the south.

Ship hands at work on the Ernestina.

Between Steamship and Leonard's sits the industrial complex of **Merrill's Wharf,** occupied by seafood-processing companies. In the mid-nineteenth century, this wharf was practically afloat in whale oil, its expanse covered with barrels draped in seaweed to keep the sun from shrinking the staves and spilling their valuable contents. In 1848, the whaling king Jonathan Bourne Jr. established his offices in the granite-block building at the head of the wharf. He remained there for forty years, his tenure effectively bookending the heyday of the whaling industry. From the bay window on the second floor of the building's south side, Bourne—who owned more whale-ship tonnage than any other American—could stare out to the mouth of the harbor and watch his fortunes riding on the tide.

A New Bedford cooper puts a head on a cask, circa 1870.

THOUGHTS OF HOME

Born in Georgia in 1889, Conrad Aiken was orphaned at age eleven and grew up on New Bedford harbor at the end of the city's sailing era. In his letters and memoirs he often recounted his wistfulness at seeing tall ships depart to distant ports, an experience on which he drew for this passage in his 1927 novel Blue Voyage.

These sails, which the men were now breaking out one by one, and which now gently filled with the following wind, and shifted a little with a settling creak of spars long unused, these sails would carry the *Sylvia Lee* all the way to Tierra del Fuego, and round the Horn to Valparaiso. What would Union Street seem like then, with its little green streetcars? Would the men remember Buttonwood Park, and the bears, and the motor-paced bicycle races at the bicycle track? Would they talk about these things, or long for them, these things which were now so commonplace and real? Would these things then seem as distant and incredible as Valparaiso seemed now?

—Conrad Aiken, *Blue Voyage,* 1927

■ HISTORIC DISTRICT   *map page 50*

In late August 1924, the bark *Wanderer* became the last whaling ship to sail from New Bedford harbor. She anchored off Martha's Vineyard to wait out an approaching storm, but the anchor let go during the night and the ship foundered off Cuttyhunk Island, fourteen miles from port. It spelled an ignominious conclusion to the saga of New Bedford's whaling hegemony.

Just above the waterfront, the thirteen-block **New Bedford Whaling National Historical Park** (33 William Street; 508-996-4095) preserves much of the port city's golden age. The bloodthirsty and nasty business of whaling seems almost incomprehensible in this present era of "Save the Whales" bumper stickers, but displays at the park's visitors center illuminate the harsh necessity of the enterprise.

The whalers were on a quest for the grease and oil of the leviathans. The waxy fat (spermaceti) in the heads of sperm whales was extracted for candles; the thick layer of blubber on almost all whales was rendered and processed into fine lubricating oils for the clock industry and heavy machine oils for the metal wheels of factories. But most of all, whale oil burned brightly in millions and millions of lamps: from 1830 until petroleum derivatives replaced whale oil shortly after the Civil War, New Bedford was the City that Lights the World. As frivolous as it now sounds, fashion kept the whaling industry going even after the introduction of petroleum, because whalebone, usually taken from the baleen of the right whale, remained in demand for skirt hoops, collar and corset stays, and umbrella ribs.

Park rangers and volunteer guides lead walking tours through the historic district daily in July and August, less frequently the rest of the year. The past remains embedded in the present; you can stumble along the same granite pavers where sailors of every creed, color, and language once swaggered, and wander past Greek Revival structures where the stay-at-home merchants and investors counted their money. New Bedford was the Houston of the mid-nineteenth century: an oil

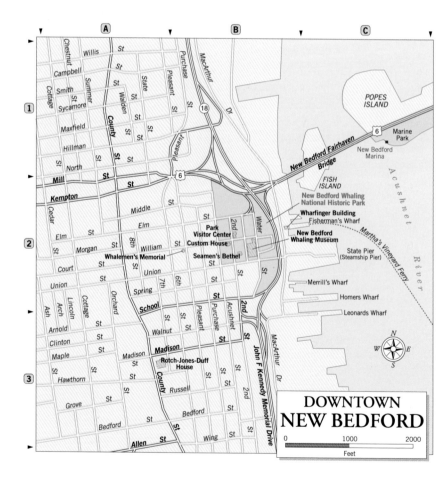

DOWNTOWN
NEW BEDFORD

0   1000   2000
Feet

town used to living large, and dominated by energy and refining industries. In 1857, more than half the American whaling fleet—329 vessels—was registered in New Bedford.

Just west of the historic district, two bronze statues flank the towering public library at 613 Pleasant Street. The dynamic **Whalemen's Memorial** by Bela Pratt, dedicated in 1913, depicts a whaler in the prow of a small whale boat with his harpoon poised to strike. The base carries the do-or-die legend "A dead whale or a stove boat." The bronze on the south side of the library lawn is a likeness of Lewis Temple, a blacksmith born in Richmond, Virginia, probably in slavery, who settled in New Bedford in 1829. Temple's invention of the toggle harpoon tip in 1848 revolutionized whaling and "made the fortunes of many men," a plaque declares. Temple wasn't one of them—he didn't patent the design.

As the whale-oil barrels piled up on Merrill's Wharf, the wealth accumulated along Water Street, often called the Wall Street of the whaling port. In the mid-nineteenth century, four of New Bedford's five banks and its half-dozen principal insurance companies all lined up along **North Water Street,** between Union and Rodman Streets, like sugar maples on a farmhouse driveway. Equally important in the local economy, **Rodman Candleworks** (72 North Water Street) opened in 1810 and operated as a candleworks until 1890. The company was among the first to produce the dripless, smokeless, long-lasting spermaceti candles—the standard for measuring illumination in "candle power." Today the Candleworks building holds offices and a popular fine-dining restaurant also named Candleworks.

Directly across Rodman Street stands the most impressive structure on North Water Street, the so-called **Double Bank Building,** which speaks with a hubris that New Bedford has long since shed. The great white building (some might say great white elephant) aspires to be the Parthenon of Buzzards Bay, its row of eight graceful columns departing from the Greek original only in their decorative capitals. Built to proclaim New Bedford's prosperity, longevity, and acumen, it served as the chief depository for more than forty late-nineteenth-century millionaires.

The Bourne Whaling Museum, founded in 1903 by the daughter of Jonathan Bourne Jr. to memorialize her father's achievements, long ago metamorphosed into the **New Bedford Whaling Museum,** a memorial to a vanished industry. Two whale skeletons float in the air of the entry hall, both ghostly and graceful, hinting at the museum's shift of emphasis—from the men whose purses were fattened by the slaughter to the conservation of a species hunted nearly to extinction. The

---

BADLY BRUZED. . . SLITLY STOVE

Friday, June 3rd 1853

All of these 24 hours Calm pleasant Weather. Ship Close in by the Ice plenty of Whales in the Ice all four boats in the Ice a Whaleing at 6 P.M. the Starbord and Waist boats struck one Whale at the Same time the Captain was nocked out of his boat by the Second Iron and taken under the Ice for Several Minutes but by Good Luck We succeeded in Saveing him although badly bruzed and took him too the Ship. Lost two Lines and got the boats Slitly Stove at 3 A.M. the Larbord boat Lowered and Struck the Whale ran under the Ice and Cut Line in a few minutes the Whale Came out of the Ice and went on and Struck again he ran under the Ice and the Iron drew. So Ended these 24 hours.

—Logbook of the Ship *Niagara*, as quoted in *Fairhaven, Massachusetts*, 1939

---

ordinary sailors who chased the whales also get their due. One of them was the twenty-one-year-old Herman Melville, who shipped out aboard the *Acushnet* on January 3, 1841, bound for the Pacific Ocean. The museum displays the crew list that young Melville signed, noting that he received an eighty-four-dollar advance against his future earnings to equip himself with "necessaries" for the voyage. Typically, a man stowed all his worldly possessions in a trunk that measured eighteen by eighteen by forty-two inches, spent days scrubbing decks and repairing sails between whale sightings, and slept below in the foc'sle under conditions described by an anonymous seaman in terms Melville could not have improved on: "a compound of foul air, tobacco smoke, sea chests, soap kegs, greasy pans, tainted meat, foreign ruffians and seasick Americans." Melville would not return to the shores of New England until 1845, and another six years would elapse before the masterpiece his voyage inspired would see print. On January 3 and 4 each year, the New Bedford Whaling Museum sponsors a twenty-five-hour marathon reading of *Moby-Dick*.

Jonathan Bourne Jr.'s favorite whaleship, the *Lagoda*, made twelve voyages in forty-eight years, bringing home the equivalent of $16 million. One wing of the museum is filled with an eighty-nine-foot half-scale model of the bark, displayed

A contemporary scrimshander plies an old craft in New Bedford.

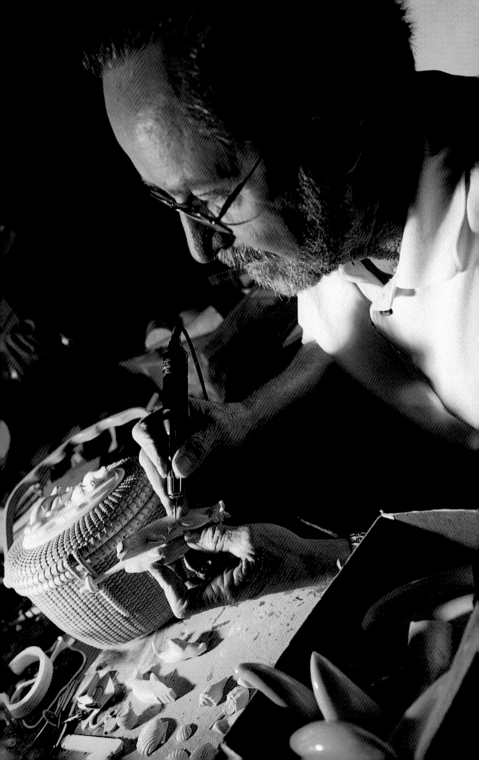

with her square-rigged sails open as if she were ready to turn to the breeze and head for the Antarctic. Beside her rest full-size whale boats—little more than a cup of air on the ocean from which men struck home their spears and held on for dear life as the whale took them on a "Nantucket sleigh ride." *18 Johnny Cake Hill; 508-997-0046.*

The walls of the **Seamen's Bethel,** across the street from the museum, attest that the whale wasn't always the loser. Marble cenotaphs memorialize New Bedford sailors lost at sea, including many "lost from a boat while in pursuit of a whale." The chapel's bowsprit pulpit was installed in 1959 to match Melville's description of the nondenominational Christian chapel in *Moby-Dick.* The pious citizens of the New Bedford Port Society for the Moral Improvement of Seamen erected the bethel in 1832, wrote Leonard B. Ellis in his 1892 *History of New Bedford,* that it might be a haven "free from the demoralizing influences to which sailors are too often exposed" and keep the young men away from the "licentious literature of the tap-room and brothel." It certainly made the appropriate impression on Melville, who wrote, "In New Bedford there stands a Whaleman's Chapel, and few are the moody fishermen, shortly bound for the Indian Ocean or the Pacific, who fail to make a Sunday visit to the spot. I am sure that I did not." The bethel remains a place of worship, with vespers on the third Sunday of each month, weddings and baptisms, and the Festival of Thanksgiving for the Harvest of the Sea in November, when fresh seafood is displayed on the altar. *15 Johnny Cake Hill; 508-992-3295.*

Just as the bethel continues to render unto God, the **Custom House** of Melville's time continues to render unto Caesar. Seafarers from around the globe still register their papers and pay duties and tariffs in the 1836 Grecian temple structure. The oldest continuously operating Custom House in the country, it was designed by Robert Mills, the architect of the Washington Monument. During the Civil War, the plaza in front of the Custom House was the recruiting station for the first Union Army regiment of African-American soldiers. About fifty black New Bedford men enlisted in the Massachusetts 54th and its overflow regiment, the 55th. Between 1861 and 1865, an estimated 350 New Bedford African-Americans—some of them escaped slaves—served in the Union Army and Navy. *37 North Second Street; 508-994-5458.*

The New Bedford Whaling Museum preserves a vital slice of maritime history.

New Bedford was well known among abolitionists as one of the best asylums for fugitive slaves. Liberal Quaker and Unitarian citizens embraced the cause of abolition, and the increasingly wealthy city hungered for laborers. A fugitive could find both work and, by percentage, one of the largest free African-American communities in the north. Between the mid-1840s and the outbreak of the Civil War, an estimated three hundred to seven hundred fugitive slaves lived in New Bedford; not one was known to have been recaptured. Perhaps the most famous was Frederick Douglass, who became a thundering voice for abolition. "On the wharves of New Bedford I received my first light," he recalled in his autobiography. "I saw there industry without bustle, labor without noise, toil—honest, earnest, and exhaustive without the whip. . ."

Douglass and his wife, Anna, arrived in New Bedford in September 1838 and were taken in by Nathan and Mary (also known as Polly) Johnson at **17/19 Seventh Street.** The Johnsons, who were among New Bedford's most active black abolitionists, owned both sides of the duplex where they lived, as well as the larger building next door at **21 Seventh Street.** They frequently housed fugitive slaves in both structures. The building at 21 Seventh Street was built as a Quaker meeting-house in 1785 and moved to its present spot in 1822, when the Quakers outgrew it; in 1828, it served as the site of New Bedford's first public antislavery lecture. The two buildings at 17/19 and 21 Seventh Street are under development as a historical museum of New Bedford's African-American heritage.

West of the historic district, the ridgeline street on the heights above New Bedford harbor predates the founding of the town in 1787. Originally a Native American trail, it was laid out in 1717 as County Road to link the farming community of South Dartmouth to Plymouth. As New Bedford's whaling trade burgeoned after the War of 1812, the newly wealthy began to build mansions on County Road—high enough to keep an eye on their ships, and sufficiently removed from the dirt and bustle of the port.

Follow Spring Street west to what is now County Street, then turn south for a tour through the vernacular architecture popular with the moneyed classes of the nineteenth century. The **Rotch-Jones-Duff House and Garden Museum** captures the lifestyle. In 1833, Quaker William Rotch Jr. had his architect, Richard

The Seamen's Bethel, in New Bedford, where Melville's Ishmael attends a Sunday service in Moby-Dick, *remains a house of worship today.*

SEAMEN'S BETHEL

SEAMEN'S BETHEL

"IN THE SAME NEW
BEDFORD THERE STANDS
A WHALEMAN'S CHAPEL
AND FEW ARE THE
MOODY FISHERMEN,
SHORTLY BOUND FOR
THE INDIAN OR PACIFIC
OCEANS WHO FAILED
TO MAKE A SUNDAY
VISIT TO THIS SPOT."

Say Dec.

THE WHALEMAN'S
CHAPEL
OF
HERMAN MELVILLE'S
MOBY DICK
OFFICE
MARINER'S HOME
→

Madeirans Make Merry

Thank four Mannies from Madeira for New Bedford's annual **Feast of the Blessed Sacrament** (www.portuguesefeast.com), which claims to be the largest Portuguese festival in the world and the largest ethnic festival in New England. After a harrowing crossing from Madeira to the United States in 1912, Manuel d'Agrella, Manual d'Agrella Coutinho, Manuel Sardinha Duarte, and Manual Sebastiao Santinho pledged to re-create their village's Festo de Santissimo Sacramento in their new homeland. What began as a modest religious feast in 1915 has grown into a four-day event, held on the first full weekend in August, that attracts up to two hundred fifty thousand participants. An estimated thirty-five hundred area residents claim Madeiran descent, and tens of thousands more trace their ancestry to other parts of Portugal. The feast site on Hope Street (off Belleville Avenue) has stages for musical performers, a full kitchen, and a barbecue pit. Food plays a large role. Revelers at one recent festival consumed 5,000 pounds of pork, 3,500 pounds of linguiça, 10,000 pounds of beef, 400 pounds of goat, 350 pounds of rabbit, 400 pounds of cod, 425 kegs of beer, and 13 barrels of Madeira. The tiny Museum of Madeiran Heritage (1 Funchal Place; 508-994-2573) sits on the feast grounds; it's open on Sundays from April through November.

Upjohn, cover the brick mansion with clapboards to make it appear more modest while still maintaining airy spaces and fine interiors. Before the property became a museum, it was owned by another whaling family and, in the twentieth century, by a businessman; the interior reflects a century and a half of social history and domestic style. The museum also preserves the original luxuriant gardens and grounds. Melville, who visited New Bedford often when his sister lived here, lauded the horticultural bent of the city's merchants: "Nowhere in all America will you find more patrician-like houses; parks and gardens more opulent, than in New Bedford," he wrote in *Moby-Dick*. "Yes; all these brave houses and flowery gardens came from the Atlantic, Pacific, and Indian Oceans. One and all, they were harpooned and dragged up hither from the bottom of the sea." *396 County Street; 508-997-1401.*

Mrs. Duff's bedroom, in the Rotch-Jones-Duff House, which was built with money made in the whaling trade.

■ FAIRHAVEN & ONWARD *map 7, A-4*

County Street intersects Route 6, which funnels downhill to cross the Acushnet River on a swing bridge that sticks open about once a week in the summer, backing up traffic for miles. Fairhaven sprawls along the not-so-distant shore, a community that shares New Bedford's harbor and its maritime roots yet stands apart because its bellicose citizens seceded from pacifist New Bedford over the War of 1812.

Ironically, petroleum wealth transformed the erstwhile whaling port. In 1861, twenty-one-year-old native son Henry Huttleston Rogers sought his fortune in Pennsylvania, where he started his own oil refinery. He eventually served as president of six Standard Oil Trust companies and vice-president of thirteen. Rogers married his high-school sweetheart and built an eighty-five-room summer home at the southern end of town. In 1884, he began funding the buildings that gave Fairhaven a lasting architectural distinction, including the French Gothic **Town Hall** (40 Center Street), the English Gothic **Unitarian Church** (102 Green Street), and **Fairhaven High School** (12 Huttleston Avenue). His greatest gift may have been the **Millicent Library** (45 Center Street; 508-992-5342), an 1893 Italian Renaissance Revival gem named for Rogers's daughter, who had died at age

GUESS WHO'S COMING TO DINNER

At a time when most of America was looking inward, the coastal towns and villages of Cape Cod and Buzzards Bay were surprisingly worldly, even cosmopolitan, forging links with peoples halfway around the world. In addition to its striking architecture and fine books, Fairhaven's Millicent Library also displays memorabilia of the town's unusual connection to Japan. In 1843, Captain William H. Whitfield of the whaleship *John Howland* returned to port with fourteen-year-old Manjiro Nakahama, a young Japanese fisherman who had been shipwrecked and stranded on a remote Pacific island. Fairhaven claims Nakahama as the first Japanese person to live in the United States. He studied English, mathematics, and navigation for three years before returning home. His familiarity with American customs and the English language assisted his rise in governmental circles in the 1860s, when Japan opened to Western trade. Fairhaven has not forgotten him, holding a Manjiro Festival in October of odd-numbered years to celebrate the bond with its sister city, Tosashimizu, Nakahama's birthplace.

seventeen. The exterior ornamentation—molded terra cotta reliefs, tiled roof, and stained-glass windows—hints at the even greater opulence inside.

Beaches begin at the south end of town on Sconticut Neck, at the mouth of the Acushnet River. Follow Main Street south until it becomes Fort Street, and continue to **Fort Phoenix.** A sandy beach with free parking is just south of the fort. Modest Fort Phoenix was built between 1775 and 1777 to protect the harbor, but British forces overran it in 1778. It did manage to ward off a British attack in the War of 1812.

The fort's cannons are fired each year after the July 4 American History Costume Parade, and guides dressed as Revolutionary War soldiers are stationed at the fort during summer and early fall afternoons. The small gun emplacement offers a sweeping view of New Bedford harbor. For even better views, walk or skate along the top of the **Hurricane Barrier,** a ninety-one-hundred-foot stone barrier completed in 1966 by the Army Corps of Engineers to protect the harbor from violent storms. The barrier stands twenty feet above sea level, with a 150-foot opening for ships. Whenever severe weather threatens, gates close off the harbor from high waves and storm surges.

Return through Fairhaven village to Route 6, which hugs the coastline as it winds along the north side of Buzzards Bay. The smell of the ocean fills the air, yet the waters lie tantalizingly just out of sight behind a band of shoreline homes, camps, and the canopies of the swamp maples and the scrubby pines that tolerate the brackish soils. Pause to bid the whaling world adieu in **Mattapoisett,** where Shipyard Park flies the American flag atop the mizzen mast of the *Wanderer,* the last ship built in Mattapoisett (in 1878) and the final New Bedford whaler. Suddenly, just east of Marion, all the signifiers of Cape Cod begin when Route 6 crosses the town line into Wareham, a community of marshy lowlands dissected by innumerable creeks and streams. The road leads on, bearing ever eastward to Provincetown: land's end.

CAPE COD CANAL REGION

"Cape Cod Canal Tunnel Permit No. 1034" reads the bumper sticker on the ne
car in the sluggish crawl of traffic three miles north of the Sagamore Bridge o
Route 3. "Aha!" you think. "Where do I get one of those?"

At almost any tacky souvenir shop. The permit is an inside joke on newbies, lik
sending a tenderfoot out to buy twenty feet of shoreline. Instead of a tunnel, tw
bridges built in the 1930s span the Canal, and summer traffic inevitably clogs o
their approaches. Bridge backups are a fact of Cape Cod life, on the order of sea
gulls, saltwater taffy, and drag queens on in-line skates.

The Canal made Cape Cod an island, rewriting history and geography. Until
was constructed, Cape Cod's upper delimitation was fuzzy. When the regio
became a tourist destination in the late nineteenth century, Cape Cod was said
extend as far north as Plymouth and as far west as New Bedford. It began in th
marshy lowlands where the outfall plain became, as Henry James put it, "mild an
vague and interchangeably familiar with the sea." Once the Canal was finished, th
world was divided between "on Cape" and "off Cape."

This chapter begins on the mainland side, on the approaches to the Bourne ar
Sagamore bridges. On the south side of the Canal begins Cape Cod proper, whe
real-estate prices rise another twenty percent. Most vacationers rush to the wi
dunes of the Outer Cape or the long strands of Nantucket Sound, leaving Ons
and Sagamore, Bourne and Sandwich free from the full frontal assault of tourisr
The villages seem to languish, perhaps even luxuriate, in a quieter era—when vis
tors made family outings to the beach, wandered mossy woodland trails am
scrub pines, and listened to the silky voice of Patti Page crackling on the Atwat
Kent radio in a seaside cottage where the wind blew salt breezes through th
tongue-in-groove walls.

■ CAPE COD CANAL *map page 7, B-3*

Perspective makes all the difference. From shore, Cape Cod's interstice of land ar
sea has a lyric majesty. But an open-water sailor sees treacherous currents and hi
den shoals, where a ship can easily run aground. For the mariner in a hurry, Cap

The blue view from Onset Point on a lazy summer's day.

The Sagamore Bridge across the Cape Cod Canal, high enough for tall ships to clear.

Cod is in the way. It adds 135 miles of tricky passage between Boston and New York. As ocean trade expanded between the two ports in the 1880s, shipwrecks became routine—an average of one vessel every two weeks. Mariners and engineers agreed: better to go through Cape Cod than around it.

It wasn't exactly a new idea, as the **Cape Cod Canal Visitor Center** (Town Marina, Sandwich; 508-833-9678) makes clear. Capt. Myles Standish, the military leader of the Plymouth colony, observed that Wampanoags living on Buzzards Bay would paddle canoes up the Manomet River, portage across to Scusset Creek, and follow it to Cape Cod Bay to trade with the settlers at Plymouth. In 1623 he proposed linking the waterways with a navigable channel to facilitate trade with the native peoples of Buzzards Bay and with the Dutch in what is now New York.

But the Pilgrims had more pressing matters to deal with. The idea of a canal surfaced now and then—the Massachusetts General Court ordered a feasibility study in 1697, and George Washington had the route surveyed during the Revolution. But the Canal remained a pipe dream until the New York financier August Perry Belmont hired William Barclay Parsons to make it happen. Parsons had been an overseer on the Panama Canal project and chief engineer of the newly completed

New York subway system; by contrast, chewing through Cape Cod looked like a piece of cake. Work began in 1909. Crews dynamited glacial boulders that weighed up to a hundred tons, relocated a Bournedale graveyard, and ultimately removed twenty million cubic yards of earth. It was one of the great engineering feats of the era, and the canal, one hundred feet wide and fifteen feet deep (it was dredged to twenty-five feet deep two years later), opened for business on July 29, 1914—seventeen days before the opening of Panama Canal.

Belmont and Parsons had built a better mousetrap, but ships kept getting caught in it. The slender, shallow channel created swift currents, and many captains dreaded the narrow bridge openings. As a result, the canal was a money-loser at first. Recognizing the waterway's strategic importance, the U.S. Army Corps of Engineers bought out Belmont in 1928 and proceeded to make the channel navigable. Between 1935 and 1940, the Corps removed another thirty million cubic yards of earth, to widen the canal to 480 feet and bring the minimum low-tide depth to 32 feet. At the same time, the Corps constructed the Bourne Railroad Bridge and the highway spans at Bourne and Sagamore. By 1940, even the tallest and widest oceangoing vessels could use the new Cape Cod Canal.

They still do. Any ship under its own power can cruise through the Canal without charge. A single Army Corps controller manages the marine traffic, both in the Canal and along the 9.6-mile channel approach through Buzzards Bay. The control room at the **Cape Cod Canal Field Office** (Academy Drive; 508-759-4431) in Buzzards Bay is closed for security reasons, but a full-scale model at the Visitor Center in Sandwich (see above) shows the sensors and tools at the controller's disposal, including five radar screens, twelve closed-circuit video cameras, three wind and tide sensors, and multi-channel VHF-FM radio communications. The Buzzards Bay office has a smaller mockup of the control room as well as a model of the Canal that pinpoints landmarks and some of the best fishing spots.

Anglers use the Cape Cod Canal as avidly as boaters do. Tides average five feet higher on Cape Cod Bay than on Buzzards Bay, and, because there are no locks, the complex tidal currents flush the Canal every eighteen hours, encouraging a diversity of marine life. Some fishing experts claim that the Canal offers the best saltwater fishing, mile for mile, on the Cape, and savvy fishermen know they'll have their best luck on the changing tide. Bluefish and striped bass are the chief quarry, and every fisherman has a different strategy, some preferring cut bait, some live bait, and others artificial lures. Stripers of up to fifty pounds have been caught in the Canal, though most anglers are happy just to land a fish big enough to keep (usually at least twenty-eight inches). Fishing from boats within the Canal is prohibited, but some commercial lobstermen set traps along the rocky banks.

Bicycling is far and away the most popular Canal-side activity, and paved seven-plus-mile bike paths line both shores. The mainland side, however, offers both the longer uninterrupted pedaling and the greater variety of activities. **P&M Cycles** (29 Main Street, Buzzards Bay; 508-759-2830) rents bicycles. Allowing for frequent stops to watch tugboats, pleasure craft, glitzy yachts, and maybe even an ocean liner pull slowly past, the pedal from Buzzards Bay to Scusset Beach takes about an hour. Gulls and terns skim along the water. Every lamppost seems to sport a cormorant, wings spread in the sun to dry.

At the midpoint of the north shore is the seasonal **Herring Run Recreation Center,** a favorite fishing spot, named for the last remnant of the Manomet River, which drains from Great Herring Pond, about a mile north. Before the Canal was dug, this stream yielded five thousand barrels of herring during the spring spawn. Although development decimated the run, it's still a remarkable sight to behold in May, when a half-million alewives make the water roil. Walking trails follow the shrubby banks of the Canal, cross the highway, and mount Bournedale Hill. Remnants of stone pasture walls hint at the farms destroyed in constructing the Canal. The tame woods that have grown up over former pastureland hold a wealth of trees and flowering plants, including the invasive trumpet creeper vine, whose orange blossoms festoon the forest in July. Dozens of wild mushroom varieties sprout from the forest floor in the fall. *Route 6 Scenic Highway, Bournedale; no phone.*

The bike path ends at Scusset Beach Reservation (see Mainland, below), but the trailhead for **Sagamore Hill** appears a few hundred yards to the west. The roughly half-mile walking trail up the seventy-two-foot hill is punctuated with tunnel entrances and concrete Panama mounts for 155-millimeter artillery pieces operated in World War II by the 241st Coastal Artillery Battery C. The emplacement guarded against German submarines—none of which ever entered the canal. A half-century of lush growth has obscured water views from the path. But the brush suddenly parts at the summit and a broad vista spreads out below: houses, salt marsh, the dark sand below the high-tide line on the littoral, and the blue waters of Cape Cod Bay. On a clear day, the spire of Pilgrim Monument in Provincetown pokes up on the horizon.

THE MYSTERY OF BEACH PLUMS

When I pick beach plums I go into the field beside the marsh, or drive out into the woods where I know there will be unadulterated little stands of plum. I'm seldom ahead of the deer, who love the sour purple things. And beach plums are not prolific bearers; they are fussy about the weather during the weeks when they set fruit. So even in a good year I am unlikely to come home with enough to make much of a batch of jelly. Two or three small jars at most.

So where does all the beach plum jelly come from? It is as iconic here as lobsters and lighthouses. It even sits on the counter at the video store. Everyone sells little jars of jelly the color of very good amethysts, capped with a circle of lavender gingham and a label which says "Product of Cape Cod." Is there a secret beach plum forest on an undiscovered, unmapped invisible offshore atoll? The bushes resist cultivation. They hate to be moved. There are no beach plum farms or beach plum cooperatives or beach plum consortiums . . . .

In any event, when the beach plums flower, the air is so sweet and heavy with the scent of bloom that you try hard to remember if there is something which they remind you of, but have forgotten.

—Carol Wasserman, *Swimming at Suppertime*, 2002

Making beach plum jam.

■ MAINLAND *map page 7, B-3*

The mainland side of Route 6 marks the western beginnings of Cape Cod, starting in the Victorian seaside village of Onset (part of the Town of Wareham), skimming along the north shore of the Canal, then giving way to a local road to connect to the dunes of Scusset Beach on Cape Cod Bay.

Cruises on Cape Cod Canal sail out of **Onset,** a tranquil resort that blossomed when the train was extended from Boston in the mid-nineteenth century. In the 1880s, Onset hosted the largest summer community of Spiritualists on the East Coast—one of many places in New England where religious proselytizing and sea-side frolic proved utterly compatible. When automobile touring became wide-spread, vacationers chose to bypass Onset, leaving the village to flourish in obscurity, its miles of sandy beaches a local secret.

Onset sits at the head of a pocket bay just north of the entrance to the Canal, a geography that produces long beaches of powdery sand but little surf, and rich oys-ter beds that can be harvested in waders. A plaque on Onset Bluffs memorializes

Exploring Onset Bay, by kayak...

the Wampanoags, who used Onset Bay as a summer fishing grounds for generations. The village green, planted on a promontory, is crowned with a Victorian bandstand, site of summer concerts and dramatic performances.

The land falls from the bluff down to Town Pier, where public beaches spread east and west of the central parking lot and wharf. The beaches are anchored by **Kenny's Salt Water Taffy** (Town Pier; 508-295-8828), established in 1895. The staff here still pulls taffy in an endless variety of flavors and sells other classic summer foods: hot dogs, fried-fish sandwiches, burgers, and soft-serve ice cream.

From the calm waters of Onset Bay, kayakers can explore about sixty-five miles of coves and inlets. **Onset Kayak & Canoe** (Town Pier and Onset Avenue East; 508-291-1333) rents single and double sea kayaks. Apart from the buoy-marked navigation channels, the waters are shallow and powerboats move slowly. Geese and ducks share the shoreline salt marshes with gulls, terns, and sandpipers. Narrated **Cape Cod Canal Cruises** (508-295-3883) depart from Town Pier, along with fishing charters and, on the *Onset Chief II* (508-759-7100), one or two whale-watching trips each week.

...and by tour boat.

Onset's ocean-contour street, Onset Avenue, curves east to meet Route 6 at the mouth of Buttermilk Bay. The highway toward Provincetown crosses a short drawbridge into the village of **Buzzards Bay** (technically part of the Town of Bourne), where dealers in antiques, collectibles, and castoffs largely occupy the downtown strip of low-rise older buildings. The village's sole traffic light marks the turn-off to Academy Drive, which leads to the head of the Cape Cod Canal. Along the road, behind the old railroad station turned visitors center, is Buzzards Bay Park, where the annual Bourne Scallop Festival is held in early September. The Cape Cod Canal Bicycle Trail begins behind the park in the shadow of the **Buzzards Bay Railroad Bridge.**

Built by the Army Corps of Engineers in 1935 to replace an old drawbridge, this dramatic span is among a handful of vertical-lift bridges still operating. The soaring open-steel construction recalls the can-do era of engineering; the stainless-steel balls atop the decorative tower cones are its sole ornament, but they're effective. Two 1,100-ton counterweights balance the 544-foot center lift span, enabling the controller to raise and lower it in just two and a half minutes with a pair of small electric motors. Alas, regular passenger trains to Cape Cod are extinct, so this glory of engineering is pressed into service on an irregular schedule (usually early morning and again around 6 P.M.) to accommodate the "trash train" as it hauls Cape Cod's garbage to a mainland incinerator.

Main Street of Buzzards Bay continues as an old-fashioned strip of family restaurants, gas stations, and small lodgings until the Bourne traffic circle—which offers the choice of crossing the Canal on Route 28, on the Bourne Bridge, or continuing along the Canal's north shore. Immediately east of the traffic circle, **Bourne Scenic Park** (508-759-7873) is a combination picnicking and camping facility in the woods along the Cape Cod Canal. Founded in 1951, the park has 465 campsites, and its old-fashioned facilities are particularly tent-friendly. Day-use passes are available.

Route 6 keeps rolling eastward until it feeds into the Sagamore traffic circle, a bottleneck par excellence below the arch of the Sagamore Bridge. While Route 6 doglegs over the bridge to become the Mid-Cape Highway, a local road continues east for four miles to the surf-pounded **Scusset Beach Reservation.** Beachgoers often stop to watch the anglers casting from the huge granite blocks of the breakwater—the last remnant of Belmont's 1914 canal—or from the fishing pier, both accessible from the parking lot. The popular swimming beach adjoins an equally popular state-run campground (877-422-6762). The ninety-eight sites, with electric hookups and shared water connections, are best suited to trailers or RVs.

THE CAPE COD HOUSE

Apart from a penchant for eating codfish and corn bread, the most lasting contribution of the first European settlers might be the colloquial architecture of the Cape Cod house, called simply a Cape in abbreviated parlance. You don't have to stick to historic districts to find the little houses, first erected in Plymouth but soon spreading all across Cape Cod. The Cape is ubiquitous, as likely to appear in a new subdivision as along a country lane.

The English workman's cottage evolved to suit Cape Cod's sandy soils, readily available species of lumber, and strong winds. The Cape hunkers close to its cellar hole, battened down with shingles of white cedar bleached silver in the salt air, flinging the steep pitch of its roof toward the sky to let snowfall and gull-dropped clams slide off with equal ease.

The original Cape was the "half" Cape—its front door and chimney on one end, with rooms sporting two windows off to the other side. As family fortunes grew, many half Capes became "full" or "double" Capes, with another wing of rooms completing the symmetry: two windows, door, two windows. Full Capes continued to evolve, often by adding a story, to become the prototype "Colonial" house. Some owners added a second story on the front but carried the eaves on the back to the first-floor level, creating the saltbox, so called for its resemblance to the packaging in which salt was once sold.

Capes tend to be covered in shingles on every wall except the front, which, by convention, faces the world with clapboards. This inconsistency dates to rulings by the Plymouth founding fathers. Fearing that newcomers would build ostentatious homes unfitting to the Pilgrims' pious austerity, they outlawed clapboards on any surface but the front. It was Cape Cod's first, but by no means last, aesthetic zoning law.

■ ON CAPE *map page 7, B-3*

Drivers headed to Cape Cod sometimes play "bridge roulette," trying to guess whether the Bourne or the Sagamore bridge might have the shorter traffic backup. Given that 125,000 vehicles cross the spans daily in high season, neither provides smooth sailing. As a general rule, the Sagamore Bridge is best for drivers headed to any destination reached by the Mid-Cape Highway, while the Bourne Bridge makes more sense for travelers headed to the Bourne and Falmouth villages along Route 28 on Buzzards Bay, or to Woods Hole to catch the ferry to Martha's Vineyard. Either

route is a passage as much psychological as geographic. "It is roughly an hour from Boston to Cape Cod," Paul Theroux once wrote, "but once I have crossed the Sagamore Bridge everything is different. It is then that summer begins."

The **Town of Bourne,** which includes Buzzards Bay and Bournedale on the north side of Cape Cod Canal, is broken into at least three seaside villages along the coves and inlets south of the Canal. From Bourne bridge, the south end of the Trowbridge Road heads west to connect to Shore Road, the unofficial main street of Bourne's resort towns. Follow the signs at Perry Avenue to visit the **Aptucxet Trading Post Museum.** When the Pilgrims bought out their English backers in 1626, they secured exclusive trading rights with the region's native peoples. They also saw great opportunities for trade with the New Amsterdam Dutch and built a trading post at the mouth of the Manomet River. A replica was constructed in the 1920s on the original foundation. Here the Dutch, English, and Wampanoags traded, using polished bits of quahog shells, called wampum, as their common currency. *24 Aptucxet Road, Bourne Village; 508-759-9487. Open May–mid-Oct.*

Settled in 1640, Bourne was called Monument until it split from the town of Sandwich in 1884; the original moniker persists in the stretch south of Aptucxet called **Monument Beach,** reached by Emmons Road off Shore Road. The marina accommodates pleasure craft of all sizes and forms, and the small sandy beach is a favorite of families with young children. The water is very shallow, even at high tide, and the beach is well sheltered from wave action. Those same conditions also make Monument Beach an outstanding area to dig clams.

Sedate Route 6A runs along the south side of the Cape Cod Canal, connecting Bourne Village to the crossroads of Sagamore and the more substantial community of **Sandwich,** the oldest town on Cape Cod. The first English settlers, a group of "ten men from Saugus" (now Lynn, Massachusetts) under the leadership of Edmund Freeman, arrived in 1637. The attraction of Sandwich was simple. Here the salt marshes meet the sea, and salt hay grows in abundance. This was of no small concern to the Pilgrims, who could barely clear forest fast enough to plant vegetable and grain crops, let alone grow enough hay for their animals. Moreover, the site had adequate timber a short distance inland, a stream with a substantial herring run, and a spot where another stream could be dammed to provide water power for a gristmill.

A cooling leap from the planked boardwalk in Sandwich.

The historic village center, which lies between Route 6A and Main Street (Route 130), juxtaposes the symbols of commerce in this world with the hopes for the hereafter in a compact district easily explored on foot. Shawme Pond marks the heart of the village. The first gristmill was constructed here in 1637; the current **Dexter Grist Mill** (Town Hall Square; 508-888-4910) is a 1961 restoration of a mill constructed on the site in 1654. With a fifty-four-inch French millstone, it remains operational, and is open daily in the summer, with more limited hours in the fall.

The setting is irrepressibly picturesque. Mallard ducks and Canada geese paddle around the glassy surface of Shawme Pond. Travelers are welcome to fill their bottles at a free-flowing artesian spring, Sandwich's original water source, between the mill and Town Hall.

The oldest house in the village proper is the equally picturesque **Hoxie House,** sometimes called the oldest house on Cape Cod—based on the discovery of the date 1637 on one of the chimney bricks and on the frequent repetition of the claim until it acquired the mantle of fact. Best modern estimates suggest the house was built in 1675. The slope-roofed saltbox, covered in shimmering silver shingles, was inhabited until the mid-twentieth century despite its having no electricity, central heat, or plumbing. Now a museum, the interior shows the house as it was when the Reverend John Smith, his wife, and their thirteen children lived here in the 1680s. Call for hours. *18 Water Street; 508-888-1173.*

Sandwich's church was gathered in 1638, allowing for the incorporation of the town the following year. The successor congregation to those initial worshippers is the **First Church of Christ,** which meets in one of the town's most architecturally distinctive buildings. The Greek Revival church was built in 1847 by the architect Isaac Melvin of Cambridge, who used designs by Christopher Wren—hence the misleading identification of the building as a Christopher Wren church. The bas-relief columns on the front demonstrate proper decorum in a church with Calvinist roots, but the conical steeple supported on eight fully rounded and decorated Corinthian columns reveals an inimitably nineteenth-century pride of primacy. *136 Main Street; 508-888-0434.*

Sandwich recalls one of its best-loved native sons at the **Thornton W. Burgess Museum.** Burgess, who was born on School Street in 1874 but left town after he graduated from Sandwich High School, published 171 books of nature stories for

The Aptucxet Trading Post Museum is a replica of what could be called the New World's first shopping mall.

HOT FISH

On a wall of the closed-in woodshed opening off the kitchen, hung one above another, were sticks of smoked herring, preferably those smoked by the Mashpee Indians. Each stick held a dozen fish, the stick thrust through the gills. Grandfather would lift the back covers of the stove, lay the fish on top of the oven, and replace the covers. With the draft of the stove open, most of the smell went up the chimney. When the skin had burned off and tails and heads had become charred, the fish were ready to take out, scrape and serve. A Mashpee smoked herring, especially one plump with roe, and good bread and butter—what a breakfast!

—Thornton W. Burgess, *Now I Remember*, 1960

children. The house the museum occupies, which was owned by Burgess's Aunt Arabella, sits adjacent to Shawme Pond, and it's not much of a leap to see the backyard as the playground of Mrs. Snapper the Turtle, Blacky the Crow, Honker the Goose, Sharpshin the Hawk, and Chatterer the Red Squirrel. The museum's exhibits emphasize Burgess's work as a proto-environmentalist and nature educator. *4 Water Street; 508-888-4668. Open Apr.–Oct.*

Although Burgess's stories show a naturalist's vision of Sandwich, he grew up during the peak of the town's stint as an industrial center. The same salt hay and ready timber that attracted the first settlers also drew the industrialist who would make the town's name synonymous with glass manufacturing. On a hunting and fishing vacation, Deming Jarves was impressed by Sandwich's location, only fifty miles by water from Boston. He saw in the nearby forests a potential source of fuel and of marsh hay for the packing of his fragile wares; he also noted the ready availability of sand. Jarves instructed an agent to buy up land secretly from area farmers. In 1825, he founded a small factory that was incorporated in 1826 as the Boston & Sandwich Glass Company. Not until he fired up his furnaces, on July 4, 1825, did he discover that Sandwich sand contained so much iron oxide that it was useless for making fine, clear glass, and so he had to ship in sand from as far away as Florida and New Jersey. Still, by the middle of the nineteenth century he had built Boston & Sandwich into one of the country's largest glass factories, employing five hundred workers. In a single generation, he transformed Sandwich from a farming community into an industrial center. The Boston & Sandwich Glass

The brick-encased furnace of the Sandwich Glass Museum.

Company closed in 1888, after producing $30 million worth of glassware, but other firms continued making glass in Sandwich until the 1920s.

Boston & Sandwich produced blown, mold-blown, and pressed glassware. Jarves actively pursued pressed-glass technology, winning a series of patents. His enthusiasm for the less skill-intensive technique did not endear him to his artisans. "The glassblowers," he wrote, "on discovery that I had succeeded in pressing a piece of glass, were so enraged for fear their business would be ruined by the discovery, that my life was threatened, and I was compelled to hide for six weeks before I dared venture into the street or in the glass house, and for more than six months there was danger of personal violence should I venture in the street after nightfall."

But pressed glass became Sandwich's signature, avidly sought by collectors in the first half of the twentieth century. One highlight of the collections at the **Sandwich Glass Museum** is the array of more than eight hundred cup plates, one of the most collectible forms of pressed glass. Exhibits survey glass production in Sandwich, including that of some of the small art-glass studios. In 2003, the museum fired up a glass furnace to demonstrate techniques of forming, blowing,

(following pages) The Sperm Whale in a Flurry (1852), by Nathaniel Currier.

and pressing glass. The new brick chimney, nestled among the village church steeples, re-creates a skyline element missing for more than a century. The gift shop sells reproductions of historic Sandwich glass as well as contemporary glass by artisans from Cape Cod and around the country. The museum's Cape Cod Glass Show & Sale in September is a major draw for serious collectors. *129 Main Street; 508-888-0251. Open Feb.–Dec. (days and hours vary).*

Less than a mile from the village center, down Grove Street, the hundred-acre **Heritage Museums & Gardens** marries Cape Cod's fascination with antiques with its veneration of horticulture. Charles Owen Dexter, a New Bedford textile merchant, purchased the property in 1921 and spent the next twenty-two years hybridizing rhododendrons. His breeding program developed extremely resilient plants that bloom in brilliant colors. He produced thousands of seedlings each year and planted many of them on his estate of glacial hillocks and sudden dells, where some specimens now tower far above visitors' heads. The famous collection blooms in a profusion of electric pinks, reds, purples, and even yellows from the last week of May through the first two weeks of June, only to be followed by a similarly flashy display of more than fifteen thousand hybrid daylilies in July and August. More than ten thousand labeled flowers and shrubs line the trails through the rolling woodlands. The winter landscape is more subtle—shades of brown and tan, a few red berries, and fluffs of snow nestling in the prickly cups of holly leaves.

Josiah K. Lilly III and his wife, Josephine, bought the Dexter estate in 1967 and opened it to the public in 1969. An heir to the Eli Lilly pharmaceutical fortune, Lilly wanted to display his father's collections of military miniatures and firearms as well as his own collection of antique automobiles, and so he built several structures modeled on marvels of Northeast rustic architecture.

The **Antique Automobile Museum** resembles the round Shaker barn in Hancock Village, in western Massachusetts, but instead of cows it houses thirty-four perfectly restored automobiles on two levels. Visitors can climb up and sit in a 1915 Model T Ford, and a staff member will even offer to snap a photo, but otherwise all exhibits are hands-off. Lilly's cars rank among some of the most beautiful ever made: a green and yellow 1930 Duesenberg Model J Derham Tourster owned by Gary Cooper, a black and chrome 1932 Auburn Boattail Speedster, a silver 1962 Corvette, a yellow 1937 Cord 812 Phaeton, and a royal blue 1922 Rolls Royce Silver Ghost Pall Mall Phaeton built in Springfield, Massachusetts.

The complex's **American History Museum,** constructed of hand-hewn timbers, is modeled on a Revolutionary War–era building in New Windsor, New York. Among the permanent exhibits are antique firearms (including an 1883 Freund-Sharps .45-caliber rifle that belonged to Buffalo Bill Cody) and the military miniatures commissioned by Lilly's father to represent regiments from Colonial times to the Spanish-American War. The "Baseball by the Beach" exhibition tells the story of the Cape Cod Baseball League and its Hall of Fame.

The **Art Museum** mounts two exhibitions a year from the permanent collections, which include extensive holdings of Currier & Ives lithographs, many of unusual whaling scenes. The folk-art gallery fairly bristles with shop signs, decoys, cigar-store Indians, and carved sailors. Glass cases contain exceptional examples of scrimshaw and Nantucket Lightship basketry. Perhaps the museum's most remarkable holding is a functioning 1912 carousel manufactured by the Charles I. D. Looff Company of East Providence, Rhode Island, and displayed in its own glassed-in pavilion. This exuberant example of the Looff carvers at the height of their powers is best appreciated in a whirling ride astride the black-painted lead horse, Thunder.

The grounds also hold **Old East Mill,** built in 1800 in Orleans and moved to the museum in 1968. When the wind reached twenty miles an hour, the mill could grind three bushels of corn, rye, barley, or salt per hour. Old East Mill closed down in 1889, because consumers found it cheaper to purchase Western grain that had already been ground. *Heritage Museums and Gardens, 67 Grove Street; 508-888-3300.*

Route 6A east of Sandwich Village leads past the **State Fish Hatchery** (Main Street and Route 6A; 508-888-0008), where the state raises a half-million trout each year to stock ponds and streams, to the **Green Briar Nature Center and Jam Kitchen** (6 Discovery Hill Road; 508-888-6870). Operated by the same society that runs the Thornton W. Burgess Museum in the village, the nature center sits on the shores of Smiling Pool, adjacent to the Briar Patch of Burgess's stories. Used throughout the year for environmental education, Green Briar has natural history exhibits and a wildflower garden. Its trails wind through a fifty-seven-acre conservation area. The town has acquired an additional hundred-sixty-six acres behind the center. Graceful beeches line the shore of a pond, and swamp blueberries and Norwegian maples provide an extraordinary flare of color during fall foliage. Dense briar thickets provide cover and food for wildlife.

(following pages) A bike excursion along Cape Cod Canal at Scusset Beach, Sandwich.

Birds and field mice aren't the only creatures who like bramble berries, and the jam kitchen evokes an era when every Cape Cod road was lined with farm stands where ladies sold homemade beach-plum jelly. Ida Putnam began making jams and jellies in 1903, and opened a tea room at the Green Briar property that Burgess often visited while he was growing up. He sent this note of appreciation to Putnam in 1939: "It is a wondrous thing to sweeten the world which is in a jam and needs preserving." The Burgess Society continues to operate the jam kitchen, selling jams, jellies, preserves, and chutneys and offering jam-making classes for adults and families. The center is open daily from April through December, with more limited hours in the winter.

But Sandwich, like all of Cape Cod, ultimately returns to the shore. The broad and winding marshes of Scorton, Old Harbor, Mill, and Factory Creeks still wave with the high grasses of salt hay that first drew Edmund Freeman and the other nine men of Saugus. Tides and currents conspire to seal the marshes from the sea

STUCK IN THE MUCK

I paddled into the great marshes of Barnstable Harbor with the laughable idea—taken directly from a topographic map—of poking all the way through a winding slough called the Scorton Creek to Scorton Harbor over in Sandwich. I knew beforehand that it was an unlikely proposition; Scorton Creek is only a foot wide and sharply winding when it passes under West Main Street (Route 6) at the town line. My kayak, on the other hand, is seventeen feet long, two feet wide in the middle, and inflexible. But as a guiding principle, Scorton Creek served my purpose: according to the best estimates of my global positioning system and myself, it got me six winding miles up into the grass, up into the mud. Up finally to my knees in the muck trying to see over enough grass to figure out where in creation I was. Maps will tempt you to madness.

At the moment the prickly mud oozed over the tops of my water shoes and down around my ankles I was glad not to be one of those earliest Europeans attracted down to the Cape by the chance to harvest salt hay from this expanse. I wondered who among them it was that thought of putting snowshoes on horses and people. Who among them said it would never work, and who ate his words when the wagons of hay rolled home.

—Paul Schneider, *The Enduring Shore*, 2000

Collecting marsh specimens from the Sandwich Boardwalk.

with towering dunes that can assume a Saharan majesty. These barrier beaches at once protect the swampy marshes from storm surges and offer miles of sand for summer gambols. Most of the shore frontage in Sandwich is private, and the lack of public parking makes the beaches de facto private as well. The major exception, however, couldn't be a more pleasant beach or have a more beautiful approach: **Town Beach,** east of the Town Marina and the Cape Cod Canal Visitor Center, has its own parking lot at the end of Town Neck Road, where a fee is extracted from nonresidents during July and August.

The better access, however, is from the **Sandwich Boardwalk.** Beginning at another pay lot at the end of Jarves and Harbor Streets, this thousand-foot walkway crosses Mill Creek and its surrounding marshes, where redwing blackbirds make their cheeky calls from tall reeds at the marsh's edge and the waters skitter with small crabs and minnows. Saltmeadow cordgrass covers the land, its ropy strands bending into the mud, and the view from the boardwalk looks downright primeval. Such sludge and muck was where life began. The planked walkway angles up to the crest of the dunes to provide an ecologically sound passage to the sandy beach. At the top, the sudden view of Cape Cod Bay and the undulating stretch of sand marks an instant passage into a quintessential Cape Cod experience, as if the horizon had been pushed back to make way for summer.

KING'S HIGHWAY

The road signposted today as the King's Highway has a long history. Wampanoags established a trail between their villages on the Cape Cod Bay shore; colonists found it useful for their wagons. Around 1660, they designated it the King's Road, though the name fell into disuse after the Revolution. The state legislature stirred up old resentments in 1920, when it slapped the name King's Highway on the by then paved thoroughfare. Cape towns took umbrage at what they considered the state's historical revisionism, and the new road signs began to disappear, one by one. Locals simply referred to the road as the Cape highway. When the official Mid-Cape Highway was built in the 1950s, the shore route was demoted to footnote status as Route 6A.

But the King's Highway nomenclature gradually gained respectability, and today no one seems outraged enough to rip down the road signs. In fact, the name has a felicitous ring, suggesting something of this quieter shore of Cape Cod, where vast salt marshes and shallow harbors present a gentle topography filled with more nuance than drama. So many seventeenth- and eighteenth-century buildings dot the settled landscape that few bother to announce their date of construction. Majestic sea captains' mansions punctuate a roadside of small Capes and boxier Colonials, where white picket fences and stone walls enforce the boundaries between neighbors, and high-spired white churches announce the centers of villages past and present. Wherever a church stands (or used to stand), a cemetery is planted nearby. Bits of the past are always for sale at the antiques dealers, who line the roadside with the profligacy of daisy fleabane. This sedate, contemplative side of the Cape has proved especially amenable to potters, glassblowers, and other artisans, many of whom sell their goods at their studios.

Properly speaking, the old King's Road stretched from Bourne village to Provincetown. In modern usage, the King's Highway usually refers to Route 6A from Sandwich to the Orleans traffic circle. This chapter deals with the village communities of the Bay shore along Route 6A from Barnstable east through Brewster, where an almost continuous line of sandy beaches is known for its gentle waves, long flats at low tide, and water that's up to four degrees warmer than on the Cape's Atlantic beaches.

Time-worn items at an antiques shop on the King's Highway.

■ **BARNSTABLE** *map page 7, C-4*

Barnstable begins in Sandwich, or at least Sandy Neck Road does—just two-tenths of a mile west of the town line. The nondescript road is the sole vehicular access to **Sandy Neck,** a six-mile-long barrier beach peninsula of wave-like dunes backed by marshlands and pockets of maritime forest. The Wampanoags called the vast marshland of Sandy Neck and the adjoining mainland shore Moskeehtuckqut, which translates as "Great Marshes." The area is so extensive that it's hard to pin down. Various sources calculate it as covering three thousand, five thousand, or eight thousand acres—"Great" by any count. As Cape Cod wags are fond of pointing out, somehow the Pilgrims never got around to changing the name to Grassy Views, Goose Vistas, Duck Hollow, or some other development-friendly moniker. Hence the region remains known as the Great Marshes to this day, and peacefully condo-free.

The north-facing strand of **Sandy Neck Beach** is probably the most popular swimming beach on the bicep portion of the Cape's arm, and its huge parking lot often fills early on a summer's day. Because the Neck is so stable (it has grown slowly eastward over the last few thousand years rather than eroding away), off-road vehicles are permitted in a narrow zone on the outer beach, adding to the human throng in fine weather.

No vehicles are allowed on the **Marsh Trail,** Sandy Neck's road less traveled. The packed-sand lane on the back side of the dunes follows the interstice of marsh and dune the full length of the Neck, although the east end of the point is private and the last mile of the trail is restricted to property owners. It departs from the town ranger station on Sandy Neck Road, about half a mile before the beach parking lot.

Some faint traces of human use persist along the Marsh Trail. Archaeologists point to small shell middens as evidence of seasonal shellfishing by the Wampanoags. On occasion, winds reveal the tips of whale bones in the sands, a testament to the era when try-yards extracted blubber from whale carcasses. Even scrap metal from World War II bombing practice sometimes surfaces. But the Great Marshes have healed themselves swiftly since the state awarded them protected status in 1978. Where hunters once bagged geese and ducks by the thousands (some hunting is still permitted), more than eighty species of songbirds, shorebirds, and waterfowl abound. In midsummer, the Marsh Trail can compete with the boomboxes on the beach, as the avian population emits a cacophony of grunts, rasps, whistles, trills, and chortles.

Salute to a Salt Marsh

The marsh is one of the most receptive environments on earth. It is always open to the sky and all the winds and weather that flow in and recede like tides in endlessly recurring motion. In its own, self-generating body it accommodates innumerable forms of life all responding to that common sea. The centuries pass, and its patience deepens. Even in winter when it looks dark, brindled in color like a day that is as dark as evening, it never sleeps.

All the passing winters vary in their temper. Last year the ditches looked snow-blind, covered with ice, for many weeks. This year, they have been relatively free of it. As spring begins to come on, the minnows dart in the ditches, and at the right time, the fiddler crabs emerge from their burrows. The surface waters dance like a colt frisking in a meadow. The new light is an invitation to that dance and ritual that accompanies the freedom to be. And the male redwing lifts its epaulettes in a gesture of praise. We can thank the marsh for its transformations, and above all, for its constancy.

—John Hay, "The Way to the Salt Marsh," 1998

Sandy Neck is also the northernmost breeding range of the diamondback terrapin turtle. Now endangered in this habitat (though rebounding), the terrapin was once so prized as a soup base that turtle hunters in the Great Marshes harvested ten thousand a week to ship to eager restaurateurs. Throughout the summer, turtles crawl out of the marshes, cross Marsh Trail, and climb onto the dunes to lay their eggs. The tiny hatchlings reverse the route, somehow knowing to seek the swamp when they poke through their rubbery shells. The turtles are easily startled and disoriented, and should be observed only at a distance.

The dunes along the north side of the trail have been stable for so long that beach plum and beach grass have given way in places to pockets of maritime forest, which provide shelter and sustenance to a substantial deer population. At the end of the public trail, take an overland cut north to the open beach for a pleasant return hike.

Even drive-by tourists get a sense of the extent of the Great Marshes, which wrap around the western end of Barnstable harbor and extend along the north side of Route 6A for another five miles. Roadside growth obscures parts of the

marshes, but when a clear vista opens up, the great salt prairie is an impressive sight. Distant clumps of maritime forest stand amid the marshes like islands, and raptors circle low, pausing to roost in the trees.

Barnstable was incorporated in 1639 as one of the four original Cape Cod settlements. With the only deep-water harbor along this coast, it became a major shipping port for both the Boston packet trade (coastal mail and cargo vessels) and for overseas vessels in the nineteenth century. As the most centralized and prosperous town on Cape Cod, it was a natural as the shire town for Barnstable County, which includes all of mainland Cape Cod.

A handful of old buildings marks the village of **West Barnstable,** just off the King's Highway on Route 149. The principal point of interest is the 1717 **West Parish Meetinghouse** (2049 Meetinghouse Way, Route 149; 508-362-4445), often called the Rooster Church for its five-and-a-half-foot-wide gilded rooster weathervane, cast in England in 1723. The weathervane even upstages the half-ton Paul Revere bell in the boxy bell tower. The church traces itself back to the Reverend John Lothrup's Congregational Church, established in London in 1616, and hence claims to be the oldest Congregational church in the western hemisphere. Lothrup must have been a charismatic preacher. Many of his parishioners followed when he emigrated to Massachusetts in 1634 and again when he uprooted from Scituate to Barnstable five years later.

Barnstable seems to have a genuine enthusiasm for its past, which consists principally of centuries of normal living rather than any memorable events. On the western outskirts of Barnstable village, the **Olde Colonial Courthouse** now serves as home base for Tales of Cape Cod, a group formed in 1949 to collect oral history and folklore. The organization opens the courthouse for lectures and special events and produces a Cape folklore show that airs twice weekly on C3TV, the local cable-access channel. *Rendezvous Lane and Route 6A, Barnstable Village; 508-362-8927.*

Various strands of history entwine at the **Sturgis Library,** named for William Sturgis, a Barnstable sea captain who was among the first Americans to engage in the Pacific Northwest fur trade. The Henry Crocker Kittredge Maritime History Collection honors the author of the definitive *Cape Cod: Its History and Its People* (1930), as well as of *Shipmasters of Cape Cod* (1935), a celebration of the region's iconic sea captains. Ordinary folk aren't forgotten, either: the library is noted for its deep genealogy and local-history collections, open to anyone tracing family roots.

Summer construction on the beach along the King's Highway.

The front portion of the library—the house built around 1645 for the Reverend John Lothrup, who served as minister of Barnstable from 1639 to 1653, and is buried west of town in the cemetery named for him—is one of the oldest standing structures on Cape Cod. The Tuesday and Saturday book sale is held in what must have been the main public room of Lothrup's house, where the very width of the pumpkin-pine floor planks testifies to the age of the building. The sale is a perfect place to pick up a bag of reading material for the beach. *Route 6A, Barnstable Village; 508-362-6636.*

High on a hill overlooking the harbor, the **Barnstable County Court House,** built of solid granite in 1832, is a magisterial public edifice that looks entirely out of place in the quiet seaside town that Barnstable Village has become. There may be more stone in the building than in all the township's land. During the War of 1812, teams of oxen hauled the cannons in front to Barnstable to defend the town's extensive saltworks from British depredation. Though the British never showed up, the cannons remain. *Route 6A.*

Drivers pass so quickly through the village center they often think they've missed it. Indeed, part of the appeal of Barnstable is that it seems hardly there. The author Kurt Vonnegut lived near the courthouse for twenty years, and, despite the lack of adult company, stuck it out because it seemed such a safe place to raise a family. "I had a large house with lots of kids in it—three of my own and three adopted," he has written. "And Cape Cod was a padded cell where children couldn't possibly hurt themselves when they were growing up."

A true appreciation of Barnstable requires a visit to its harbor, down Mill Way. The large foreign trade ships don't put in here these days, but the channel remains deep enough to accommodate excursion vessels. **Hyannis Whale Watcher Cruises** (Mill Way Marina, Barnstable Village; 508-362-6088 or 800-287-0734) offers the only whale-spotting cruises from the mid-Cape, using high-speed vessels to converge on Stellwagen Bank with boats from Provincetown and Cape Ann. A fleet of sportfishing vessels docks at the marina as well, each offering a variety of trips: laid-back mackerel or flounder fishing, adrenaline-pumping angling for bluefin tuna, or trolling for muscular striped bass and bluefish (a streaky pursuit: a lot will bite in a short time, and then, suddenly, none). At **Mill Way Fish & Lobster** (275 Mill Way, Barnstable; 508-362-2760), the chef-owner, who trained at the Culinary Institute of America, has transformed a basic clam shack and seafood market into a gourmet destination. Locals have been known to spread a tablecloth on a wooden picnic table on the deck and lay out china and crystal for a high-style feast.

It tastes better than it looks: Mill Way Fish & Lobster, Barnstable.

East of the harbor, the **Donald G. Trayser Memorial Museum** occupies a striking red-brick hilltop building constructed as the U.S. Customs House in 1856, when Barnstable was a significant port of entry. After trade diminished, the building served as the post office from 1913 to 1959. Now it houses the collections of the Barnstable Historical Society. Named for a local historian often remembered for his studies of grisly Cape Cod murders, the museum displays what might have been the pride of a hundred attics—ship models, China trade artifacts, farm tools, paintings, and Native American objects. *Route 6A, Barnstable; 508-362-2092. Open mid-June–mid-Oct.*

About a mile east of Barnstable Village, the **Cape Cod Art Association** (Route 6A, Barnstable; 508-362-2909) supplies something of a preview of the intense visual-arts activity on the Outer Cape. The small facility has four exhibition galleries and offers drawing and painting classes with an emphasis on realistic landscape and portraiture. On the east end of Barnstable, the village of Cummaquid has improbably assumed the Wampanoag name for the Sandy Neck peninsula. Largely residential, it's home to the **Cummaquid Golf Course** (Marstons Lane, Cummaquid; 508-362-2022), which, dating from 1895, claims to be the Cape's first private golf club.

■ **YARMOUTHPORT** *map page 7, C-4*

The other villages of Yarmouth may contain more of the town's population than quiet, tidy Yarmouthport, but they would be hard-pressed to compete for finest domestic architecture. Yarmouthport is still proud of the fact that fifty sea captains, active or retired, lived in town at the same time in the late nineteenth century, and their homes remain an attraction. At least four of the sprawling properties serve as hostelries, doing business as the Village Inn, the Wedgewood Inn, the Liberty Hill Inn, and the One Centre Street Inn.

On the way into town from Barnstable, **Hallet's Store & Museum** records the progression from necessity to tourist trap to bona fide attraction. Built in 1889 as a drugstore, Hallet's long ago shifted its primary trade to its breakfast and lunch counter and its shelves of souvenirs. Relics of the drugstore days are said to be housed in the upstairs museum—open, apparently, by whim. But the store itself, open from April through November, is worth a stop anyway. You can enjoy an ice-cream soda at the fine old marble soda fountain, or pick up a mixed four-pack of the store's own birch beer, cream soda, sarsaparilla, and raspberry lime rickey. *139 Hallet Street, at Route 6A; 508-362-3362.*

The two house museums on the town common couldn't be more different. The **Edward Gorey House** puts on display a shy and quirky individual who became a cult artist. The author of illustrated, often rhyming, and always bizarre books such as *The Gashlycrumb Tinies, The Doubtful Guest,* and *The Hapless Child,* Edward St. John Gorey gained his broadest fame for the animation that opens the PBS *Mystery* series. While growing up, Gorey summered with cousins in Barnstable, and he chose to spend the last fourteen years of his life with a gaggle of cats in this two-hundred-year-old house, which has become a museum displaying Gorey memorabilia, his books and Broadway set designs, and information about his favorite animal-rights charities. *8 Strawberry Lane, Yarmouthport; 508-362-3909. Open Mar.–Jan.*

The other museum on the common, the **Captain Bangs Hallet House,** stands in for an era. The original house was built in 1740 and vastly expanded a century later. When Capt. Bangs Hallet retired from the China trade in 1863, he bought it from another deep-water captain, Allen H. Knowles. The guided tours (from Thursday through Sunday between June and mid-October) emphasize the wealth accreted in Yarmouthport from far-flung world trade.

GOREY TALES

E was for Edward who lived on the lane
(Strawberry, it's said—he did not speak its name).
With masterful pen filled with black ink he drew
Macabre little stories and odd vignettes too.
He pictured the auk and drew Eliot's cats,
Elephants, gravestones, detectives, and bats.
The house still recalls old Edward St. John,
Who lived fourteen years there before he passed on.
Each morning, ensconced at Jack's Outback, he'd dream
Over Wheaties, strawberries, and a bowl of whipped cream.
His ode to Jack's toe is still there on the wall,
And his skewed way of seeing the world got to all
Of the people in Yarmouthport. Each has a story
To tell you of some strange encounter with Gorey.
His ashes were scattered at one of the beaches,
But his spirit lurks on in the shadowy reaches
Of Parnassus Books, where it squats on the floor,
Reading and chuckling and reading some more.

The **Edward Gorey House** is open year-round (though not daily, so call ahead) except February. **Jack's Outback** (Route 6A, Yarmouthport; 508-362-6690) is open daily for breakfast and lunch. **Parnassus Book Service** (Route 6A, Yarmouthport; 508-362-6420) remains a bibliophile's heaven, where readers can paw through thousands of books old and new.

— P.H. & D.L.

A one-and-a-half-mile nature trail through woodlands and meadows is open from dawn to dusk and is very popular with dog owners. Along the trail are Kelly Chapel, a small nineteenth-century Quaker chapel moved here from South Yarmouth, and Hallet's Blacksmith Shop, relocated from the common. Access to the trails is via a narrow lane next to the Yarmouthport post office, on Route 6A. *11 Strawberry Lane; 508-362-3021.*

The massive Carpenter Gothic–style **Church of the New Jerusalem,** across from the village green, was one of the largest Swedenborgian churches built in the region. The congregation is no longer active, but local history buffs are working to preserve the church. No such aid is necessary for the **Strawberry Hill Meetinghouse** (Church Street, off Route 6A), where an active Universalist congregation continues to worship in the 1836 building. Bow-arch windows, an elegant clock tower, and elaborate scrollwork make the building impressive at close range, but its hilltop location must have also made it a landmark for sailing ships at sea.

Although Yarmouthport never had a deep harbor, **Bass Hole,** at the mouth of Chase Garden Creek, provided a channel for one of the Cape's earliest large shipyards, established around 1750 to craft the 50- to 150-ton schooners characteristic of the Cape's early Grand Banks fishing fleet. Turn north off Route 6A onto Centre Street to reach the extensive parking lot for **Grey's Beach,** a well-protected sandy beach with extensive marshes behind it. The 2.4-mile **Callery-Darling Trail** includes a boardwalk across the salt marsh at Grey's Beach, a place many locals recommend for watching the sunset. The nature trail winds through both wetlands and wooded uplands. Entrances are at the Grey's Beach parking lot and at the corner of Centre Street and Alms House Road.

■ **DENNIS** *map page 7, C-4*

Originally the east parish of Yarmouth, Dennis incorporated in 1793, taking the name of its longtime minister. His 1736 saltbox home, the **Josiah Dennis Manse Museum** (77 Nobscusset Road; 508-385-2232), displays artifacts of local history on Tuesday mornings and Thursday afternoons from June through September. The Maritime Room contains a scale model of the Shiverick Shipyard, which built eight clipper ships between 1850 and 1861 at Sesuit Harbor—the only clippers built on the Cape. Dennis is a good destination for a rainy day. While rain pelts

Once a drugstore, now a tourist attraction, Hallet's has been a Yarmouthport fixture since 1889.

the beach in sheets, vacationers can happily sort through linens, teapots, old photographs, and costume jewelry at the antiques shops at the corner of Route 6A and South Yarmouth Road, or visit the summer theater, art museum, and old-fashioned cinema at the **Cape Playhouse Center for the Arts,** a twenty-seven-acre complex along Route 6A.

Founded in 1927, the **Cape Playhouse** (508-385-3911) claims to be America's oldest professional summer theater. In a real-life story that seems made for the stage, Bette Davis rose from usher to ingénue during the 1928 season. Henry Fonda was also a player that summer, and he returned in 1956 to appear with his daughter, Jane. Over the years, many film and television actors have trod these boards, including Humphrey Bogart, Gregory Peck, Paul Robeson, Art Carney, Richard Thomas, and Cybill Shepherd. Betty White and Allen Ludden met while performing at the Cape Playhouse in 1962 and later married. Generations of summer playgoers have packed the former Nobscusset Meeting House (moved here from Barnstable), sitting happily in the dark oak pews in hopes of catching a rising star.

The **Cape Cod Museum of Fine Arts,** the newcomer of the lot, was established in 1981. The collection is strongest in artists of strictly local renown, but the museum also owns a few works by more widely known artists who spent at least some time on the Cape. Landscape painting dominates, and the canvases invariably invoke a sense of déjà vu, for many take familiar scenes as their subjects. The spacious central gallery, a triumph of contemporary design, nods to Dennis's shipbuilding past—the ribbed vault of the ceiling recapitulates the curvature of an inverted hull of a deep-water vessel. The museum is open year-round. *Cape Playhouse Center for the Arts; Route 6A, Dennis Village; 508-385-4477.*

The **Cape Cinema** (508-385-2503), one of the smallest movie houses on the Cape, opened in 1930 and screens art films and documentaries from mid-April through October. With a facade copied from a Federal-era Congregational church in Centerville and a ceiling that incorporates a vast mural designed by Rockwell Kent, the building is a delightful example of decorative themes run amok.

It's hard to match Kent's fanciful universe, but the views are rather more encompassing from **Scargo Tower.** At the gazebo and church on the old village green, turn south onto Old Bass River Road and immediately left onto Scargo Hill Road. The glacial drumlin of Scargo Hill stands only 160 feet above sea level, but, as

A stunning sunrise above the sand flats in Dennis.

An artisan puts the finishing touches on an intricate piece at Scargo Pottery.

Josef Berger (writing as Jeremiah Digges) observed in his 1937 classic *Cape Cod Pilot,* "on this low-lying peninsula every foot of 'up' means miles of 'out.'" The twenty-eight-foot brick tower, constructed in 1902 to replace an earlier wooden structure, has a claustrophobia-inducing circular stairwell with a century's worth of scratched and painted graffiti inside, but it leads to views that sweep from the Pilgrim Monument at Provincetown to the power plant stacks at Sandwich. On the clearest days, the white cliffs of Plymouth gleam to the northwest, and the faint outline of Nantucket appears on the southern horizon.

Below the tower is the blue oblong of **Scargo Lake,** which has a pleasant fresh water swimming beach. Although almost certainly a glacial kettle pond, local legend contends that it was created for the Indian princess Scargo, daughter of Sagauw, sachem of the Nobscussets. In *Legends of the New England Coast* (1957) Edward Rowe Snow recounts that a neighboring chief gave the young girl some fish, which she placed in a small pond. When the pond dried up she was able to save a few fish in a bowl, but she was so sad at the loss of the others that she began to waste away. Sagauw promised to create a pond as wide as an arrow's flight so that it would never dry up—and set his people to work on it. The excavated dirt became Scargo Hill, the depression Scargo Lake. The princess revived and released her fish into the pond, where their descendants still flourish. It's an uncharacteristically cheerful legend, as Indian maidens in New England tales usually end up dying from thwarted love or from threats to their virtue by unchaste Europeans. The Scargo Lake beach can be reached off Dr. Lord's Road from Route 6A.

The unpaved Dr. Lord's Road continues uphill into the pine woods to **Scargo Pottery** (508-385-3894), where Harry Holl first started making clay sculpture, vessels, and tiles in 1952 and is now joined by family members and other artisans. Their work, ranging from ceramic castles to raku vessels to dinnerware, is available in the shop. During warm weather, the artists leave their studio doors open so that visitors can watch them work.

A northward turn off Route 6A down Sea Street takes you past the former homes of many Dennis sea captains, en route to Sesuit Harbor, the site of Shiverick Shipyard. Here too was what the locals called Sears' Folly, though you could argue that John Sears had the last and most profitable laugh. During the Revolution, the British blockade kept American fishermen from acquiring salt to cure their catch. In 1776, the retired sea captain invented a solar evaporation apparatus with shutters to shelter the hundred-foot-diameter evaporating pan from the rain. The neighbors jeered, but Sears eventually won a lucrative patent on his saltworks, which became the prototype for a multimillion-dollar industry on the Cape.

The shipyard and saltworks are long gone, but **Cold Storage Public Beach** remains at the east end of the mouth of Sesuit Creek, a wide strand for gentle swimming, excellent clamming, and long walks. Cold Storage Beach can be breathtakingly beautiful, especially when low tide occurs at sunrise and the long sand flats glisten red and gold. And it can be heartbreaking, for pilot whales often strand themselves on this beach. Volunteers turn out and wash them down with seawater to keep their skin from burning when exposed at low tide, and to help them float as the tide rises. Rescuers usually coax many of the small-toothed whales into deeper water, but more often than not the pods return ashore to die. Recalling his first experience with a stranding, the naturalist John Hay wrote, "The silent insistence of the animals was stunning."

Clam Dinner

If you do find clams, make the most of them. There are three kinds—clams, qua-haugs and sea clams. You may steam or bake them if they are really clams; if they are quahaugs (pronounced, God knows why, "ko-hogs," and if anybody asks you how to spell it, reply that the quahaug was invented to be eaten, not spelt) take them to your landlady, if she is a native, and tell her she may have them. Then start talking about clam pie. Tell her you have heard how good it is, but you think the stories must be a little exaggerated. She won't be able to resist baking one, and the chances are you'll come off with all you can eat. And a cut of clam pie is worth taking any chances.

If you have no landlady, sit down to your quahaugs and call them "little necks" or "cherry stones," which they are, eat the small ones raw and enjoy yourself. If what you have dug up is a mess of sea clams, which is less likely, try similar maneuvers to get your Cape Cod cook to build you a chowder—offering to supply the clams, of course, and a "junk" of salt pork. If this can't be engineered, restore your treasures to the sands whence they have come.

—Josef Berger, writing as Jeremiah Digges, *Cape Cod Pilot*, 1937

■ **Brewster** *map page 7, D-3*

Settled in 1656 as the "north parish" of Harwich, Brewster did not incorporate as a town until 1803, by which time its sea captains were already ranging far and wide. Convention has it that Brewster was home to "more than ninety-nine captains." Perhaps lingering Pilgrim or Quaker modesty (for many early settlers were Quakers) kept the anonymous accountant from claiming an even hundred. At any rate, Brewster calls itself the Sea Captains' Town, and many of the large Federal and Greek Revival homes along Main Street (Route 6A) represent the profits of the sea trade. At least two of them, the Old Manse Inn and the Isaiah Clark House, have second lives as B&Bs.

Like all the towns along the King's Highway, Brewster has been hospitable for artisans working on the edge between crafts and fine arts. In the 1960s, Bill Sydenstricker developed a technique akin to enameling to produce a line of exquis-itely pictorial fine glass. He died a few years back, but the artisans of **Sydenstricker Galleries** (490 Main Street; 508-385-3272) reproduce his designs and add new ones to the portfolio.

The gray-shingled **Old Higgins Farm Windmill** and **Harris Black House** stand in Drummer Boy Park. Both windmill and house were built around 1795 and were moved to the park in 1974. The historical society calls the house "possibly the last remaining primitive one-room house" on Cape Cod, excepting perhaps the accommodations at an Outer Cape dune shack. The windmill and house are open limited hours from mid-June through mid-September. The bandstand at Drummer Boy Park gets a workout when the Brewster Town Band, a group of amateur and professional musicians ranging in age from their teens into their eighties, plays concerts every Sunday evening in July and August. *785 Main Street; 508-896-9521.*

Many of the exhibits at the **Cape Cod Museum of Natural History** are aimed at schoolchildren, but even the most jaded adult is likely to come away with a fresh appreciation for the forests, marshes, bays, and shores of Cape Cod. Some displays are unapologetically didactic, such as the catalog of creatures found on tidal flats. Others—like the skeleton of a minke whale, fossil shark teeth, a fossil walrus skull, and a piece of whale baleen that museum-goers are invited to touch—retain a more nineteenth-century air of wonder. A collection of purple bottles that Shirley

(above) Horseshoe crab at Calm Flats, Brewster. (following pages) Paine's Creek, Brewster.

Nickerson found in a lifetime of beach walking on Cape Cod is meant to illustrate both the longevity of refuse and the photochemical effect of sunlight on glass containing manganese, but it's more likely to make you want to head to the beach to find your own patent-medicine bottle.

For the vacationer turned random naturalist, the downstairs exhibits amount to a crib sheet on the creatures of the Cape. Taxidermic examples of several dozen bird species are crammed beak by jowl into a pair of glass cases, offering a most unlifelike opportunity to study the differences between the house sparrow and the white-eyed sparrow or between red-tailed and red-shouldered hawks. A quick study can soon identify the white-winged scoter, common merganser, bufflehead, and oldsquaw in an estuary instead of shouting, "Look! Ducks!" The marine tanks, meanwhile, are more than just a bunch of pretty fish. Children tend to watch in utter amazement, while their parents grow queasy as a volunteer explains that what looks like a congealed mass of tar is actually a whelk that has crawled out of its shell to commit mollusk-cide on a sea clam. Museum lessons in identifying flora and fauna can be put to immediate use on the two short nature trails that depart from the lower level. The museum was cofounded in 1954 by the naturalist John Hay, whose works (along with many other fascinating and often rare volumes) can be found in the museum's lending library. *869 Main Street; 508-896-3867.*

Heading east on Route 6A, turn south on Paine's Creek Road and west on Stony Brook Road for a detour to **Stony Brook Grist Mill and Herring Run** (Stony Brook and Satucket Roads; no phone). In late April and early May, the fish ladder flashes with herring making their spawning run to Mill Pond and Upper Mill Pond. The gristmill, which is open for tours from Memorial Day through Labor Day, was constructed in 1873 of boards from a dismantled saltworks, but there's been a gristmill on this site since 1663. The water wheels on Mill Pond also powered early industry, from a seventeenth-century fulling mill (which rendered homespun, loom-woven cloth denser) to shoe and furniture factories.

Stony Brook Road leads eastward to rejoin Route 6A less than a mile west of the **New England Fire & History Museum,** a six-building complex that houses antique firefighting equipment, from fire engines to home-fire buckets. The late Boston Pops conductor Arthur Fiedler was a firefighting buff, and the museum owns his collection of fire helmets. *1439 Main Street; 508-896-5711.*

The 4th of July at the Brewster Store.

OLD SALTS OF THE GENTLE SHORE

The exploits of sea captains may no longer be the talk of the taverns, but every historical society (and every owner of a sea captain's house) has a briny yarn or two to spin.

THE CAPTAIN AND THE DAUPHIN

Davy Nickerson, it is said, brought a baby home from Paris during the French Revolution, a lad he named René Rousseau but who everyone was certain was the infant Dauphin. (Candidates for the Dauphin, the lost heir to the French throne, were as common in the eighteenth century as candidates for White Russia's Anastasia in the twentieth.) The boy grew up to be a sea captain, and Brewster's contender for the French Restoration perished at sea at age twenty-five. Nickerson outlasted him but five years. Their names share a stone over an empty grave behind Brewster's First Parish Church.

FEATHERY FORTUNE

Capts. Barnabas Wixon and Ezra Howe of Dennis took the prize for ingenuity by turning a bad summer of fishing off Labrador into a fortune. Ashore to repair their gear, they were surrounded by eider ducks in full molt. Whapping the ducks with spruce-branch brooms, they plucked a shipload of feathers that found a ready market in Boston.

SPEED RACERS

Capt. Asa Eldredge of Yarmouthport sailed the *Red Jacket* on her maiden voyage from New York to Liverpool in 1854, setting a record of thirteen days, one hour, and twenty-five minutes despite inclement weather for the whole trip. In 1853, Capt. Frederick (William F.) Howes of Yarmouth (inventor of the double topsail) raced the clipper *Climax* from Boston to San Francisco against Capt. Moses Howes of Dennis aboard the Shiverick-built clipper *Competitor.* Both finished the voyage in 115 days. Capt. Joshua Sears skippered another Shiverick ship, *Wild Hunter,* on her maiden voyage to Calcutta, from 1855 to 1856—though fighting his way through a flotilla of Chinese pirates to complete his voyage slowed him down somewhat.

DRESS CODE

Brewster's Capt. John Higgins captured the prudishness prize by dressing the natives of the Caroline Islands (now Micronesia) in pants lest they offend Christian eyes.

From the road, the **Brewster Ladies Library** appears quaintly anachronistic, its Victorian style and name suggesting an institution where glove-wearing ladies sip tea whilst discussing the latest potboiler by that rakish George Eliot. The library, founded as a subscription institution in 1852, occupies an 1868 building that was the first dedicated library structure built on the Cape. The original rooms have been refurbished to overstuffed Victorian style to encourage lounging and reading. But the institution functions as the public library for Brewster, and the remainder of the complex is completely current in style, books, and information technology. Men and boys are welcome—and always have been. *1822 Main Street; 508-896-3913.*

At the junction of Route 6A and Route 124, the **Brewster Store** is a slice of vintage village life, where you can get a cup of coffee and a newspaper, buy a clam knife, or fill a bag with penny candy. The upstairs "museum" includes the former post office, a cranberry-separating machine, and other curiosities sporting the patina of age. *1935 Main Street; 508-896-3744.*

Perhaps the best known golf course in Massachusetts, the semiprivate **Ocean Edge Resort & Golf Club** (2907 Main Street; 508-896-1885) frequently hosts USPGA tournaments, including the Massachusetts Open. Duffers who'd rather play one of the top ten public courses in the country (according to *Golf Digest*) can opt for **The Captain's Golf Course** (1000 Freeman's Way; 508-896-1716), about two miles south, where the fairways do not have ocean views.

From Route 6A, well-signed roads lead north to the **eight Brewster beaches,** more famous for their tidal flats than for swimming. Brewster sits at the conjunction of two glacial outwash plains, and the beaches taper very gradually into the ocean, exposing as much as a mile of flats at low tide. These flats are rich with clams, and nonresident shellfishing licenses are inexpensive, making Brewster one of the best places on the Cape to dig your own.

Nickerson State Park (508-896-3491; campground reservations 877-422-6762) is a nineteen-hundred-acre respite for Cape Cod visitors who have had enough of beaches, salt marshes, dunes, and open vistas. Originally the baronial summer estate of railroad magnate Rowland Nickerson, this tract represents the Cape's largest patch of contiguous woodlands. Donated to the state by his widow in 1934, it opened as the state's first park in 1937, with fervent promises to avoid both commercial exploitation and unnatural prettifying with concrete statuary and the like. The state has kept its word, and Nickerson is beloved by campers, hikers, canoeists, and cyclists.

U P P E R   C A P E

Spanning the realms of both myth and science, the Upper Cape towns of Mashpee and Falmouth nonetheless fly beneath the radar of travelers who aren't passing through to catch a ferry to Martha's Vineyard. It's not as if this southwestern quadrant of Cape Cod is deserted. The eight villages of Falmouth make it the second most populous town on the Cape, and Mashpee is the fastest growing. Yet the best-known parts of Falmouth are the ferry parking lot and the docks at Woods Hole, and even some Cape Codders might be hard-pressed to point out Mashpee on a map.

These towns diverged from the typical pattern of settlement by Plymouth Pilgrims. The initial English homesteaders at Falmouth were Quakers. Mashpee was created for Native American converts to Puritanism; the sole town of Praying Indians to survive, it remained predominantly Wampanoag well into the mid-twentieth century.

Even the geography differs from the rest of the Cape. High rocky headlands meet the ocean at Woods Hole and West Falmouth, while inland Mashpee and East Falmouth are pocked with old-growth forest, ancient kettle ponds, and some of the Cape's most productive agricultural land. The south-facing coast, on the other hand, consists of long, narrow peninsulas dribbling down to a network of powder-sand barrier beaches on Vineyard and Nantucket Sounds.

Although the Cape's first planned resort was built in Falmouth Heights in the 1870s, the Upper Cape has never been quite so inundated with tourists as its neighbors eastward on Route 28. Apart from the Vineyard ferry, the biggest draw in the region is the Falmouth village of Woods Hole, a onetime whaling port that has evolved into a renowned marine biology research center. As a result, the Upper Cape has not been remade in the image of what entrepreneurs hope tourists will want. Nor does it need remaking. The electric sunset views from Old Silver Beach on Buzzards Bay, the steady cross-shore breezes that send kite surfers into paroxysms of delight, the Gitchegumee pines-and-shining-water of the Mashpee lakes, the lighthouse headland of Nobska Point, the rafts of waterfowl on Waquoit Bay—they're all reason enough to visit.

At the Mashpee Wampanoag Indian Pow Wow, held every July.

■ MASHPEE   *map page 7, B-4*

In the *Cape Cod Pilot,* Josef Berger wrote of Mashpee, "The 'town' is more wood than village; and its story is in its full pines as well as its people." There's still a ker nel of truth in his observation, for Mashpee's original settlement pattern was mor Wampanoag than European, with small clusters of dwellings dispersed through th landscape. In effect, there are three centers to the town. Entering Mashpee from Sandwich on Route 130, travelers first encounter small **Mashpee center,** with it veterans' garden, country store, town archives, Baptist church, Dunkin' Donuts and town hall. Nearby, although barely marked, are the town landing on Mashpe Pond, the herring run on the trickling Mashpee River, and the **Flume** (Route 130 508-477-1456), a restaurant where knowledgeable gourmets descend in the sprin; to enjoy Earl Mills Sr.'s preparation of shad roe breaded in cornmeal and sautéed i butter. Both herring and shad run up the Mashpee River in front of the restauran to spawn in Mashpee Pond. Mills is an elder of the Mashpee Wampanoag tribe which limits the taking of herring to those with either a tribal identification card o a tribal permit.

Due south, Great Neck Road descends past the Mashpee Wampanoag India Tribal Council offices to the Mashpee Rotary—the intersection of Routes 28 an 151—and its modern developers' essay at creating a town, **Mashpee Commons** Essentially a large shopping center straddling both sides of Route 151, Mashpe Commons has its own branch library and post office and is being "built out," wit plans to surround the generic olde New England village architecture of the shop with olde New England condominiums and town houses—exactly as a Hollywoo set designer might imagine Cape Cod.

The spiritual anchor of historic Mashpee lies east of the traffic circle on Rout 28, where Meeting House Road branches left to return to Mashpee's municipa center. The small church at the corner and its surrounding graveyard of eigh teenth- and nineteenth-century markers bear dignified witness to Mashpee's origi as a town of Praying Indians.

Although the Wampanoags sold the land that would become Mashpee t Plymouth Colony in 1648 for two brass kettles and a bushel of corn, in 1660 th missionary lay preacher Richard Bourne got 10,500 acres set aside for his Nativ American converts to Christianity. His zeal at preaching the gospel was so success ful that Mashpee became the strongest of the towns of Praying Indians, weatherin; the vicissitudes of King Philip's War (when most native bands were killed or drive away) through a studious neutrality toward both the English and the Wampanoag warlord Metacom.

The Mashpee Wampanoags assimilated rapidly into English colonial society and fervently supported the American Revolution. Throughout their history they welcomed outsiders to the tribe, absorbing refugees from other tribes, runaway slaves, and other people of color who wanted to lead a free life. Beginning in the mid-nineteenth century, many immigrants from the Azores and Cape Verde islands settled in Mashpee. As a result, the tribe became an all-American stewpot of many racial and cultural strains, all sharing the common cultural thread of Wampanoag tradition.

Although the people of Mashpee now evince all manner of faiths, the **Old Indian Meeting House** functions as the wellspring of the town. Built around 1684 at Santuit Pond, it was soon moved to its current location, remodeled in 1717, and rededicated in 1923. The simple structure follows the Cape Cod model of white clapboards on the front and weathered cedar shingles on its other walls. Its clear glass windows—arrayed in twelve over twelve sashes and flanked by black shutters—flood the interior with light, as does a large arched window behind the pulpit. A plaque dedicates the building, "that it may stand in all future years the indestructible record of a rugged race to be governed by the word of the Lord in all things." Like the church, the graveyard has a simple grace, with

THE MASHPEE COMPASS

Each of the directions has its own spirit. The east is significant because this is where we are as well as who we are. The southwest is where all the good souls go when they pass on to the next world. The sun goes out of the way or is lost in the west; this spirit combines with north and south to create violent or peaceful weather, respectively. The south is warm with no rain and combines with west and east to create ideal weather or dry, hot weather, respectively. The north brings the time for conferring one's blessings and preparing for the ongoing life cycle. The warm rains and winds come east from the southwest and nurture our beans, squash and corn—the Three Sisters—the basics of our early existence. The most essential direction, of course, is the one inside each of us.

—Earl Mills Sr., Chief Flying Eagle of the Mashpee Wampanoags,
Cape Cod Wampanoag Cookbook, 2001

modest stones noting the surnames so familiar from the crew rolls of eighteenth-century whaling ships and modern cranberry-picking crews. *Intersection of Meetinghouse Road and Route 28.*

Mashpee was perhaps the quietest spot on Cape Cod until developers began to create condominium and town house complexes along its small saltwater coastline. By 1960 the Wampanoags had become a minority in their own town. Accelerating residential development of the shore region is balanced, however, by large areas of conservation land and parks in the woodsy interior.

North of the municipal center, on the peninsula that divides Mashpee Pond from Wakeby Pond, the Trustees of Reservations operate the 135-acre **Lowell Holly Reservation,** with four miles of trails and former carriage roads that criss-cross the peninsula and the adjoining shore. The summer entrance (across from the "Carpe Diem" sign on South Sandwich Road) leads to a parking lot with a small swimming beach. Another pull-off, farther up the road, provides year-round access to the woodland trails. Huge American holly trees have grown wild on the property for centuries, and Abbot Lawrence Lowell augmented them with exten-sive plantings of rhododendrons and mountain laurel. After his death, caretakers planted yet another fifty varieties of American holly selected for their shiny foliage and vigorous fruiting. Most of the forest on the reservation has not been cut for at least two centuries, and walking through extensive stands of beech, black gum, black birch, red maple, pine, and oak feels positively druidic. Mashpee and Wakeby ponds support extensive populations of trout, smallmouth bass, chain pickerel, and bluegills—making them a handy larder for ospreys and golden eagles. *South Sandwich Road; 781-821-2977.*

The boundaries between Mashpee and Sandwich on the north and Falmouth on the west are fluid—it's common to pass in and out of corners of both while driving a seemingly straight road. Traveling west from the Mashpee Rotary on Route 151 to reach John's Pond, you'll cross briefly into Falmouth. At the town line is the **Barnstable County Fairgrounds,** where the organizers of a nine-day agricultural fair in late July claim it to have been "a Cape Cod family tradition" since the 1860s. Like most rural fairs, it has musical entertainment and tractor displays, but it also keeps alive some of the Cape's gentler farm practices, with bee exhibits, spin-ning demonstrations, and 4-H rabbit shows. *Route 151, Falmouth; 508-563-3200.*

The Barnstable County Fair.

The fairgrounds are also the site of the **Mashpee Wampanoag Indian Pow Wow** (508-477-0208), a July event at which songs, dances, and tales perpetuate Wampanoag traditions. After generations of assimilation into the broader culture, the Wampanoag seize on the pow wow as a reaffirmation of their identity. Although the tribe failed to garner federal recognition in the 1970s, they know who they are: the "people of the first light," as their name translates from the Algonquian. Traditional food plays a major role in the pow wow, which concludes with a Wampanoag-style clambake on Sunday.

Just after the fairgrounds, turn right on Currier Road. The **Ashumet Holly and Wildlife Sanctuary** of the Massachusetts Audubon Society comes up quickly on the left. Much smaller than the Lowell Reservation, this forty-nine-acre property surrounds a small glacial kettle pond where fluctuating water levels have encouraged the growth of rare species of wildflowers. Among them is the endangered Plymouth gentian, which blooms in August only when the summer has been dry enough for the pond to recede. Its large pink flowers have bright yellow

Traditional dance at the Wampanoag Indian Pow Wow.

centers edged in red. Eight different species and sixty-five varieties of holly (producing berries in five different colors) grow on the reservation, along with the rare Franklinia tree discovered in the wild in Georgia in 1770 and declared extinct in the wild by 1790. About 130 species of birds frequent the reserve, of which robins are particularly numerous, holly berries being their favorite winter food. Iridescent blue-green barn swallows skim the contours of the land; they have nested since 1935 in the barn at the trailhead. *286 Ashumet Road, off Currier Road; 508-563-6390.*

Currier Road turns into Hooppole Road, where signs direct travelers through a woodsy trailer park to **John's Pond,** a 329-acre kettle pond so wide-open that a strong wind can whip up whitecaps and surf. Mashpee provides a lifeguard on the broad sandy beach in the summer. Four miles of walking trails and cranberry-bog roads surround the pond, providing pleasant nature hikes through town conservation land. *Hooppole Road; 508-539-1400.*

Perhaps Mashpee's most dramatic conservation property, however, is the South Cape Beach complex, which includes **Mashpee National Wildlife Refuge, South Cape Beach State Park,** and the town's own seventy-seven-acre **Jehu Pond Conservation Area.** Ultimately, the National Wildlife Refuge will be the umbrella for this complex of nearly ten square miles. From the Mashpee Rotary, follow Great Neck Road South to Great Oak Road. Continue about a mile to the Jehu Pond parking lot to explore the inland portions of the refuge. More than four miles of walking trails track through pine and oak woodlands; across saltwater and freshwater marshes filled with ducks, frogs, and turtles; and around several abandoned cranberry bogs that blush crimson in the spring as the vines come out of hibernation. Walk quietly and you may come upon a deer sipping from one of the small ponds or a red fox hiding in the grasses, waiting to pounce on an unsuspecting vole.

The road continues past marshes and through bayberry barrens to the barrier beaches of South Cape, where separate areas are set off as state beach, open to anyone, and town beach, open only to Mashpee residents. Offshore shoals undercut the power of incoming waves, and the migration of sand along the shore produces a long shelf extending into the ocean. As a result, the water is not very deep and is definitely warm, reaching seventy degrees on a sunny August day. South Cape Beach State Park also has about three miles of packed-sand roads and trails for exploring the wetlands that have formed behind the barrier beaches.

Risk Measurement

The Cape Cod that people write about I seldom recognize. I constantly think about the place. It is my home, so it is in my dreams, a landscape of my unconscious mind, perhaps my mind's only landscape. Paddling between islands in New Guinea, I often think, *That's no worse than Falmouth to Oak Bluffs.* Swimming in a bad chop or a swift current anywhere, I think of Woods Hole or the harbor entrance at Lewis Bay. Living on the Cape has given me a good notion of wind speed and air temperature. This complex landscape has taught me ways of measuring the world of risk.

—Paul Theroux, "The True Size of Cape Cod,"
in *Fresh Air Fiend: Travel Writings 1985–2000,* 2000

■ **FALMOUTH** *map page 7, B-4/5*

Just west of the Mashpee town line on Route 28, the headquarters of the **Waquoit Bay National Estuarine Research Reserve** provides the first hint that scientific inquiry often trumps relaxation on the Upper Cape. Wide and shallow Waquoit Bay is nearly closed off from the sea by barrier beaches, and its marshes and flats are particularly sensitive to environmental degradation. Scientists treat the bay and its watershed as a laboratory to study the effects of human habitation on fragile ecosystems and make recommendations for environmental policy. Educational displays at the center also encourage homeowners to do their part—exhorting them for example, to cut back on fertilizing lawns, because excessive fertilizer promote algae blooms in streams and rivers, which kill off fish. *Route 28; 508-457-0495.*

The long, narrow harbors west of Waquoit Bay sheltered coasting schooners in the eighteenth and nineteenth centuries, and many a captain spent the months between voyages tilling the soil on the peninsulas between the harbors. Railroad obviated the need for the small freight vessels before the twentieth century began and simple farmhouses soon gave way to grand estates as Falmouth Heights and nearby peninsulas developed into one of Cape Cod's first exclusive summer communities. For a taste of both eras, turn south from Route 28 down Davisville Road Drive through the stately center of East Falmouth, cross the bridge on Menauhant Road, and stop at **Green Pond Seafood** (366 Menauhant Road; 508-540-1901), a

Clams on the scale at Green Pond Seafood.

small fish shack on the road's west side that has become locally famous for its stuffed quahogs. Acapesket Road returns north to Route 28.

Route 28 enters Falmouth Village on its eastern end, passing shopping centers and roadside motels en route to the almost picture-perfect triangular town green that marks the largest of Falmouth's eight villages. Falmouth did all the usual Cape Cod things in the eighteenth and nineteenth centuries—drilled its militia on the green, staved off British incursions in the War of 1812, and engaged in coastal trading, salt-making, inshore fishing, and even a bit of whaling. Well-to-do merchants' and sea captains' mansions, many transformed into B&Bs and inns, surround the green, and a tall flagpole marks the center.

On the green, Falmouth's past is never far away. The modest private house at 16 Main Street is the **birthplace of Katharine Lee Bates,** author of "America the Beautiful." A block up Palmer Avenue, a pair of eighteenth-century houses separated by a formal boxwood garden constitute the **Falmouth Historical Society** (65 Palmer Avenue; 508-548-4857). The society's Conant House contains, among its other exhibits, a good history of Falmouth's limited career as a whaling port (with most ships sailing from the village of Woods Hole), while the Julia Wood

The Falmouth Historical Society...

House pays tribute to its first owner, Dr. Francis Wicks, a pioneer in promoting vaccination against smallpox.

Much of Falmouth's history is writ in less intentional terms a few blocks south of the town green, along Mill Road at the **Old Burying Ground.** This small cemetery from the town's early days filled up a century ago. It retains the quiet poignancy of a seafaring village burial ground, with tombstones without graves for the men lost at sea, and graves without tombstones for the unidentified bodies that washed ashore.

Although the Falmouth green bears the hallmarks of inland New England, the ocean is within sniffing distance. **Surf Drive Beach** begins less than a mile away at the foot of Shore Street, which heads south from Main Street. The beach changes names several times on its course nearly five miles southwest—a continuous series of sandy barrier beaches lapped by warm water.

Quakers founded Falmouth around 1660, but the town soon enough fell in line with mainstream Congregationalism. In 1796, the imposing **Congregational Church** was constructed right in the middle of the town green. Half a century later, it was jacked up and rolled to its present location. Other faiths managed to erect their houses of worship on or around the green as well, including the

...and historical Falmouth. (following pages) A golden sunset over Old Silver Beach, Falmouth.

Romanesque Revival edifice of Episcopalian **St. Barnabas Memorial Church,** which hosts the town's strawberry festival each June.

In the early twentieth century, Falmouth made credible claims to being the strawberry capital of the world. Predominantly Portuguese immigrant farmers grew vast quantities of the fruit on the sandy soils of East Falmouth, Teaticket, Waquoit, and Hatchville villages. The Hatchville area of East Falmouth (from Route 28 east of the village, turn north onto Sandwich Road) remains a major agricultural area. **Tony Andrews Farm** (394 Meetinghouse Road; 508-548-4717) and **Coonamessett Farm** (277 Hatchville Road; 508-563-2560) sell pick-your-own strawberries in June. The promising **Cape Cod Winery** (681 Sandwich Road; 508-457-5592) also sits in this East Falmouth fruit bowl, producing eminently drinkable white wines from its mature plantings of French-American hybrid seyval and vidal blanc grapes. The winery's more recent plantings of cabernet sauvignon, cabernet franc, merlot, and pinot grigio vinifera grapes should serve as a basis for varietal wines in the coming years.

You can reach Falmouth's west-facing beaches on Buzzards Bay by following Route 28 north from its dogleg at the Falmouth Village green. But to get an appreciation of the little cove communities, the sweeping views from the glacial heights, and the windswept barrier-beach systems, it's better to stick with the old slow road, designated Route 28A, as it passes Colonial and early Federal farmsteads in West Falmouth and North Falmouth. The barrier-beach system on **Chapoquoit Peninsula** in West Falmouth has big swells and crashing surf when the wind is blowing out of the southwest, as it usually is. Windsurfing (and, by extension, kite-surfing) is permitted in the summer only before 9 A.M. and after 5 P.M., but the wind and waves are so terrific that kite-surfers in full wetsuits turn out in all but the dead of winter.

Perhaps the most famous of the Falmouth beaches is **Old Silver Beach,** so-called for its powdery sand, which glistens with a silver sheen. A circuitous route to

■ WOODS HOLE *map page 7, B-5*

Apart from the sea route, there are two ways to cover the four miles between Falmouth village and the town's quirkiest hamlet, Woods Hole, which squats at the extreme southwest corner of Cape Cod, where Vineyard Sound meets Buzzards Bay. The logical choice is Woods Hole Road, which is essentially the southward extension of Route 28 on the west side of Falmouth Village. As it enters Woods Hole, the road passes **The Dome** restaurant, a twenty-seven-foot-high igloo of a geodesic dome built in 1953 under the supervision of the inventor Buckminster Fuller. The more scenic (often faster) route involves pedaling along the **Shining Sea Bikeway**, which begins in Falmouth southwest of the green at the intersection of Mill and Locust Streets, across from the Steamship Authority Parking Lot. Nearby **Corner Cycle** (115 Palmer Avenue, Falmouth Village; 508-540-4195) is the most convenient place to rent some wheels. One of the early rails-to-trails projects, Shining Sea plunges through the countryside to Surf Drive Beach at Oyster Pond, where pairs of wild mute swans nest, blue herons and white egrets patiently fish, and ducks paddle around in small, noisy flotillas. The path veers inland to skirt the rocky hump of **Nobska Light,** but it's worth detouring on Nobska Road to visit the squat little light and partake of sweeping views of the passage between Martha's Vineyard and the mainland. The rail trail is nearly flat and well-paved its entire length. It concludes at the ferry loading dock in the heart of Woods Hole.

The now-abandoned rail line was extended to Woods Hole in 1872 at the behest of the Pacific Guano Company, a fertilizer enterprise founded by Boston shippers to give their South Seas trading vessels something to bring home; that something was bird droppings rich in phosphate of lime from Pacific islands off South America. In 1863, the company built a plant at Penzance Point in Woods Hole to combine the guano with ground-up menhaden and fish scraps in order to make a rich fertilizer. When wind blew from the west, the entire village of Woods Hole smelled extremely ripe. But whaling had become unprofitable after the discovery of petroleum, and Woods Hole has never been ideally suited for commercial fishing. The fertilizer factory may have stunk, but it was the smell of money.

The novel use of trash fish as fertilizer intrigued Spencer Baird, the first federal fisheries commissioner, who established a summer research station at Woods Hole in 1871 and a year-round facility in 1875, thereby launching the village's marine research industry. In 1888, the Marine Biological Laboratory (MBL) was established, and the following year Pacific Guano went bankrupt, freeing up a lot of real

estate and clearing the air in Woods Hole once and for all. The biologists came in ever greater numbers, making Woods Hole one of the preeminent scientific villages in the world. In 1930, with initial funding from the Rockefeller Foundation, the Woods Hole Oceanographic Institution (WHOI) opened with a mandate to study all aspects of marine science. The big three of WHOI, MBL, and the National Marine Fisheries Service have been joined in more recent years by the United States Geological Survey, the Sea Education Association (an undergraduate college program), and the Woods Hole Research Center, which studies the structure and function of natural ecosystems.

Perhaps the first thing to be noted about Woods Hole is the absence of a barber shop. Few places in America are as hirsute; the whole village could be an Oak Ridge Boys concert. Mullets and ponytails abound on the young men, who often affect T-shirts that are more holes than fabric. Their elders, by contrast, sport the white-peach look of hair and full beard in a consistent half-inch length both fore and aft. The congenitally bald hide their pates beneath Greek fishermen's caps. In other words, the inhabitants of Woods Hole look uncannily like the grad students and faculty in the marine science department of any large research university, which is essentially what Woods Hole is. MBL alone occupies more than 170 buildings in a village not much larger than a couple of Manhattan city blocks.

As in all good coastal villages—especially those situated on narrow peninsulas—the main drag in Woods Hole is called Water Street. It begins just above the Steamship Authority docks and parking lot. Across the street, the tiny **Woods Hole Historical Museum** (578 Woods Hole Road; 508-548-7270; open mid-June to mid-Sept.) deals largely in the secular (i.e., nonscientific) side of the village, with a maquette of Woods Hole in 1895, models of ships built in its yards, and examples of small watercraft.

The Woods Hole Oceanographic Institution grew so huge in the 1960s that it relocated most of its facilities to a campus outside the village, but the **WHOI Exhibit Center** offers a dramatic overview of the research institution's programs. In the semiotics of New England village architecture, the white clapboard building with a belled cupola and brass weathervane should be either a school or a church, and, in the ways of Woods Hole, it's a little of both. The exhibits inside the newly renovated center bespeak cutting-edge science, with an emphasis on technologies

Pedaling along the Shining Sea Bikeway in Woods Hole.

Before the Dinosaurs

One of the planet's most successful creatures, the horseshoe crab was swimming the world's oceans about 200 million years before the dinosaurs appeared, and it hasn't changed a whole lot since. Cape shellfishermen detest them—one adult horseshoe crab can devour thirty soft-shell clams in a day—but scientists and shorebirds love them. Sanderlings, sandpipers, dowitchers, and American oystercatchers gobble up the eggs and larvae. Indeed, horseshoe crab eggs and larvae seem to form the base of the food pyramid on North Monomoy Island (see the Nantucket Sound chapter), accounting for the concentration of birds, fish, and, by extension, seals, which eat the fish that eat the spawn.

Researchers at the Marine Biological Laboratory have other reasons to like the critters, having adopted them as an unofficial emblem on all the outdoor signage. Horseshoe crabs have ten eyes of varying sensitivity that help scientists decipher the neurobiology of vision. (One MBL scientist, H. Keffer Gartline, was awarded the Nobel Prize in 1967 for his work on horseshoe-crab vision.) Like some other primitive creatures, horseshoe crabs have blue blood that uses copper rather than iron to bind oxygen molecules. In the 1970s, Frederick Bang, an MBL researcher, was studying blood circulation in horseshoe crabs when he accidentally discovered that even the tiniest amount of bacterial contamination caused the blood to coagulate. By extracting the substance that reacts to bacteria, scientists were able to create a hypersensitive test to ensure the purity of all kinds of medical products, including injectable drugs and vaccines.

Associates of Cape Cod, the MBL spin-off that commercialized the test, reportedly sells $50 million worth of horseshoe-crab reagent a year. The company pays collectors to bring in live horseshoe crabs, which are bled and released unharmed into the Vineyard Sound shallows: 200 million years and counting.

for exploring inner space, that is, the depths of the world's oceans. WHOI operates three large oceangoing research vessels as well as the three-person deep submersible the *Alvin*. Of the various research concerns in Woods Hole, WHOI has an Indiana Jones personality—seeking out the frontiers of the deep ocean, recording life forms never seen before, scouring the ocean floor to uncover the wreck of the *Titanic*. The introductory video hits some of the highlights in what feels like an abbreviated *National Geographic* undersea special, complete with the French intonations of narrator Jean-Michel Cousteau, of the famed diving family. The glamour bits include stunning footage of pulsing jellyfish, sulfur-eating worms around hydrothermal vents, and a broken *Titanic* teacup on the ocean floor. Visitors can climb into the claustrophobic confines of a cutaway model of the *Alvin* to be reminded that beautiful pictures and new discoveries also take years of hard work under less than luxurious conditions. *15 School Street; 508-289-2663. Open Apr.–Dec.*

Woods Hole isn't much of a shopping village, although a handful of souvenir shops do punctuate the lineup of sporting-goods shops, restaurants, and bars along Water Street. If you're after local color, you can find plenty at **Pie in the Sky** (10 Water Street; 508-540-5075), a bakery where substantial cookies come in ten versions, or the funky **Fishmonger's Cafe** (56 Water Street; 508-540-5376), where the plain wooden tables look out on the harbor and the interior decor consists primarily of materials recycled from Otis Air Force National Guard base, just north of Falmouth. Otherwise, just check any watering hole with draft beer and a raw bar.

Of all the Woods Hole scientific institutions, the **Marine Biological Laboratory** has the largest physical presence in the village, as its campus engulfs most of the lower two-thirds of Water Street. One historic building of note, the Candleworks, a former spermaceti candle factory from Woods Hole's whaling days, sits at the narrow channel connecting Eel Pond and Great Harbor. The two bodies of water are effectively the village's inner and outer harbors. One of the big events of any given day is the lifting of the drawbridge on Water Street to allow vessels to pass between them. Both harbors are anchorages for Woods Hole's community of houseboats, most of which are occupied only in the summer, and many of which are little more than ramshackle shacks on Styrofoam rafts. By and large, their inhabitants are the nonscientists—fishermen, musicians, ex-hippies, carpenters, and other characters more interested in being than in becoming.

The **MBL Robert W. Pierce Visitors Center** hints at the scientific riches of the institution's research programs, where more than forty Nobel laureates have either studied or taught. About two hundred fifty people work at MBL all year, augmented in the summer by an additional thousand researchers and students who come from around the globe to study the organisms in the waters around Woods Hole. Remarkably few are marine biologists per se, but they take advantage of the facilities to study more general life processes in convenient marine models. Displays in the center hit a couple of highlights—the use of transparent sea-urchin eggs to study how cells differentiate into specialized body parts, and the long-running studies of vision using horseshoe crabs, which have vision cells far larger than human rods and cones. One of the early profitable products to come out of MBL was a protein found in horseshoe-crab blood that can detect bacterial contamination in serums, drugs, and the circulatory systems of dialysis machines. *100 Water Street; 508-289-7623.*

The **National Marine Fisheries Service Aquarium,** at the foot of Water Street, claims to be the oldest public aquarium in the country, and at least until recent renovations there was little to doubt in the boast. The research program here seeks to keep New England's fisheries healthy and productive. Dozens of tanks hold specimens of everything from codfish and lobsters (including a rare blue lobster) to plug-ugly toadfish, sculpins, and eels. This being Woods Hole, educational exhibits abound, but they're so well done that you might actually catch yourself studying the Georges or Stellwagen Banks displays to understand just how critical they were (and, for all their problems, still are) to Cape commercial fishermen. Some of the old-fashioned exhibits survive on the upper level of the building, perhaps because they were just too satisfying to update. Touch tanks for youngsters hold such curiosities as live starfish, horseshoe crabs, the elegant channeled whelk, and several feisty lobsters (claws clamped closed with rubber bands). Ghastly

A stalked jellyfish at the Marine Biological Laboratory.

> **MBL Beach**
>
> At Stony Beach the water is regarded as primarily interesting, even by small boys. On weekends, in hot midsummer . . . it is so crowded that one must pick one's way on tiptoe to find a hunching place, but there is always a lot of standing up anyway; biologists seem to prefer standing on beaches, talking at each other, gesturing to indicate the way things are assembled, bending down to draw diagrams in the sand. By the end of the day, the sand is crisscrossed with a mesh of ordinates, abscissas, curves to account for everything in nature.
>
> You can hear the sound from the beach at a distance, before you see the people. It is that most extraordinary noise, half-shout, half-song, made by confluent, simultaneously raised human voices, explaining things to each other.
>
> —Lewis Thomas, "The MBL" from *The Lives of a Cell,* 1974

medusas in jars have a B-movie appeal, and a text panel explains that, when stung, you should remove any tentacles clinging to your skin so they'll stop discharging venom. Folk remedies for jellyfish stings, it further relates (without endorsing any of them), include meat tenderizer, sugar, vinegar, plant juices, and baking soda. *Albatross Street; 508-495-2001.*

During the summer, **OceanQuest Discovery Cruises** (Woods Hole dock; 800-376-2326) give passengers the chance to play oceanographer in a manner that improves on the old television science show *Watch Mr. Wizard* while keeping the same sense of gee-whiz. Complex-sounding descriptions ("operating the instrumentation and equipment useful to study physical and meteorological oceanography") translate into such tasks as reading a thermometer submerged at different depths and figuring out how hard the wind is blowing and from which direction. A little basic chemistry reveals that seawater is full of salt. The favorite for most passengers is hauling nets and examining the catch, complete with a full profile on every critter that comes aboard (and the ubiquitous horseshoe crabs that are already aboard). The grade-school science lessons prove to be infectious fun for adults as well as kids, and there's the bonus of spending ninety minutes on the water in Woods Hole harbor, where evolution has wrought not only the horseshoe crab and the flounder but also the marine biologist and the curious traveler.

NANTUCKET SOUND

No one loves Nantucket Sound better than an eleven-year-old. This is Cape Cod for the *Mad* magazine crowd, where giant trampolines sit up the road from pirate mini-golf and bumper cars, where voracious travelers find themselves having to choose between a slab of chocolate fudge and a soft-serve sundae swimming in hot butterscotch. Vacationers let down their hair, drop their inhibitions, shelve their diets, and just plain give up and have a good time.

The communities of Nantucket Sound are vacationland at its most brazen, where human artifice and natural beauty are locked in a contest from which neither escapes unscathed. The crawl of traffic along Route 28 at high season is legendary. Drivers slump over their steering wheels as they motor past gas stations, souvenir stands, roadside attractions, sweets shops, and ice-cream shacks on their way to cedar-shingled summer cottages and pastel-painted motel complexes. The ocean is nowhere in sight, and yet . . . the open light of the shore appears in tantalizing glimpses, a brightness at the end of every narrow southward road. Beyond the tacky detritus of a half century of unbridled development lies the unwavering dream of a Cape Cod vacation.

Laid out at the heart of the Cape, the communities of Nantucket Sound circle in the orbit of Hyannis, with its seaport, airport, and shopping malls. The little villages strung like beads along the shoreline exist almost entirely for summer, all but closing down from Columbus Day to Memorial Day. Only Chatham, the eastern anchor of Nantucket Sound, goes about its tidy business all year, as its fishermen fish and its self-anointed squires clip the coupons of their Treasury bonds.

The Mid-Cape Highway, Route 6, forms the northern border for this area, but the only thoroughfare through the settled landscape of Nantucket Sound is Route 28, which enters from Mashpee on the west and bids adieu along the shores of Pleasant Bay, en route to the Cape Cod National Seashore.

■ HYANNIS   *map page 7, C-4*

The cautious and gradual way to approach the maelstrom of Hyannis is from the west on Route 28, with a looping detour through the very proper and exclusive village of Osterville to the quintessential summer strand, **Craigville Beach.**

Craigville is the people's beach. Local tradition holds that even the youthful John F. Kennedy considered it his Cape Cod favorite—but Craigville is clearly *not* the beach on which the mature JFK walked, lost in thought, in the famous photograph. A narrow strand with extensive parking lots on both sides of the access road, Craigville is a family shore with few peers along the Sound. Its long crescent of sand remains unbroken by the jetties that punctuate so many other beaches, and the warm and shallow waters invite swimmers by day and fishermen by the light of the moon. The east end of the beach is famous for mid-August fishing for Spanish mackerel and bonito. When the west wind is blowing on a slack high tide, they cruise in large numbers close to the shore.

From the beach, Old Craigville Road connects to Hyannis proper at pine-flanked West Main Street. The bucolic quality of the countryside can convince the unsuspecting traveler that Hyannis might be just another sleepy Cape village. But then comes the traffic circle and the **Cape Cod Melody Tent,** which is pretty much what it sounds like: an outdoor music venue under a big top. With its

The sandy strand of Hyannisport contrasts with the bustle of downtown Hyannis.

twenty-three hundred seats in the round, the Melody Tent is the music industry's equivalent of summer stock, with stars in eclipse playing their greatest hits to aging fans. *21 West Main Street, Hyannis; 508-775-9100. Performances mid-June–Aug.*

Hyannis lurks a few hundred yards east. If it didn't exist, Cape Codders would have invented it, for Hyannis is as necessary to Cape Cod as the Capitol Building is to Washington. However messy the process, it's where things get done. As Paul Theroux (for many years a part-time Cape resident) once observed, "Cape Codders forgive Hyannis its gimcrack look, because Hyannis is so useful a place— it's where you rent things, buy things and get things fixed and go to the movies. You can't have movie theaters and charm any more than you can have condominiums and rusticity."

Despite the asphalt meadows of the shopping malls along Route 132 north of town, Hyannis has managed to keep its Main Street more or less intact. A domestic drama of competing identities plays out there daily. The old-line Puritan of Cape Cod clothing store proffers surprisingly fashionable couture for women alongside men's wear that ranges from this month's *GQ* styles to the time-honored blue blazer and plaid pants. Colonial Candle, launched nearly a century ago when Mabel Kimball Baker started making bayberry tapers in her kitchen, holds forth with not one but *two* factory stores on Main Street, selling as much the idea of old-time Cape Cod as the appeal of eating dinner by candlelight.

Colonial Revival's counterpoint in Hyannis is glamour by association—specifically, by association with the Kennedy clan. The antiques and collectibles stores have a seemingly unlimited supply of 1960 presidential campaign buttons, cheap JFK portraits lithographed on gray cardboard, and yellowing November 1963 newspapers. Bookstores carry *PT-109* in the books-on-tape section. One restaurant serves a "Jackie O Jus" roast beef sandwich, while another plays up JFK Jr.'s preference for its bar. A clothing designer speaks of the late Kennedy prince with a mixture of pride, admiration, and aggravation: "God, he was gorgeous. His dog used to pee on the roses in front of my shop."

The Kennedy family began summering in Hyannisport in 1926 and bought the house that forms the heart of the modern compound in 1928. Exactly at the heart of Main Street, in the former Town Hall, the **John F. Kennedy Hyannis Museum** "remembers the happy times," as the director puts it. Certainly the images support

A sailboat plies the waters of Hyannis Harbor.

Patriotically decked out, Hyannis's shrine to its favorite son.

that contention—a 1931 family snapshot on the beach, a 1944 photograph of PT boat veterans playing touch football on the lawn, a formal portrait of the extended family on the day after JFK's election as president. A Kennedy family tree takes up an entire wall of the museum, and a film narrated by Walter Cronkite contends that Cape Cod shaped JFK's dreams of adventure. While the photos of Kennedy sailing are widely familiar, it is less well known that he often shot in the low eighties on the golf course at the Hyannisport Country Club, adjacent to the family compound. The official image of John F. Kennedy at Hyannisport is a sunny one. Brother Edward is quoted: "The time President Kennedy spent in Hyannisport during his youth and his presidency were among the happiest days of his life." *397 Main Street; 508-790-3077. Open Feb.–Dec.*

But the seaside town didn't escape the Kennedy sorrows. When Rose Kennedy was at the compound, she attended Mass daily at **St. Francis Xavier** (347 South Street)—including the day after JFK's assassination and the morning after Robert Kennedy was shot. All four of her sons were altar boys, and in 1946 the family dedicated an altar at St. Francis in memory of Joseph P. Kennedy Jr., who died in World War II.

One-way streets and unhelpful signage discourage the curious from even trying to find the Kennedy family compound at Hyannisport, but at the Ocean Street dock in Hyannis, **Hy-Line Cruises** (508-228-3949) offers a seasonal harbor cruise so visitors can gawk at the compound from the water. The docks are a busy place, with sportfishing vessels, a handful of commercial fishermen, and Hy-Line's high-speed catamaran to Nantucket all sharing the facilities. The larger, lumbering car ferry to Nantucket leaves from nearby docks off Pleasant Street; the catamaran, leaving a few minutes later, usually overtakes it at the mouth of the harbor.

A combination recreational and memorial complex stands near the foot of Ocean Street. The **John F. Kennedy Memorial** is a classic example of high emotions and good intentions trumping taste. An awkwardly executed bas-relief medallion of JFK is mounted on a stone wall facing the harbor. The placement takes on a certain logic if you read the inscription around the fountain in front of the wall: "I believe that it is important that this country sail and not lie still in the harbor," JFK wrote. Coins pitched into the fountain support the JFK Memorial Scholarship Fund and the town's youth sailing program. The memorial stands, appropriately enough, adjacent to **Veterans Park,** where a monument praises the men of the "forgotten war" in Korea. Both memorials open onto the broad sandy beach of **Kalmus Park,** well protected from all but the gentlest waves.

KENNEDY INCOGNITO

Yet Hyannis Port always brought a certain sense of informality that was missing elsewhere. Mrs. Kennedy dressed more casually, in old slacks and her orthopedic shoes. She washed and set her own hair most of the time, and, in fact, it often didn't matter what her hair looked like because she covered it with a big scarf to protect her against the strong winds of the Cape. No wonder tourists sometimes stopped her to ask the way to the Kennedy compound. She did indeed look like someone's faithful servant or impoverished relative when she got bundled up in her usual walking attire of a heavy sweater and grandmotherly babushka. It never fazed her when people did approach her, and sometimes she brought amazed tourists back to the house with her, posing for snapshots on the front lawn and graciously signing autographs. Once she got on a tour bus and rode with the crowd right up to her front door.

—Barbara Gibson, *Life with Rose Kennedy*, 1986

Although better known for White House touch-football games, John F. Kennedy also enjoyed rounds of golf at the Hyannisport Country Club, next to the Kennedy family compound.

■ **YARMOUTH SOUTH COAST** *map page 7, C-4*

Within a mile of leaving Hyannis heading east ("south" by the road sign) on Route 28, three landmarks suddenly appear in West Yarmouth: the faux waterfall of Thunder Falls Mini-Golf, the white whale of Putters Paradise Mini-Golf, and the silver-shingled **Baxter Grist Mill,** restored and presented to the town of Yarmouth in 1960. The mill structure is so modest that at first glance it appears to be only another water hazard on a mini-golf course. But it's the real thing. Built shortly after 1700, it operated with an external water wheel until about 1860, when it was fitted with an interior water turbine. The mill went out of business around 1900, when electricity and cheap flour made it uneconomical and tourism began to overtake subsistence farming in the community. *Tours on a limited summer schedule; call the Old Yarmouth Historical Society at 508-382-2231 for hours.*

Never terribly successful as a farming community, West Yarmouth gave itself wholeheartedly to tourism in the late nineteenth century. As a result, vacation homes and cottage colonies cover the land like brambles, from the south side of

Route 28 to the shore. The boggy land on the north side of the highway, by contrast, has some of the lightest development on Nantucket Sound, leaving room for large attractions like the open pavilion of **Jump on Us! Trampoline** (260 Route 28, West Yarmouth; 508-775-3304).

While most agriculture vanished beneath the onslaught of tourism, cranberry cultivation survived. A huge working bog lies just west of the turnoff down Berry Avenue to **Englewood Beach,** one of the few beaches on the south side of Cape Cod with free parking (albeit at a distance from the beach itself). It is an excellent spot for small children, because the water drops off very gradually and Great Island shelters it from large waves.

Back on Route 28, the **ZooQuarium** has long since evolved from its origins as a roadside spectacle to a charmingly low-key nature attraction that delights small children and leaves their parents relieved by its sheer wholesomeness. Indoor aquariums and terrariums hold some strapping examples of local fish and amphibians, especially turtles. ZooQuarium works with the state Division of Fish and Wildlife to hatch out Plymouth Red Belly Turtles for release into the wild as part of a program to bolster this endangered species in its native habitat of Plymouth County. Outdoors, children are encouraged to pet the llamas, fallow deer, pygmy goats, Navajo churro sheep, and Icelandic sheep, which are all identified by cute names. "Please wash your hands before eating," a sign implores. The ZooQuarium is also home to rehabilitated wildlife that would be unable to fend for themselves if released into the wild; on one recent visit, the residents included a red-tailed hawk, a barn owl, a bobcat, and a red fox. Once upon a time, Aqua Circus, the predecessor to ZooQuarium, presented Acapulco-style high divers in its indoor pool, but nowadays visitors view the antics of performing sea lions. *674 Route 28, West Yarmouth; 508-775-8883. Open mid-Feb.–late Nov.*

Turn south down Sea View Avenue to reach Yarmouth's long strand of Nantucket Sound beaches along South Shore Drive. To control sand migration and erosion, rock jetties punctuate the long barrier beach. The jetties also seem to separate public beaches from private ones, while providing great access for surf fishermen looking to cast their lines beyond the swimming zone. Swirling currents around the jetty points are particularly good spots to catch bluefish on the surface by fishing with sand eels—or striped bass swimming a few feet deeper as they feed on the bluefish leavings. **Sea View Beach** has limited parking, while **Parker River Beach** offers both more spaces and bathhouses.

At the east end of South Shore Drive, **Bass River Town Landing** and **Bass River Beach** make good use of the mouth of the river. The landing has its own parking lot with long spaces for boat trailers, and the channel is lined with stone jetties to provide a complete separation from the adjacent sandy beach. Between the two, a boardwalk and planked deck provide a walkway, observation point, and picnic spot for boaters and bathers alike.

South Street turns northward from the beach and landing complex. Follow it to Willow Street and turn east to reach the little waterside park dominated by the towering **Judah Baker Windmill,** at the corner of Willow and River Streets. Windmill Park has a few dozen parking spaces, but it's also a favorite stopover for touring cyclists, who come to enjoy the small sandy bathing beach and postcard views over the tufted marshes of Bass River. The 1791 mill, restored in 1999, is open for tours on an irregular basis in the summer; call the Yarmouth Historical Commission (508-382-2231, ext. 237) for hours. If you're traveling with your own kayak or canoe, Windmill Park Beach is a good spot to put in to explore the Bass River estuaries.

Both River and South Streets lead north into South Yarmouth, one of the rare New England villages organized around a Quaker meetinghouse rather than a Congregational or Unitarian church. The land was set aside in 1713 as a reservation for the Pawkunnakwut band of Wampanoags, but all but one member of the tribe died in a 1763 epidemic. Quaker David Kelley bought much of the land, built a rope works, and donated the parcel where the **Quaker Meeting House** was built in 1809. For much of the nineteenth century, the district went by the name of Friends Village—despite the presence of Baptist and Methodist meetinghouses—and the village prospered as a mercantile center. Small shipyards and many saltworks opened up on the banks of the Bass River, along with a magnesia factory to process the byproducts of saltmaking. Remnants of the era of commercial prosperity survive mainly in the handsome, foursquare merchants' houses along Pleasant Street.

■ **DENNIS SOUTH COAST** *map page 7, C-4*

Dennis doesn't go out of its way to alert travelers to its beaches. There is no sign, but four-tenths of a mile east of the Bass River bridge, Fisk Street leads south to

Angling for bluefish at Bass River in Yarmouth.

ROLLING DOWN THE RAIL TRAIL

While the crowds are at the beach, cyclists can freewheel past Cape Cod's inland vistas on the 25.8-mile Cape Cod Rail Trail. The asphalt path follows the former Old Colony Railroad right-of-way between Route 134 in Dennis and LeCount Hollow Road in South Wellfleet, passing through inland corners of Harwich, Chatham, Brewster, Orleans, and Eastham along the way.

Leave Dennis in the early morning and you'll be chowing down on fried clams at Capt'n Cass in Orleans' Rock Harbor for lunch—with plenty of time for a swim at Hinckleys or Long Pond in Harwich. New paving and overpass bridges at highway crossings have made the trail safer and easier to ride than ever. It traverses piney woods, skims past several cranberry bogs, and winds up on towering headlands above the ocean. At the South Wellfleet end, cyclists can walk their bikes across the highway and keep going on Cape Cod National Seashore trails or shoot down LeCount Hollow Road to the beach. Nickerson State Park, at approximately the midpoint, has several additional miles of trails and the only public restrooms on the route.

Travelers who haven't brought their own bicycles can rent them at **Barbara's Bike Shop,** at the western trailhead (Route 134, Dennis; 508-760-4723), and adjacent to the trail outside the main entrance of Nickerson State Park (Route 6A, Brewster; 508-896-7231).

West Dennis Beach, a powder-sand barrier beach and marsh system at the mouth of Bass River. By coincidences of geography, the waters off West Dennis Beach tend to enjoy a steady southwesterly breeze with only light gusts, making the area as close to perfect for windsurfing as Cape Cod waters get. Back on Route 28, **Inland Sea Windsurf Co.** (888-465-2632) sells all the necessary gear.

In the same mini strip mall, **Howlin' Howie's Kayak Rentals** (40 Route 28, West Dennis; 508-398-0060) has the supreme advantage of being on Grand Cove, part of the Bass River system. Bass River is one of the largest cuts into the interior on the south side of Cape Cod. Draining from the glacial Dennis Highlands, the river connects several kettle ponds, forming a miniature inland bay with marshy coves. The scent of peat fills the air amid green marsh grasses on the upper reaches of the Bass River system—a paddling antidote to the hubbub of summer. It's as if another world has opened up, with only egrets and herons for company.

To bypass the Route 28 traffic snarl, follow the shoreline on Lower County Road east from West Dennis Beach into Dennisport. This is a particularly good route if you're hungry, as **Swan River Restaurant** (508-394-4466) **& Fish Market** (508-398-2340) is at 5 Lower County Road, at the mouth of Swan River. The affiliated enterprises are open from spring to Columbus Day. The main dining room of the restaurant has huge windows overlooking the marshy mouth of Swan River, a modest stream that dissects Dennis's Nantucket Sound coast.

East of the river, Lower County Road continues inland, while Old Wharf Road loops southward to Dennisport's two best public beaches, **Glendon-Darling Beach** and **Sea Street Beach.** Both have large parking lots, restrooms, and, in the summer, food vendors. Tiny beach cottages of World War II vintage line Old Wharf Road, and both foot and auto traffic is heavy and slow in July and August. Long stone jetties divide the beaches into discrete areas. The beach at Sea Street descends precipitously from the parking lot, and the view from the top of the rise takes in the islands of Monomoy and, on a clear day, the faint outline of Nantucket in the distance. Old Wharf Road ends at Depot Street. One block north, a right turn onto Lower County Road continues the shore route into the town of Harwich.

The shopper's alternative is to follow Sea Street back to Route 28 in tiny Dennisport center. Just west of the Harwich town line, the small village storefronts have become a de facto shopping center for antiques and collectibles. The range of goods is broad, from absolute junk to fine-quality English and American furniture, art pottery, and glass. Representing about a hundred dealers, **Main Street Antique Center** (691 Main Street, Dennisport; 508-760-5700) stocks the most merchandise of local interest, including Sandwich glass, vintage shell art, and Cape Cod souvenir china.

■ HARWICH   *map page 7, D-4*

Harwich is one of the most fragmented of Cape Cod towns, with seven villages representing what were once seven churches. There's a Harwich for each of the four main compass points, as well as Harwich Center, Harwichport, and Pleasant Lake. The distinctions are of more import to those who live here than to travelers, who tend to stick to the waterfront southern tier of West Harwich, Harwichport, and South Harwich. Both Portuguese immigrants and New York summer people began arriving around 1890, but an old Yankee tang still clings to the villages.

SWEET TART

Cranberries have covered Cape Cod since time immemorial, and candy makers have been satisfying the sweet tooth of Cape vacationers for decades, so it's surprising that chocolate and cranberries didn't really come together until the late twentieth century. Although confectioners had dabbled in cranberry creams, it took Raymond Hebert of **Stage Stop Candy** (411 Main Street, Dennisport; 508-394-1791) to perfect the whole-berry cranberry cordial in the mid-1980s. Picking his berries from a wild bog, he experimented and, he later recalled, "got it right on the third try." The cordial resembles a cherry cordial—fruit surrounded by syrup in a chocolate shell—but is less cloying, with the distinct tang of fresh cranberries.

Dorothy Cox's Chocolates (115 Huttleston Avenue, Fairhaven; 508-996-2465) started experimenting with cranberries and chocolate at the request of the Ocean Spray Cranberry Cooperative in the 1970s. Cox's struck gold in the early 1990s by "panning" sweetened dried cranberries in dark and milk chocolate and their yogurt-based white confectionery, becoming the first producer of the (syrupless) chocolate-coated cranberry. A year later, the company sold fourteen hundred two-pound bags on the QVC shopping channel in four minutes.

Raymond and Donna Hebert of Dennisport's Stage Stop Candy.

A handful of sandy beaches with good wave action lie at the end of the roads dribbling southward from Lower County Road. Braced on each side by stone jetties, they're short and blunt, shaped like clam hoes or cranberry rakes with the jetties as the outer tines. The ocean paws at the beaches, creating a scoop in the sand just below the low-tide line. The best of the West Harwich group are the **Earle Road Beaches.**

Lower County Road rejoins Route 28 in Harwichport, a briny little village that flourished as a whaling port and shipbuilding center in the eighteenth century, turned to codfishing in the nineteenth, and has largely devoted itself to tourism in the twentieth and twenty-first. The village center still holds a passel of shops, including the showroom of the **Cape Cod Braided Rug Company** (537 Route 28, Harwichport; 508-432-3133), which has produced machine-braided wool rugs since 1910.

A southward turn on Bank Street leads down to Nantucket Sound at **Bank Street Beach,** perhaps the most commodious of the Harwich beaches. If the substantial parking lot is full, the beach will be too. The public portion of the beach is not very long, but the sand stretches far toward the water at low tide. Fences on each side clearly mark private beaches attached to the inns on the west side and to private homes on the east.

Bank Street leads north from Route 28 to the **Harwich Conservation Trust cranberry bogs.** Park in the Harbormaster's workshop parking lot and follow the short trail southward to hike the perimeter of these sixty-two-acre working bogs, said to be the oldest commercial bogs on the Cape. (They've been farmed continuously since the 1880s.) The darting birds with iridescent backs greedily snapping up mosquitoes over the bogs are tree swallows.

Some of the bog's cranberries might find their way to **Sundae School** (606 Main Street, Route 28, Harwich Port; 508-430-2444), a Cape institution with a parking lot larger than those at most of the area beaches. In addition to traditional toppings of hot fudge and butterscotch, the ice cream parlor serves fresh seasonal fruit, including blueberries, peaches, raspberries, and, of course, cranberries. In season, a real Bing cherry tops the whipped cream.

Harwichport's historic Wychmere and Saquatucket harbors lie along Route 28 a short distance farther east. Wychmere has become principally a private preserve for yachtsmen and wealthy retirees, but Saquatucket retains some of its old-fashioned workaday grit. Fishing trawlers and tuna harpooners anchor here, and the

Freedom Cruise Line (702 Main Street, Harwichport; 508-432-8999) operates a ninety-minute ferry service to Nantucket with free parking for day-trippers. Operating from the same driveway across from the harbor, **Monomoy Island Excursions** (508-430-7772) runs sightseeing cruises to view seals and sea birds at the tip of Chatham's South Beach and on the two halves of Monomoy Island, protected as a National Wildlife Refuge (see "For the Birds," on page 152). Several sportfishing boats also sail from Saquatucket, ranging from thirty-foot light tackle boats to party launches twice the length.

■ CHATHAM   *map page 7, D-4*

The lyric-minded sometimes call Chatham the first stop of the east wind, because nothing but ocean lies between this elbow of Cape Cod and the west coast of Portugal. But wind has less to do with Chatham than waves, for the ocean keeps making and remaking the land, as if each shoreline were little more than another draft to be erased in a fall hurricane and refashioned like a sand-castle fantasy the following summer. The edges of Chatham are mutable and evanescent, changing not just in detail but in design as perplexed landowners look on with dismay. Yet this country of shoals and bars, of barrier islands and breaches, has a permanence as well. Amid the changing landscape, the people cultivate a Cape Cod constancy.

On the Route 28 approach to Chatham from Harwich, Barn Hill Road leads down to **Hardings Beach,** the first hint of the massive barrier beaches on the Cape's Atlantic face. Two large parking lots accommodate hundreds of automobiles, yet the one-and-a-half-mile beach backed by low, rolling dunes seems to swallow the crowds like a sandstorm. The moody seaside stroll to the decommissioned Stage Harbor Light is the stuff of which personals ads are made—and it's a popular romp for dogs and their owners after September 15 and before April 1. Strollers caught far from the parking lot by the rising tide can walk back on the boardwalk behind the dunes. Humans and canines aren't the only fans of Hardings Beach: signs warn not to molest the basking gray and harbor seals that sometimes haul out here to catch some rays.

Although still marked "south" on the road signs, by the compass Route 28 doglegs north at the traffic circle on the west end of Chatham village to effectively

The value of the catch at the Chatham Fish Pier often tops that of much larger ports, partly because expensive scallops and bluefin tuna form a big part of the haul.

bypass the community and its more than sixty miles of shoreline. Better to turn south onto Stage Harbor Road, which passes by the placid children's beach at **Oyster Pond** along the way to Stage Neck peninsula.

The **Old Atwood House Museum** is home to the Chatham Historical Society. The rooms of the 1752 house are filled, sometimes to overflowing, with items of local interest—such as an entire room devoted to Chatham author Joseph C. Lincoln, a prolific early-twentieth-century fiction writer who set most of his stories and novels on Cape Cod, many in Chatham. First editions of his books are on display, as well as several oil paintings that illustrated them. Frederick Wight, a Chatham native who later headed UCLA's Fine Arts Department, painted portraits of many Chatham sea captains between 1928 and 1935, while his mother, Alice Stallknecht, recorded their reminiscences of the seafaring life. These portraits and transcripts occupy another gallery.

But Stallknecht's own artwork—murals of Chatham life, which she painted between 1932 and 1945—made a bigger splash. Her expressionist style and her penchant for blending biblical and modern scenes caused quite a sensation when they were unveiled. Locals professed particular shock at her mural of townspeople surrounding a Christ depicted as a clean-shaven Cape Cod fisherman. Her candid character studies of Chatham townsfolk at a church supper may have a more lasting appeal; aged volunteer guides delight in pointing out relatives and former neighbors, mostly passed on. However scandalous they were when first painted, Stallknecht's murals have acquired the respectability of age—just part of the Chatham story.

It's a disjointed tale with many chapters. A bronze tablet set into a stone on the front lawn of the Atwood House offers the observation that "Somewhere within gunshot of this stone lies the remains of Squanto, Indian guide, friend and counselor of the Plymouth Colony who died in 1622 on the sloop *Swan* in Stage Harbor." *Open June–Sept. 347 Stage Neck Road, Chatham; 508-945-2493.*

Stage Harbor landing provides extremely well-protected moorings for small craft. **Stage Harbor Marine** (508-945-1860) operates sportfishing charters, seal-watching cruises, and trips to Monomoy. The "harbor" itself is a semicircular tidal inland waterway protected from the Atlantic by the reaching arms of Hardings Beach and Morris Island. The swirling, drifting sands of the Chatham shore lie east across the corduroy surface of the wooden drawbridge, which leads to Chatham Light.

A Chatham windmill takes advantage of marine breezes.

A right turn down Morris Island Road leads south across a causeway to the ritzy preserve of newly built McMansions, on the same island with the headquarters of the **Monomoy National Wildlife Refuge.** At or near low tide, many locals park on the causeway to dig for quahogs in the shallow waters of the surrounding flats. On a good day, clammers say, they can harvest between eighty and ninety large clams in an hour.

For walkers, drivers, and boaters alike, the principal landmarks of the Chatham shore are the **Coast Guard station** and adjacent **Chatham Light,** a key warning signal of the town's treacherous shoals. The lighthouse blinks with two quick flashes, an obscure reference to the fact that it was a double light until the second tower was moved up the coast to replace Nauset Light in 1923.

A dozen U.S Lifesaving Service stations used to be spread out along the forty-mile Atlantic beach of Cape Cod between Monomoy Point (now at the southern tip of South Monomoy Island) and Race Point in Provincetown, and lifesavers stalked the beaches day and night to watch for ships in trouble. The patrols would meet at halfway houses, turn around, and retrace their steps. Time and again they went into the surf with boats and lines to haul hundreds of sailors to safety. But the

surfmen didn't always prevail. A tall granite obelisk next to the light memorializes the lives lost on March 17, 1902, when the lifesavers of Monomoy Station attempted to rescue Capt. William Mack of Cleveland and his crew on the barge *Wadena*, which had run aground on Shovelful Shoal off Monomoy Point. When the rescue boat overturned, seven lifesavers and four of the barge's crew drowned, along with Captain Mack, whose family erected the monument.

Many a ship has run aground off Chatham, for the shoals shift constantly. Park across the street from the light and behold the land and sea in a constant dance as first one leads, then the other. The shore here keeps changing in human rather than geological time. During most of the twentieth century, the southern reach of Nauset Beach stretched across the harbor, and Chatham Light stood on an inside passage. But a hurricane in fall 1987 breached the barrier beach in front of the light, truncating Nauset and creating the island of **South Beach.** Waves pounded, sands swirled, and the shore currents deposited great swaths of sand at the north end of South Beach. An isthmus soon connected the island to the mainland, creating vast new mussel beds in the process.

Boats at Mill Pond in Chatham and (above) beachcombers on South Beach.

FOR THE BIRDS

Monomoy is a place apart—apart from the mainland since a 1958 storm, apart from itself since a 1978 blizzard split the island into north and south. As a National Wilderness Area, it offers the rare chance to see Cape Cod in something like its primal state. Humans never had more than a toehold on this barrier-island strip that dribbles off Cape Cod's elbow. Fishermen lived at its southern tip to be just that much closer to the Nantucket shoals, and market waterfowl hunters built blinds in its marshes. A few rusticators took over the fishing shacks when the harbor filled with sand.

But Monomoy has always been essential for birds. Strategically located as a stopover on the migratory Atlantic flyway, the islands see as many as two hundred species of birds as regular, if seasonal, visitors. Dozens of species of warblers chirp through each spring and fall, alighting on every bit of scrubby brush on South Monomoy. Come harsh winter, pelagic species like jaegers join the geese and ducks around North Monomoy. On the remote beaches and dunes, far from most predators, endangered piping plovers and roseate terns have been staging a comeback from near extinction.

And for reasons yet unexplained, gray and harbor seals have taken to Monomoy in great numbers since the mid-1990s, with three thousand to five thousand spending at least part of the year fishing the surrounding waters and hauling out on the beaches.

For all this *Wild Kingdom* idyll, Monomoy tolerates a limited number of human visitors, who walk the slowly vanishing trails; botanize; observe birds, seals, and even foxes; and generally putter around in the way that khaki-wearing, binocular-toting, field-guide-quoting folk are wont to do.

Monomoy National Wildlife Refuge covers about twenty-seven hundred acres on North and South Monomoy islands and a forty-six-acre portion on Morris Island, which is attached to Chatham. The Morris sector has a visitors center and a small trail. It also has a dock for ferries to North and South Monomoy, where only three boat services are allowed to land passengers. Portions of the beaches are often closed between April and September as endangered species nest and raise their hatchlings.

Although private boaters or kayakers are allowed to land in the refuge, other visitors can make the most of their time by signing up for the guided tours offered by both the Massachusetts Audubon Society's Wellfleet Bay Wildlife Refuge in Wellfleet and the Cape Cod Museum of Natural History in Brewster. Sign up at, or by calling, the refuge or the museum.

Monomoy National Wildlife Refuge Visitors Center. *Wikis Way, Morris Island, Chatham; 508-945-0594. Open weekdays 8-4, sometimes weekends in summer.*

MONOMOY BOAT SERVICES
Monomoy Island Ferry (Rip Ryder). *508-945-5450, www.monomoyislandferry.com. Departs from visitors center.*
Outermost Harbor Marine. *83 Seagull Lane, off Morris Island Road; 508-945-2030, www.outermostharbor.com.*
Stage Harbor Marine. *80 Bridge Street, Stage Harbor; 508-945-1860, www.stageharbormarine.com.*

MONOMOY GUIDED TOURS
Cape Cod Museum of Natural History. *508-896-3867, www.ccmnh.org.*
Wellfleet Bay Wildlife Sanctuary. *508-349-2615, www.wellfleetbay.org.*

As a barrier system, South Beach is pounded by waves and has tricky inshore currents, making it a problematic beach for swimmers but an excellent place to walk, sun, play volleyball, or merely contemplate the power of tides and storms. It's a strenuous walk in loose sand, but the southern end of the peninsula is one of the best places to look for shorebirds and basking seals. For the curious who would rather not walk, several boats around Chatham convey sightseers to the point.

Shore Road leads north through Chatham's main harbor to the **Chatham Fish Pier,** which, unlike most of the town, shows no signs of gentrification. The possible exception is a decorative bas-relief sculpture called *The Provider*, which depicts many of the species landed here: lobster, scallop, squid, flounder, cod, crab, sea bass, pollock, skate, tuna, and mackerel. It's dedicated to "The Chatham Fishing Industry, Ever Changing to Remain the Same." On the docks, Chatham Fish & Lobster maintains its processing plant, while Nickerson Fish & Lobster sells fish by the pound as well as fried fish, boiled lobster, and other standards of the shore dinner. The Chatham fishing fleet is minuscule by New Bedford standards, but the value of the catch landed here often exceeds that at Boston's Fish Pier, in part because high-value scallops and bluefin tuna make up a large percentage of the catch. Several sightseeing boats also sail from Fish Pier.

Shore Road leads north and joins Route 28. A roadside sign offers two choices to cure what may ail you: psychotherapy and sportfishing charters. The small, gray-shingled home with a bowed roof like an upended ship's hull is the **Nickerson Family Association House** (1107 Orleans Road, North Chatham; 508-398-3183

for hours), a genealogical research center that marks the spot of the 1664 home o
William and Ann Busby Nickerson, the town's founders.

A plaque honoring the town's early families stands in front of the library, o
Main Street, which marches from the Route 28 traffic circle into the solid upland
of the village. Enumerating those Pilgrim Nickersons, Doanes, Bassets, an
Eldridges, the plaque "In Memory of the Pioneers of Chatham" proudly notes tha
William Nickerson purchased the land from the Monomoyick band o
Wampanoags. Chatham's Main Street retains the air of an old Cape Cod village, i
big churches clustered around a green dell, small independent shops lining th
streets, and pink damask roses on every lane. Town powers manage to keep touris
traffic in check by offering free parking at several central lots, thereby encouragin
strolling.

Quirky shops and boutiques dot the village. **Blue Water Fish Rubbings** (50
Main Street; 508-945-7616), for example, has found a nonculinary use for th
local catch by brushing the fish with textile inks to print piscine T-shirts, fleec
pullovers, and aprons. The gallery of **Kelsey-Kennard Photographers** (465 Mai
Street; 508-945-4800) carries stunning aerial photography of the shiftin
Chatham shores in all seasons over half a century. **Yellow Umbrella Books** (50
Main Street; 508-945-0144) sells volumes about Cape Cod and books by Cap
authors, including Paul Giambarba's 1965 children's classic, *Around Cape Cod wit
Cap'n Goody in His Magic Whaleboat.* (The used-books section is a good spot to bu
a disposable beach read.) The **Squire** (487 Main Street; 508-945-0945) has bee
around only since the late 1960s, but this tavern-cum-family-restaurant has the a
of seasoned perseverance. Police, shopkeepers, and tourists hunker down for coffe
doughnuts, and baked haddock by day; come evening, the bar morphs into th
briny domain of the clamdiggers, gill netters, tuna harpooners, and scallop dredger

During the summer, the entire town turns out on Friday nights to cluste
around the bandstand in tiny Kate Gould Park, next to the Chatham Wayside In
Bring a blanket, stop at **Chatham Candy Manor** (484 Main Street; 508-945
0825) for a bag of chocolate creams, and grab a seat on the grass. Neighbors sho
"Heidy-ho!" to each other in the gloaming until, at 8 P.M. sharp, the band star
playing "Band Time in Chatham" (to the tune of "State Fair March"): "It's Ban
Time in Chatham / With a show to hear and see. / For Band Time is a grand tim
/ 'Tis the open door of opportunity. . . ."

A fisherman shows off a trophy at Chatham Fish Pier.

THE AMERICAN GAME

Walt Whitman's America is alive and well on a summer's eve on Cape Cod, when lithe young men take the fields of the village baseball parks, the umpire cries *Play ball!*, and a baby-faced pitcher bears down on home plate. When the college junior hangs a curveball, the crisp *crack!* of a wooden bat striking the horsehide sphere resounds in the sultry air, setting the whole game in motion. "I see great things in baseball," Whitman wrote. "It's our game—the American game." And Whitman never saw the Falmouth Commodores play the Brewster Whitecaps.

The Cape Cod Baseball League represents the American game at its purest. More than half the players pack groceries, mow lawns, paint houses, or wash dishes before they turn out to play six games a week from mid-June through August in the most prestigious amateur league in the country. With ten teams stocked by some of the country's top collegiate players, Cape League games invariably attract the professional scouts. On average, more than 180 players in the Major Leagues each season are Cape Cod Baseball League alumni.

The Barnstable Townies pose for a 1953 team portrait.

Sliding in for a run.

With some help from Major League Baseball, the towns support the teams—spectators are asked to toss a dollar or two into the jug that goes around to help defer costs—and players board with families, usually at a nominal cost. Pro scouts skulk behind home plate with their radar guns, small children chase down foul balls to exchange for an ice-cream coupon, and old-timers tell anyone who will listen about the summer that Nomar Garciaparra went on a batting tear.

As Christopher Price wrote in his 1998 appreciation of the league, *Baseball at the Beach*, "The Cape League remains true to the ideal of the game of baseball—that it is simply a game, to be played with nine men on a side, four bases, three outs, and a village full of people cheering for both sides."

Box scores and listings of upcoming games appear daily in the *Cape Cod Times*, and the league's schedule is posted on the Web site www.capecodbaseball.org. The ten teams and their home fields and towns are:

Bourne Braves. *Coady School Field, Trowbridge Road, Bourne.*
Brewster Whitecaps. *Cape Cod Tech High School, Route 124, Harwich.*
Chatham Athletics. *Veterans Field, Route 28, Chatham Center.*
Cotuit Kettleers. *Lowell Park, Lowell Street, Cotuit.*
Falmouth Commodores. *Guv Fuller Field, Route 28, Falmouth.*
Harwich Mariners. *Whitehouse Field, Harwich High School, Oak Street, Harwich.*
Hyannis Mets. *McKeon Field, High School Road, Hyannis.*
Orleans Cardinals. *Eldredge Park, Route 28, Orleans.*
Wareham Gatemen. *Spillane Field, Route 6, Wareham.*
Yarmouth-Dennis Red Sox. *Red Wilson Field, Station Avenue, South Yarmouth.*

C A P E   C O D
N A T I O N A L   S E A S H O R E

In one dramatic curving stroke, the Cape Cod National Seashore limns the outline of land and sea from the elbow to the fist of Cape Cod's muscular arm. In many respects, this national park is the best and purest expression of the Cape. Pitch pine and bearberry barely cloak the graceful bones of the land, and a forty-mile strand lines the rim of the land like salt on a margarita glass. Authorized by Congress in 1961, the National Seashore became a reality five years and many millions of dollars later. The 43,569-acre preserve comprises federal, state, and town land along with approximately 600 parcels of private property. Apart from the brown-and-white Park Service signs, it can be difficult to tell where town property ends and federal jurisdiction begins. The Seashore touches Chatham and takes in large sections of the townships of Orleans, Eastham, Wellfleet, Truro, and Provincetown. Most of this chapter covers the National Seashore, but it also details areas of Orleans and Eastham that lie outside park limits. The community of Chatham is covered in the "Nantucket Sound" chapter, Wellfleet, Truro, and Provincetown in the "Outer Cape" chapter.

The Seashore was set aside first for conservation and preservation and only secondarily for recreation. Its borders encompass vast mats of salt marsh, towering headlands, horizon-stretching sandy beaches, fragile dunes, still kettle ponds, trickling brooks, maple and cedar swamps, and a handful of tiny cottages perched among the rolling inland dunes on Cape Cod's outermost reaches. Because the habitats are often fragile, visitors should treat all the land and shore as something precious—national treasure held in stewardship until, some day, the sea reclaims it.

■ NAUSET BEACH & ENVIRONS *map page 185, D-6*

Route 28 "south" from Chatham actually veers north by the compass as it skirts the western bank of aptly named Pleasant Bay, enclosed by a seven-mile barrier beach. The Cape's arm pivots at Orleans, where the land suddenly narrows, and Main Street defines the yin and yang of this slender peninsula thrust between the Atlantic Ocean and Cape Cod Bay. On the west end lies a fishing harbor dotted with glacial erratics, on the east the five-mile sandbar of Nauset Beach.

An angler at sunrise on Nauset Light Beach, one of the many strands within the
Cape Cod National Seashore.

The popularity of **Nauset Beach** for swimming and sunbathing predates the
National Seashore by a century, and the residential and motel area above the
beach's marshlands was already well established when the Seashore was created. In
keeping with tradition, the Town of Orleans administers the beach, maintaining
changing rooms and showers and providing lifeguards in the summer for the central beach area. Orleans also permits some concessions—including Liam's, locally
famous for its onion rings.

Nauset's parking lot—one of the largest on the National Seashore—can easily
fill up by 9 A.M. on a beautiful July day. A boardwalk cuts through fifteen-foot-
high dunes to the narrow beach, so long that all those bodies from all those cars
quickly disperse like so many grains of sand. Swimming at Nauset calls for stamina
and strength. When the waves wash in, they suck the sand from beneath waders'
feet. If caught unaware, the best strategy is to paddle out a little and catch the crest
of a wave to body surf to shore—and then stand up quickly before the next wave
hits. Nauset Beach waves can even challenge serious board surfers. At high tide,
they echo off the dune wall in a basso profundo growl.

An old trail inside the beach's winter berm leads southward from the sun
bathing, surf-swimming throngs toward **Chatham Light,** across the mouth o
Pleasant Bay. Surfcasters stand on this lower beach and haul back their long pole:
to throw artificial lures or hooks baited with whole clams into the breakers. They
watch the shore zone for those magic moments when mackerel swim between the
beach and the outer sandbars and voracious bluefish chase behind them, churning
the waters as they slash and feed.

Heading west on Orleans's Main Street leads you to **Rock Harbor,** nestled in
the crook of the Cape's elbow. A fleet of small sportfishing boats docks at the pier
When offshore waters are rough, they cruise the coast for mackerel and flounder
When bluefish or striped bass are making a run, they follow the schools. Don't be
fooled by the modest size of the boats. They're perfectly capable of heading to
deeper waters, where surface-feeding shortfin mako sharks and bluefin tuna spend
the late summer.

Namskaket Road, a more southerly branch off Main Street, leads to **Skake
Beach.** This town beach with calm waters is a perfect counterpoint to Nauset. The
water is so shallow that the harbor freezes in a cold winter, building up sheets of ice

LAND SAILS

Swept by unrelenting winds, the open plain at the Cape's elbow was home to the
region's greatest concentration of windmills, used both to grind grain and to pump
seawater to the evaporating pans of salt works. "The most foreign and picturesque
structures on the Cape," Henry David Thoreau observed in *Cape Cod,* ". . . are the
wind-mills—gray looking octagonal towers, with long timbers slanting to the ground
in the rear, and there resting on a cart-wheel, by which their fans are turned round to
face the wind." Orleans and Eastham still boast colonial-era windmills, now less
practical than picturesque.

The **Jonathan Young Windmill,** at Town Cove Park (Route 28 and 6A) was built
in Orleans around 1720 and moved to Hyannisport in 1897. It came full circle in
1983, when it was donated to the Orleans Historical Society, which installed it at its
present location. The Eastham mill, at **Windmill Park** on Route 6, was built in
Plymouth in 1680 and floated across the bay to Eastham in 1793, where it remained
in irregular use until the end of the nineteenth century. Restored to working condition in 1936, it was spruced up again in 1998. Tulips planted around the structure
give Eastham's park a distinctly Dutch cast in the spring.

that look like abstract sculpture. Skaket complements Nauset in another way: the sun rises over the water at Nauset and sets with golden glory over Skaket.

Back on Route 28, the **French Cable Station Museum** occupies the 1890 building where the French Cable Company operators handled telegraph traffic between the United States and France. The laying of a direct three-thousand-mile cable between France and Orleans in 1898 and another between Orleans and New York made this small building a major conduit of world news, including financial transactions of the Paris Bourse and the New York Stock Exchange. Marines guarded the center during World War I, when it served as the link between U.S. and French Army headquarters. Technologically obsolete, the station closed down in November 1959. Quaint pre-radio pieces of equipment—devices of wood and glass and brass that brought the news of Lindbergh's landing in Paris—are the chief attraction. *Cove Road and Route 28, Orleans; 508-240-1735. Open June–Sept.*

■ NAUSET MARSH & ENVIRONS   *map page 185, D-5/6*

When the French explorer Samuel de Champlain mapped Nauset harbor in 1605, it was a protected but navigable bay, with arms of sand extending from each side at its mouth. By the nineteenth century, the sandy arms had nearly met, leaving only a small inlet. Wave action decreased, marsh grasses took hold, and one of the most productive salt marsh habitats in the world was born. Even by Cape Cod salt-marsh standards, the **Nauset Marsh** system is huge, stretching more than three miles north to south and nearly two miles east to west. The system even has its own tides, running about two hours behind the Chatham tide tables, the nearest published tables on the Atlantic side of the Cape—essential knowledge for kayakers trying to negotiate the shallow passages behind Coast Guard Beach.

The best way to explore Nauset Marsh is by kayak, pushing off from Town Cove, which has one of the most navigable channels of the marsh's inner reaches. Not surprisingly, one of the Cape's largest outdoors outfitters sits right at the water's edge, just off the Orleans traffic circle. **Goose Hummock Shop** (Route 6A, Town Cove, Orleans; 508-255-0455) sells fishing and bow-hunting gear and also arranges sportfishing charters. But most people visit the store to rent canoes and kayaks or to take classes in kayaking technique.

(following pages) Nauset Light sends a signal on a foggy morning.

A stealthy paddler can almost disappear into the landscape, observing herons and egrets as they step through shallow water to suddenly spear small fish, or sneaking up on a yellowlegs sandpiper as it probes the edges of the marsh grass. The grasses clump together in what Cape Codders call hummocks—"sedge islands" to naturalists—forming great muddy mats beloved by oysters, periwinkles, and a world of tiny creatures. Fish hatch and grow to fry size in this protected environment, which is too shallow for most marine predators, and the waters teem with creatures barely visible to the naked eye. Ducks and Canada geese take advantage of the rich buffet, and in the years before this area became a refuge, human hunters would set up blinds on the hummocks and fill their larders. Today the geese are protected—too protected, many homeowners claim, as they try to rid their yards of mushy goose scat.

The tidal streams and channels that swirl in and out of the hummocks are perfect for novice and experienced paddlers alike. Shellfishermen cultivate oysters and clams in Nauset Marsh—but their aquaculture grants are strictly off-limits. From Town Cove, it's a leisurely two-hour paddle in extreme shallows to the mudflats behind Coast Guard Beach where a pair of ospreys nests on a tower. There's a kayak landing here, beside the foot trail over the sand to the beach.

Walkers can explore the northern edge of Nauset Marsh from the promontory of **Fort Hill.** Just north of Town Cove, Routes 6, 6A, and 28 converge at the Orleans traffic circle to continue to the tip of the Cape as Route 6. A right turn about one mile after the rotary leads to Fort Hill and the **Edward Penniman House** (Fort Hill Road; no phone; open in July and August). Penniman grew up on this property as a farm boy but went to sea at the age of eleven. By 1868, sixteen years later, he had risen through the ranks to become a harpooner and, finally, a whale-ship captain, and returned to build this French Second Empire mansion, complete with a whale's jawbone as a front gate. Just beyond the house, the crest of Fort Hill looks down on the grassland hummocks of Nauset Marsh, so extensive that they seem like continents viewed from a spaceship. Red-tailed hawks patrol the hillside, especially during cold-weather months, riding the low thermals generated by temperature differences between the marsh and the hill. Ducks and geese frequent the marshes below, with buffleheads and mergansers during the winter, large flocks of mallards in warmer weather, and Canada geese throughout the year.

Three interpretive trails depart from the parking lot across from the Penniman House. During the summer, resident warblers and other songbirds abound along the **Red Maple Swamp Trail,** a short wheelchair-accessible boardwalk loop through the swampy inlands. The **Skiff Hill Trail** footpath exits the scrub growth to expansive views of Nauset Marsh, where National Seashore plaques describe Champlain's 1605 visit, when he mapped Nauset Marsh and marked the area for possible colonization. The following year, one of his ships got into a scuff-up with the local Nausets, who attacked when they saw the French building what looked like a permanent camp on the shore. Champlain did not summer again on Cape Cod. Skiff Hill is also the site of a sharpening rock where the Nausets would whet their axes, skinners, knives, and arrowheads. The trail is actually a leg of the mile-and-a-half **Fort Hill Trail,** an easy journey well worth taking to enjoy the brambles and beach roses, which bloom in gaudy profusion on the bluff's edge from June through August. As Thoreau noted of the Cape's wild roses, "no Italian or other artificial rose garden could equal them. They were perfectly Elysian, and realized my idea of an oasis in the desert."

At the next traffic light north on Route 6, Samoset Road leads west to one of Cape Cod's best sunset views at **First Encounter Beach.** Like Skaket Beach in Orleans, First Encounter lines a shallow harbor with a gradual incline that makes it subject to equally spectacular ice buildups in a cold winter. A bronze plaque at the edge of the parking lot explains the name in politically correct twenty-first-century terms: "Near this site the Nauset tribe of the Wampanoag nation, seeking to protect themselves and their culture, had their first encounter 8 December 1620 with Myles Standish, John Carver, William Bradford. . ." and other *Mayflower* passengers and crew. The exchange was not exactly an "encounter," though that's how Bradford styled it in his chronicle. The Englishmen never saw the Nausets—only their arrows flying at them—and responded with musket fire into the brush. Apparently they were no better shots than the Nausets: according to Bradford, neither side sustained casualties.

The turnout to the **Salt Pond Visitor Center** (508-255-3421) of the Cape Cod National Seashore is one-half mile farther along Route 6. The facility, which recently underwent rehabilitation, is the Seashore's principal information center, open throughout the year. The small bookstore here stocks virtually every reliable field guide to and history book about the region. A free map and trail guides are readily available. Great visuals in the film *Sands of Time* make the complicated geology of Cape Cod far more palatable (and comprehensible) than it ever seemed in the classroom.

A ranger at the Salt Pond Visitor Center—the Cape Cod National Seashore's main information hub—offers guidance to tourists.

But no film can substitute for the subtleties of the environment itself. T appreciate the ever-changing landscape, walk the half-mile **Nauset Marsh Trai** which leads down to the Salt Pond, an erstwhile freshwater kettle pond that th ocean breached and transformed into a cove on Nauset Marsh. The firm shom provides a chance to observe the marsh habitat at close range. Schoolteachers lik to blindfold their pupils and take them along the quarter-mile loop of th **Buttonbush Trail,** which emphasizes smell, touch, and sound along with sigh (It's signed in both Braille and printed text.)

A third trail, often used by bicyclists, departs from the parking lot through th woods along the north coast of Nauset Marsh to **Doane Rock,** the largest glaci erratic boulder in the area and site of extensive shaded picnic grounds. A walkin trail loops from the picnic area through the pine and oak forest. Another foo path cuts a few hundred yards through bayberry and beach plum thickets e route to Coast Guard Beach.

■ THE GREAT BEACH *map page 185, D-3/5*

The first travel writer to describe Cape Cod, Henry David Thoreau, slogged across Eastham in the driving rain to walk along the beach to Provincetown. Even the difficult-to-impress Concord author was amazed. "There I had got the Cape under me, as much as if I were riding it bare-backed," he wrote in the posthumously published *Cape Cod.*

Contrary to tradition, he did not bestow the name Great Beach on the Outer Cape's Atlantic coast. But it is a great beach, with or without Thoreau's sanction. Individual strands have accreted their own names over the years, but the sandy coast continues in one great sweep up the outer edge of the Cape from Nauset Marsh to Race Point. The Eastham spit, a barrier beach built up by longshore currents spinning sand south along the shore, marks the most southerly portion of Coast Guard Beach. This unique ecosystem is among the few places where it is both safe and environmentally responsible to tread on a barrier system, walking, if you wish, all the way to Nauset Inlet, where breakers crash at the mouth of Nauset Marsh and dissipate, as the wild and violent ocean suddenly turns placid and tame.

It's not always that way. Heavy weather, even hundreds of miles offshore, can trigger surf that proves challenging for swimmers. When a massive nor'easter strikes—usually in the fall, sometimes in the winter—surging tides and nightmare waves roll across the spit at the mouth of Nauset Marsh, threatening to flatten the dunes and breach the whole system. Ultimately, the salt-marsh growth behind the dunes stills the assault, but a few famous storms have made breaches in the sandbar that have taken months or even years to heal. In the Blizzard of '78, perhaps the greatest storm Cape Cod endured in the twentieth century, the dunes on the one-and-one-half-mile Eastham spit were flattened, and the Coast Guard Beach bathhouse was rocked from its foundations. The beach shack where Henry Beston lived for a year between 1926 and 1927 and wrote his meditative book, *The Outermost House,* was smashed to splinters. It's tempting to think that Beston would have considered the demise of his dwelling the completion of a cycle, the sea's poetic and philosophic rhyme of obliteration and creation.

During his solitary year, Beston often sought camaraderie by visiting the equally isolated men at the Coast Guard Station, a red-roofed white building that squats on a bluff above the beach, from which they watched for ships in trouble.

> ### WRECK AND RESCUE
>
> To understand this great outer beach, to appreciate its atmosphere, its "feel," one must have a sense of it as the scene of wreck and elemental drama. Tales and legends of the great disasters fill no inconsiderable niche in the Cape mind. Older folk will tell you of the *Jason,* of how she struck near Pamet in a gale of winter rain, and of how the breakers flung the solitary survivor on the midnight beach; others will tell of the tragic *Castagna* and the frozen men who were taken off while the snow flurries obscured the February sun. Go about in the cottages, and you may sit in a chair taken from one great wreck and at a table taken from another; the cat purring at your feet may be himself a rescued mariner.
>
> —Henry Beston, *The Outermost House,* 1928

The harrowing currents and sandbars of Pollock's Rip, just offshore, nearly claimed the *Mayflower* when she made her North American landfall here on November 9, 1620.

But the sandbars that make navigation in these waters so treacherous also blunt the surf, turning the beach into a refuge for human recreation and for wildlife. Piping plovers nest above the high-tide line in late spring, and National Seashore rangers try to encircle them with barriers to give the threatened species a chance to reproduce. In winter, harbor seals often haul themselves out on Coast Guard Beach to loll in the sand and bask in the sun for a day or two before they lumber back into the water. Private vehicles are prohibited at Coast Guard Beach from June through Labor Day, but a shuttle bus runs from a parking lot near Doane Rock.

Nauset Light Beach lies three-quarters of a mile up scenic Ocean View Drive. The lighthouse—white at the base, red on top—is said to be Cape Cod's most photographed lighthouses, and its likeness appears on countless potato-chip bags. The Great Beach acquires a haughty majesty below Nauset Light, which sits atop a steep "glacial scarp"—a literal mountain of sand clawed by the ocean for three to four thousand years. Each year the sea takes roughly five feet during fall and winter storms, giving back two over the summer, as it slowly tunnels toward Cape Cod Bay. Longshore currents carry the missing grains of sand farther south to Nauset Beach and Monomoy Islands, or north to accrete in the Province Lands.

Beach flowers abound on the National Seashore.

Sixty steep steps descend to the beach, which is both broad and long, permitting near privacy for sunbathers willing to walk far enough. Although most town beaches ban leashed pets, they're permitted on National Seashore beaches (but not on trails), and Nauset Light is a particular favorite with dog owners. In the summer, the base of the scarp fills with soft, loose sand. In winter, the beach is lower and sometimes reveals the foundation of an earlier lighthouse, which stood well inland before the sea eroded its embankment.

The lighthouse station established here originally had three brick light towers, 150 feet apart, which were replaced by movable wooden towers in 1892. The portability came in handy when one tower was moved back from the encroaching sea and fitted with a single blinking light. When the current lighthouse was installed in 1923, the wooden structures—nicknamed the **Three Sisters**—were sold off and served various purposes, from beach cottage to hamburger stand. The National Park Service bought them back and completed a multi-year restoration in 1989, reestablishing them in their original configuration, but in an inland meadow a short walk from the beach parking lot.

STORM WATCHERS

Nauset Light parking lot was doing a brisk business. It was the first northeaster of the season and now, in mid-October, the lot was more crowded than it had been since Labor Day weekend. The heavy, gusty rains of the morning had temporarily ceased, but most of the storm watchers remained in their cars out of a wind that was still stiff and steady from the northeast at nearly fifty knots. A few, seeking more than spectator sport, stood at the railing along the top of the ocean bluff, smiling with a kind of open-mouthed, self-conscious excitement, as one does on a carnival ride.

For sheer power and visual spectacle, Nauset in a northeaster is better than a thousand Niagaras. Here we gather to peer over the edge of our land and watch our very foundations eroding away. At such times, the Cape seems no more than a low sandbar on which the ocean stumbles, momentarily, on its long, slow march toward the mainland.

—Robert Finch, "Gannet on the Bluffs," from *Common Ground*, 1981

The French Cable Company brought its first American cable to Nauset Light Beach from Île St-Pierre in the Miquelon group of French-owned islands off Newfoundland in 1879 before moving operations to Orleans. The **cable hut** remains as part of a cluster of buildings associated with the cable operation.

Four miles north, a young Italian inventor named Guglielmo Marconi nearly single-handedly rendered the transatlantic telegraph cables obsolete in 1903. Watch for National Seashore signs on Route 6 for the single turnoff to Marconi Beach, Marconi Station Site, and the National Seashore administrative headquarters. The Marconi area is one of the most desolate, otherworldly landscapes on Cape Cod. The NASA rover vehicles used on the moon and Mars wouldn't seem out of place here. The National Seashore delicately describes the ecological status as "slowly recovering from European land-use practices, which stripped the landscape of topsoil, and then further from the effects of Camp Wellfleet, which added to the impoverishment of the vegetative cover during World War II." Lovers of desert places, however, are stirred by the upland heath. Heather and creeping bearberry carpet the sand, and defiant stunted pitch pines bristle like shaggy scarecrows.

An angler might be casting for light at Nauset Light Beach. (following pages) Sun worshippers taking in the rays at Marconi Beach.

The road forks a few hundred yards in, leading off on the right to **Marconi Beach,** where the glacial scarp reaches more than forty feet above the outer beach, effectively walling off the strand from the rest of the world. A good swimming beach, it's an even better walking beach, seemingly endless beneath the sandy cliff. Offshore sandbars blunt the force of the waves, but over the centuries they have also caused many a shipwreck, including the foundering of the pirate ship *Whydah* on April 26, 1717.

The left fork passes the Seashore administration buildings and winds over the high heath to the **Marconi Station Site.** Because of construction delays at Wellfleet, Marconi originated his first transatlantic wireless test message from Glace Bay, Nova Scotia, on December 17, 1902. But he did initiate the first wireless communication between the United States and England from this spot on January 18, 1903, passing Morse code messages between President Theodore Roosevelt and King Edward VII. The huge spark-gap transmitter, which operated between 10 P.M. and 2 A.M. to take advantage of optimal atmospheric conditions, was not popular with Wellfleet residents, as the crackle of the three-foot spark could be heard four miles downwind. Nonetheless, the station operated until 1917, when erosion began to threaten its easternmost transmission towers. Over the years, the transmitter played a central role in sea rescues, none more dramatic than summoning the *Carpathia* to pluck more than seven hundred passengers from the sinking *Titanic* in 1912. Marconi deliberately chose a high point of land, but by happenstance he also picked one of the narrowest spots on the Cape. The vista from the observation platform above the station, with the outlines of the shore stretching to the horizon on both ocean and bay sides of the peninsula, is almost like the view from an airplane.

The **Atlantic White Cedar Swamp Trail,** which leads from the small parking lot at the Marconi Station, manages to reprise a whole range of Cape ecosystems, from desert to swamp, in a one-mile loop. From the rugged beach heather and broom crowberry, the sandy trail passes through shrub thickets of beach plum, bayberry, and pitch pines. As the elevation drops into moister soil, pungent checkerberry (wintergreen) and wild sarsaparilla form the ground cover beneath a sprinkling of white and black oak trees. At the edge of the swamp stand the first invading red maples, a species that, left unchecked, will pave the way for beech and oak forest. At the lowest elevation, a boardwalk crosses the swamp itself, where tannic water gathers around the trunks of Atlantic white cedar.

The first European settlers freely exploited white cedar, taking advantage of its lightness and resistance to decay to build houses and fashion barrels and even water pipes. The trail returns to its starting point via the packed-sand Wireless Road, built to haul Marconi's equipment overland to the station site.

The Great Beach continues unabated in the miles north of Marconi Beach Road. The individual ocean beaches at **Le Count Hollow, White Crest, Cahoon Hollow,** and **Newcomb Hollow** are all managed by the Town of Wellfleet. Parking requires a Wellfleet permit (available to residents, as well as overnight guests of the town's motels or approved B&Bs). Bicyclists can, and do, access the beaches freely. Even without a beach stopover, the scenery along three-mile **Ocean View Drive,** bracketed by Le Count Hollow Road on the south and Gross Hill Road on the north, can be breathtaking, especially when a northwest wind off the moors strikes the incoming waves, throwing back great manes of spray from their crests to create what Henry Beston called "sea horses."

■ HIGHLANDS & PROVINCE LANDS *map page 185, A/C-1/2*

The land narrows in a pinch north of Truro, and the character of light changes from the pleasant diffuse illumination of the seaside mainland to the suffuse light of an island, where even the shade seems to glow. However dry the day, the air remains moist and the smell of the sea is ubiquitous.

The U.S. government purchased ten acres of land on the Truro Highlands in 1792 to build the first lighthouse on Cape Cod, **Highland Light,** also known as Cape Cod Light. Today only four acres remain, the rest having been eroded by the sea. The current lighthouse, erected in 1859, was moved four hundred fifty feet inland in 1996, where it will presumably last another century and a half. The Highland House, near the light, was originally part of a late-nineteenth-century resort complex. It now houses the Truro Historical Society's collections, including many items from shipwrecks along this dangerous coast. The headlands (aptly named highlands) stand approximately a hundred feet above the sea. Below the light is another **Coast Guard Beach,** managed by Truro and not to be confused with the National Seashore beach in Eastham. The beach can be reached by Coast Guard Road, and though crazed surfers relish the wild waves, authorities discourage swimming here. A safer bet is **Head of the Meadow Beach,** where the National Seashore provides lifeguards in the summer. Head of the Meadow Road provides access just north of the Route 6A spur into North Truro.

A bicycle and walking trail crosses the highlands from Head of the Meadow to **Pilgrim Heights,** which can also be reached by its own access road off Route 6. Compared with the throngs who gather at the nearby beaches, few people investigate this picnic area. A gentle walking trail through young forest passes the spring that, according to tradition, provided the first fresh water the Pilgrims drank in the New World. After three months of sipping dank water from storage barrels, William Bradford recalled, the spring tasted "as pleasant unto them as wine or beer had been in foretimes." The bike and walking trail continues to **High Head,** which overlooks the heaped parabolic dunes above Pilgrim Lake, a former harbor now closed off to the sea, and the dense civic knot of Provincetown beyond.

Route 6 passes along the shore of Pilgrim Lake and crosses the line into Provincetown—and a landscape of sand and wind. The town hugs the harbor on Cape Cod Bay, while wild dunes range across the rounded head of Cape Cod. This great desert in the ocean, devoid of bedrock, has never been amenable to ownership. The earliest reports of habitation suggest that even the Pamet Wampanoags who lived in Truro shunned the dunelands when they visited fishermen in the harbor for gaming and carousing. The land remained the property of the Province of New England, hence the name "Province Lands," until it passed to the Commonwealth of Massachusetts at the time of the American Revolution.

When the first English settlers came to Cape Cod, the dunelands were hidden under dense forest, soon denuded to build houses and ships. Once the trees were gone, the sand made its move, and by the early eighteenth century it was already threatening to bury the Provincetown fishing enclave. The authorities leaped into action, planting scrub pines, bayberry, and beach plum to stabilize the dunes. It's a never-ending effort; you see new plantings, usually protected by fencing, every year.

Turn off Route 6 on Race Point Road to reach the **Province Lands Visitor Center** (508-487-1256), the nerve center for these far reaches of the Seashore. With exhibits and handouts similar to those at the Salt Pond center, this smaller operation is open from April through November—but its two-level observation deck is open all year. The panoramic view takes in the rolling inland dunes that form the fist of Cape Cod as well as the broad swath of beach that wraps around that fist like tape on a prizefighter's hands. Because the shore suddenly drops off to deep water at Race Point, large baleen whales, notably humpbacks and finbacks, often swim close in to feed and cavort.

The gentle path past Pilgrim Spring.

COOL KETTLES

Park Service rangers are always surprised when someone asks for directions to one of the National Seashore's kettle ponds. After all, people visit Cape Cod for the saltwater beaches. But locals love the cool recesses of these tranquil ponds, which were created when the water table rose as high as holes in the soil left by blocks of ice that broke off from the glacial sheet more than eleven thousand years ago. More than 360 glacial kettles dot Cape Cod, drawing on a few acidic aquifers that keep them clear and clean. About twenty ponds big enough for swimming lie inside the National Seashore boundaries, driving gung-ho pond lovers to spread out their topographic maps and put on their hiking boots to reach them.

Wellfleet supports town beaches on two pristine kettle ponds. **Gull Pond,** off Gross Hill Road, is one of the busiest during the summer, thanks to a well-developed facility with lifeguards, a boat launch, rental canoes, paddleboats, and floating docks. Although its beach is smaller, **Great Pond,** off Cahoon Hollow Road, makes a good alternative—and if it gets too crowded, it's surrounded by still more ponds, including 200-yard-long Turtle Pond. In Eastham's Wylie Park, another **Great Pond** (not to be confused with Wellfleet's) has one of the Cape's largest freshwater swimming beaches.

The visitors center provides perhaps the most direct access to the **Province Lands Bicycle Trail,** which is not for the casual or inexperienced rider. Steep hills, sharp curves, and blowing sand pose hazards, but it still beats coping with the auto traffic on the roads. The loop trail traverses nearly five and a half miles of undulating dunelands where the wind has scooped out hollows and built abrupt sand heaps, which are held in place by the tenacious roots of raggedy pitch pines and the creeping growth of bearberry. Separate spurs lead to Race Point and Herring Cove beaches.

The bike trail also passes the entry point for the **Beech Forest Trail,** off Race Point Road. This mile-and-a-half walking trail loops through an oasis of luxurious beech forest around a kettle pond. Migrating warblers flying up and down the coast treat the small forest as a rest stop, and it's not uncommon to spot a dozen or more species in a casual outing.

Visible from the visitors center as a wide swath of sand, **Race Point Beach** covers the northernmost tip of Cape Cod. Despite the blacktop berm that keeps the showers and changing rooms from blowing away—or being buried under drifts of

Race Point, at the northern tip of Cape Cod.

sand—it has an elemental feeling, as if you're unexpectedly being made privy to the moment of creation. The sand is slowly creeping west, and the wind walks the surface of water and land with a brisk, skipping motion, unimpeded by the continent back at the far end of Route 6. Every surface is reflective, making the light seem to tingle in the air as it bounces from mote to mote until the atmosphere itself glows. Salt spray licks tan bodies running at the water's edge, and the summer seems eternal. Waves strike the beach at an oblique angle, making this more a bathing than a swimming beach, though the waters can grow still at the changing of the tide. Race Point fills up early, as it's a favorite place for Provincetown vacationers to catch the sunrise. The beach lies three-quarters of a mile from the visitors center on Race Point Road.

Long ago sanded in, Old Harbor stands at the east end of Race Point Beach, marked by the former U.S. Life Saving Service station, now the **Old Harbor Lifesaving Museum.** The building contains shipwreck rescue equipment from its active era, from 1897 to 1944. The museum is usually open on summer afternoons, and Park Service rangers demonstrate a breeches-buoy rescue on Thursdays.

Inquire at the Province Lands Visitor Center, as the museum is the first service trimmed when funding is short.

Province Lands Road from the visitors center meets the end of Route 6 at **Herring Cove Beach,** known for its excellent wheelchair access (including wheelchair-ready showers and a beach wheelchair for transport) and for its social scene. In contrast to the wild edge of Race Point, Herring Cove is washed by gentle surf where the Atlantic Ocean and Cape Cod Bay merge. Imagine the relief of the *Mayflower's* captain when he rounded the point, after being battered by waves and currents on the Cape's eastern face, to discover these comparatively placid waters.

Many people elect to walk or bicycle the mile from Provincetown Center to Herring Cove Beach, especially if they're going to the southern stretch, which by local tradition (and contrary to federal law, which governs the National Seashore) is a clothing-optional beach. Nude sunbathers should consider that Park Service officials periodically make sweeps of the beach, issuing tickets or arresting those who refuse to put on clothes.

National Park Service literature tends to be mute about other local-use traditions at Herring Cove Beach. The long, long beach is divided by custom into sections based on sexual orientation, with the straight area north of the bathhouse and parking lot, the lesbian area just south of the lot, and the gay men's area south of that (reached by the Moors-Herring Cove Access Trail). The clothing-optional beach is on the narrow strand between the bay and tidal marsh en route to Wood End lighthouse.

Sunset knows no sexual orientation, and west-facing Herring Cove Beach offers spectacular views over the waters of Cape Cod Bay, with the mainland's Plymouth harbor in the distance.

A many-tailed kite, like an exotic aquatic bird, catches the wind at Herring Cove Beach.

OUTER CAPE

The Outer Cape is as improbable as it is seductive. This spiral knob at the end of Cape Cod is *terra infirma* built of little more than heaps of grit swept up from the ocean floor and piled into great dunes. That human beings should choose to inhabit this Sahara in the sea seems preposterous, and yet they do, cultivating oases of human comfort beneath the great arc of the sky and its open light. Lashed by the brittle salt spray of winter storms, seared in the unrelenting glare of August when the sun slaps the harbor chop with a brutal *smack!*, the little villages cling to the Outer Cape's leeward shore like mussels on a piling.

Like very plump mussels, indeed.

Wellfleet, Truro, and Provincetown are three of the physically smallest communities in the Commonwealth, especially if the lands of the Cape Cod National Seashore are excluded. They have no industry to speak of except fishing and tourism, no resources save beauty. Yet they bubble with activity, reenacting the American penchant for excess, proclaiming at once with Walt Whitman, "I celebrate myself, / And what I assume you shall assume . . . ."

The erstwhile fishing village becomes a proscenium for self-actualization, the whaling port a painter's hideaway, the mackerel seiner's shack the novelist's hole-up—complete with pencil, yellow legal pad, and laptop. It sometimes seems as if every square inch of the land, every degree of the sky, every cloud, every grain of sand, every dune shack, hollyhock, fishing boat, herring gull, damselfly, and flatfish has been described, analyzed, painted, and photographed—probably a hundred times—by the painters, poets, novelists, photographers, and practitioners of other plastic and literary arts who have been drawn inexorably to this paltry shore.

And still, every moment is as fresh and tentative as one with a new lover. The arching light and the rolling, lumpy landscape can't help but take your breath away. The sheer openness, the emptiness of sky and dune, dwarfs everything petty, banishes mundane anxieties, puts the world somehow into perspective. The Outer Cape flashes you a smile, and your heart is lost. It's only a matter of time before you give in.

This chapter is the complement to the preceding one. Establishing the Cape Cod National Seashore placed fifty to ninety percent of the acreage in the Outer

Outside Provincetown, the seemingly endless dunes of the Province Lands.

Cape's three towns under federal jurisdiction for perpetual preservation; the National Seashore chapter deals largely with that natural landscape. This chapter details the towns and the ways humans inhabit the world of the Outer Cape. For drivers, there's only one way to get here. It's not that all roads lead to Provincetown—just that Route 6 does.

■ **WELLFLEET** *map page 185, C-3*

The first Pilgrims on this section of the Cape called their settlement Billingsgate, after the raucous London fish market, and the adjacent waters Grampus Bay— "grampus" being a fine old English word for small blackfish whales, such as pilot whales and orcas. When the community broke off from Eastham in 1763, it renamed itself Wellfleet, though the villagers' reasons were obscured by their spelling. Did they mean "Whale Fleet," since dozens of ships sailed from the harbor to slay leviathans? Or were they comparing themselves to Wallfleet, in Essex, England, famed for its oyster beds? The origin of the nomenclature will never be settled to the satisfaction of adherents of either theory, because the villagers went about their business of whaling and harvesting oysters rather than explaining themselves to posterity. The whalers may be gone, but the oystermen are still very much in evidence.

Come balmy weather, the creative writing, music, studio art, and psychology departments of dozens of universities disgorge their faculties to summer in Wellfleet. Art and craft galleries open, restaurants blossom, and it becomes a challenge to get a Sunday *New York Times* before Lema's grocery store runs out. But the town itself changes little, apart from the utter unavailability of parking spaces in the village center.

By the time drivers reach the Outer Cape, Route 6 has devolved from a divided highway with clearly defined exits into a two-way free-for-all where drivers make sudden, lunging turns onto ill-marked side roads. Fortunately, plenty of warning signs in each direction mark the approaches to the **Wellfleet Drive-In Theatre and Flea Market.** One of the last icons of post–World War II American car culture left on the Cape, this 1957 drive-in, with its hundred- by forty-four-foot screen, plays first-run double features nightly, rain or shine, from early May through September, with shows beginning at dusk. From mid-April until the last tourists leave town in the fall, the flea market operates on Saturdays and Sundays on the same grounds (also on Wednesdays and Thursdays in July and August),

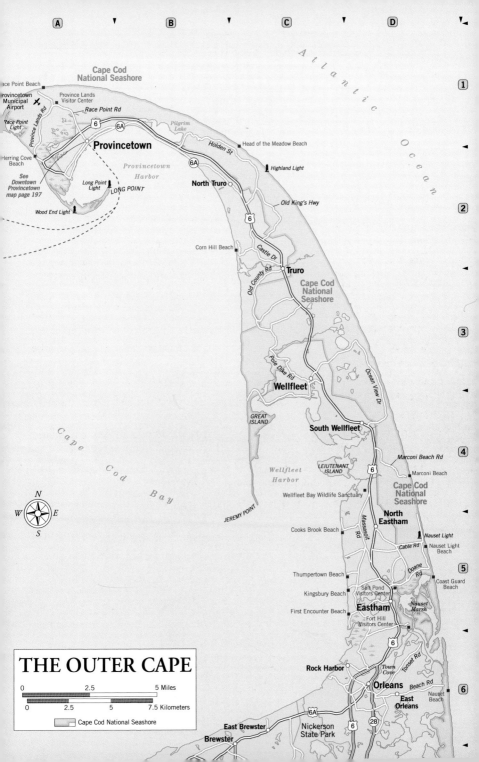

THE OUTER CAPE

Cape Cod National Seashore

with as many as three hundred vendors spreading everything from Cape Cod souvenir ashtrays to vintage furniture to bargain pantyhose on their folding tables. *Route 6 at Eastham-Wellfleet line; 508-349-7176.*

Almost neighbors with this beehive of commercial activity, the Massachusetts Audubon Society's **Wellfleet Bay Wildlife Sanctuary** covers a thousand acres of woodland, marshes, and upland grassy sands between Route 6 and Wellfleet harbor. Open the car door and you'll be met by a cacophonous chorus of birdsong—from melodic arias to chortles, cheeps, twitters, and raspy caws. About sixty species of birds breed in the sanctuary, and another two hundred, mostly migrants, have been spotted here as well. Foxes and coyotes prowl the grounds, and deer browse the uplands. Exhibits at the solar-heated nature center provide a good introduction to various habitats and resident creatures, and the center's composting toilets combine visitor service with a lesson in wetlands environmentalism. Half a dozen trails crisscross the sanctuary holdings. Among the most popular is the **Silver Spring Trail,** which passes through woodlands to freshwater wetlands. On a warm day, walkers might spot as many as forty turtles sunning on a single log. The longer **Goose Pond Trail** ventures through pine and oak stands to brackish Goose Pond, known for its concentration of herons, egrets, plovers, and oystercatchers. En route to the beach, the Boardwalk spur from Goose Pond crosses extensive salt marshes crawling with fiddler and green crabs. The sanctuary offers year-round workshops, lectures, and guided tours as well as summer field schools in ornithology, coastal ecology, and even nature photography. *West Road; 508-349-2615. Open Columbus Day–Memorial Day. Trails open daily; nature center closed Mon.*

Although Cape Cod narrows significantly at Wellfleet, several streams and creeks drain the west side of the glacial sandbank ridge, turning Wellfleet's well-protected harbors into a network of sandy shallows and estuaries. The bluepoint oyster makes itself right at home: the annual Wellfleet oyster harvest exceeds fifteen thousand bushels, with a value of more than $2.5 million. Wellfleet explicitly encourages nonresidents to gather oysters from specific, well-seeded beds—with a license, of course. Among the best areas for "recreational shellfishing" are the beds of Chipman's Cove and Indian Neck, near the tame waters of Indian Neck beach. From Route 6, a west turn onto either Pilgrim Spring Road or Cove Road will lead to a dead end at the Indian Neck Town Landing on Chipman's Cove.

Boats at anchor in Wellfleet Harbor.

Long Pond Road from Route 6 to Main Street is perhaps the most direct and least confusing approach to Wellfleet village for visitors unaccustomed to a landscape with many points and coves and very few through roads. Should you come into town with your windows open, you may hear the **Town Clock** chime from the tower of the Congregational Church. Landlubbers often check their watches and figure that the clock needs resetting, but swabbies recognize that it strikes ship's time: two bells at one, five, and nine o'clock; four bells at two, six, and ten o'clock; six bells at three, seven, and eleven o'clock, and eight bells at four, eight, and twelve o'clock. (Half hours get one additional bell.)

The lot behind **Town Hall** (310 Main Street) is not only the best bet for parking and public restrooms; from late May through late September, it's also the site of **Hatch's Fish Market** (508-349-2810) and **Hatch's Produce** (508-349-6734), which provide the freshest harvests from sea and land, respectively. One modest landmark across the street is the **Lighthouse Restaurant** (508-349-3681), where the notoriously penny-pinching artist Edward Hopper used to treat himself to

The bounty at Hatch's Fish Market in Wellfleet.

chicken à la king, the cheapest thing on the menu. Such recherché dishes are rarely part of the Wellfleet culinary repertoire these days, even at the Lighthouse, where the usual menu of fried fish, clams, and oysters is occasionally spiced up on "Mexican Night" by dishes involving hot peppers and orange cheese.

The center of Wellfleet is a trickle of restaurants, galleries, and souvenir shops along Main and Bank Streets and Kendrick Avenue. Take it all in by walking down Bank Street to **Uncle Tim's Bridge.** The small wooden footbridge crosses Duck Creek to a marsh island topped by Cannon Hill—the highest perspective on the habitations of Wellfleet village and their relation to the multiple coves of the harbor.

Kendrick Avenue, at the foot of Bank Street, skirts the water's edge to the broad Town Marina. From late May through late October **Mac's Seafood** (508-349-0404) is a good stop for sushi and deli before an evening of often challenging, sometimes uproarious theater at **Wellfleet Harbor Actors Theater,** also known as **WHAT** (508-591-1616). The theater building looks as if a good rainstorm would wash it away, but don't judge the book by its cover. Founded by Gip Hoppe and Jeff Zinn, WHAT is known for sharp cultural and political satire that sometimes finds its way from Wellfleet Harbor to Off Broadway (or at least to Somerville, Massachusetts).

The long, south-facing strand of **Mayo Beach,** adjacent to the Marina on Kendrick Avenue, is one of the few Wellfleet beaches with free parking. Many aquaculture grants abut the beach, so don't be surprised to see people in waders with clamhoes and buckets amid the sun worshippers.

The high peninsula at the mouth of the harbor is **Great Island.** Until the channel to the mainland filled with sand in 1831, it stood surrounded by water, a mass of dunes and cliffs where pirates and smugglers sometimes called and shore whalers plied their bloody trade. In a well-mannered town like Wellfleet, such a roguish past adds a bit of spice, as if to say, "We come from vigorous stock." (Ruffians in the family tree are always more enchanting if they're several generations removed.)

You might expect that condominium complexes and perhaps a golf course would have despoiled Great Island by now, but its wildness, both topographical and historical, is protected as part of the Cape Cod National Seashore. From Mayo Beach, Kendrick Avenue turns into Chequasset Neck Road (stay to the left) as it passes the country club, crosses Herring River on the dike installed in 1906, and enters the Great Island section of the National Seashore. A crushed shell path leads

(following pages) Old boat hulls grace a salt marsh at Wellfleet.

The Wellfleet Harbor Actors Theater, illuminated.

from the parking lot to the beach and the start of the Great Island Trail. One loop goes to the site of the Smith Tavern, discovered during a 1969–70 archaeological dig that has been filled back in. The excavation yielded more than twenty-four thousand artifacts, ranging from seventeenth-century tankards and wine bottles to bits of scrimshaw. Alas, no pirate hoard turned up to support the local legend that young Maria Hallett used to sneak off to Great Island to meet her lover, the pirate Black Sam Bellamy. Skeletal evidence, however, shows that some men met a violent end here, their skulls split with knives or axes. Stretches of the trail pass through loose sand, making the full circuit, with its optional loops, a four-hour trip.

■ TRURO   *map page 185, C-2*

Truro has the Gothic emptiness of an abandoned landscape newly inhabited. In the eighteenth and early nineteenth centuries, the town was the busiest spot on the Outer Cape. Its shipyards at Pamet Harbor sent coasting schooners, Grand Banks fishing vessels, and small whaling ships down the ways. When the people of Nantucket wanted to get into the whaling trade, the island hired Ichabod Paddock, a Truro man, to show them how it was done. But the whales moved offshore, Truro's harbors silted in, the fishing fleets dwindled, and the town came to have more headstones than houses.

In a bit of overstatement, a sign on Route 6 points west down Town Hall Road to "Truro Center." The village has a smattering of public buildings at the convergence of Town Hall, Meetinghouse, Bridge, and Castle Roads. The most striking is the **Cobb Memorial Library,** a 1912 shingled structure with a brass cupola and what functions as the Truro Center clock.

On Castle Road, an old squared-off windmill building (minus arms and sails) marks the **Truro Center for the Arts at Castle Hill.** The main "campus" is in the silver-shingled barn. In some respects, the Center for the Arts is Truro's true center. Spring and summer workshops draw on the creative richness of the community, with well-established artists and writers such as Joel Meyerowitz, Marge Piercy, Anne Bernays, and Justin Kaplan serving as instructors. *508-349-7511. Workshops mid-Mar.–Aug.*

Castle Road continues to Corn Hill Road, where a left turn winds downhill below the bluffs to **Corn Hill Beach**, site of the first recorded act of theft in the New World. With the *Mayflower* anchored in Provincetown harbor, a party of Pilgrims exploring the coast happened on a cache of corn stored for the winter by the Pamets, helped themselves, and named the place "Corn Hill." A 1920 plaque, on the north side of the beach parking lot, offers the Pilgrims' justification ("sure it was God's good providence that we found this corn or else we know not how we should have done") but doesn't say how the Pamets felt about the incident. An adjoining plaque reports that in 1929, Ralph S. Bellamy soared from the bluffs for an unpowered flight of fifteen minutes and six seconds, breaking the previous American record set by Orville Wright at Kitty Hawk in 1911.

All the property atop Corn Hill is private, but it's worth driving or walking to the summit to appreciate the rolling landscape, the unique light, and the stark beauty of Truro's coast. Indeed, the painter Edward Hopper, who spent summers from the 1930s to the 1960s at his studio on the bluffs south of the beach, found the beauty of Truro something of a trial. As his wife, Jo, wrote in 1942, at Truro the Cape's "special beauty is shown about in greatest richness—but he doesn't want this special beauty—too exotic, too special."

Ideally, you should drive the back roads of Truro in a 1948 Hudson with balloon whitewalls, creeping along with the windows open to the salt air. Hopper once said, "To me the most important thing is the sense of going on. You know how beautiful things are when you're traveling." And in Truro, landscapes unfold like a slow cinema of Hopper visions. The light has an oblique clarity that defines the curved volumes of lumpy moors and marshy hollows by their outlines. Many

Truro houses sit isolated on bluffs and hillsides, and they seem to glow with an aching Puritan emptiness. The singular gnarled tree, the barn weathered silver in salt air and sun, the uninhabited gas station aglow with dim lamps—they are all still there, forty years after the poet of desolation bore witness to them.

Castle Road eventually winds back to Route 6, but in less than a mile the left branch leads to Shore Road (Route 6A) and to **Truro Vineyards.** The owners of this tiny winery struggle against all odds to grow vinifera grapes in the sandy soils. Although the vineyards contain the oldest such plantings on Cape Cod, the bulk of the grapes used in the wines are imported from New York and California. Truro Vineyards manages to make very competent wines and encourages visitors to stroll through the vineyards, taste the grapes, and watch activities in the barn winery. *Shore Road, North Truro; 508-487-6200. Open Apr.–Dec. on weekend afternoons, Memorial Day–Oct. afternoons daily.*

Aging wine at tiny Truro Vineyards.

GRAINS OF SAND

In 1946, Art Costa, the self-styled King of the Dunes, fired up his 1936 Ford "woody," let most of the air out of the tires, and started taking tourists through the strange world of the "back side" or "back shore," as P'towners call the high dunes between Race Point and High Head, just over the town line in Truro. The Costa family is still at it, with a fleet of Chevrolet Suburbans and the blessings of the Cape Cod National Seashore.

A highlight of the tour is the up-and-down roll through the Peaked Hill Bars National Historic District, where the Coast Guard kept a lifesaving station into the 1920s and the lifesavers built small shacks and beach houses to shelter their wives and girlfriends. P'town artists and writers speak of these "dune shacks" with a hushed reverence, for they have a distinct cultural history. Eugene O'Neill was living in the former Coast Guard station when he learned that he'd won the 1920 Pulitzer Prize. It was hardly a shack; the socialite Mabel Dodge had gussied it up, even bringing in a couch that had belonged to Isadora Duncan. Jack Kerouac revised part of *On the Road* during his stay in one of the bare-bones shacks belonging to Hazel Hawthorne, a novelist and a cousin of the painter Charles. For all their makeshift architecture, many of the shacks have lasted for decades, riding the shifting sands like boats bobbing on the sea. Artists and writers still covet a block of the time that O'Neill called the "solitude where I lived with myself."

For a brief passage through the sandy wilds, though, anyone can ride with the Costa family's drivers. To sign up, just look for the ladies in lawn chairs at the corner of Standish and Commercial Streets. The favorite tour of the day is timed to pause for sunset on the beach at Race Point. *Art's Dune Tours; 508-487-1950 or 800-894-1951.*

The Cape's peninsula is entirely devoid of bedrock where Shore Road actually begins to follow the shore. The sky arches from sea to sea over the sand, and the landscape takes on strange, shimmering hues of blue and tan. All of a sudden, rows of Monopoly houses line the road—the beach cabin colonies of North Truro. Artists find the sudden symmetry of human presence in a world of sand and sky irresistible. In a 1977 interview, the photographer Joel Meyerowitz said suggestively, "Every life that passed through there filled up the floor boards, the siding with its history. Those little bungalows . . . [are] triangular boxes of sensations, boxes of memories."

Fishing boats at the dock in Provincetown in the early 1900s.

■ PROVINCETOWN *map page 197*

No one gets to Provincetown by accident. It lies at the edge of the continent, a village of earthly delights where the asphalt ends at the ocean. As the novelist and sometime resident Michael Cunningham has observed, "It is not en route to anywhere else. One of its charms is the fact that those who go there have made some effort to do so." And yet P'town pilgrims are inevitably surprised, for reality rarely squares with their expectations.

When Thoreau visited for the first time in 1849, the parochial inlander was astonished by the salted codfish drying everywhere in the sun. Each house, he wrote, was "surrounded by fish-flakes close up to the sills on all sides, with only a narrow passage two or three feet wide, to the front door . . ."

Had Thoreau been more conversant in the ways of working sailors, he would have expected as much. By old Breton and Basque accounts, Provincetown was a fishing village four centuries before the Concord curmudgeon arrived to declare, "One may stand here and put all of America behind him."

The modern tourist is more likely to exclaim, "Toto, I don't think we're in Kansas anymore."

Travelers today don't have to endure the olfactory assault of cod flakes they did in Thoreau's time. Instead, they face a floating carnival on aptly named Commercial Street, where high art and low comedy coexist in equal measure, where the tragically hip meets the slyly crass, and sexuality comes in as many flavors as Ben & Jerry's ice cream. Here T-shirt shops and postcard racks vie with marine supply stores, tasteful home-decor showrooms, and garden cafés. Ice cream and taffy emporia compete with fried fish and hot dog booths. You can sign up for

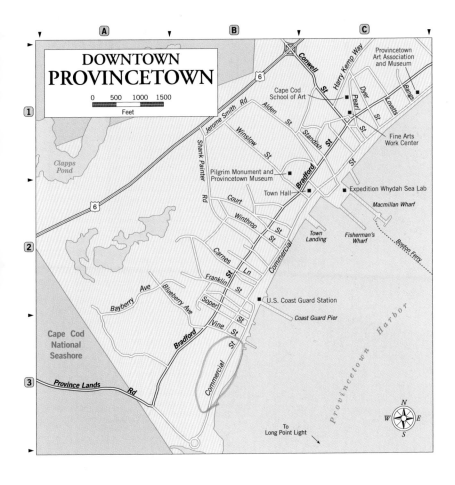

DOWNTOWN
PROVINCETOWN

0   500   1000   1500
Feet

a tour of the dunes or the innocuous modern version of a whaling expedition, rent a bicycle to escape to the seashore, catch some drag cabaret, get a tattoo or a massage, or peruse paintings, prints, and photographs at galleries large and small.

Although Provincetown still has a small fishing fleet, since Thoreau's day the town's subtext has shifted from piscine to painterly. The Portland Gale of 1898 destroyed more than half the town's wharves and most of its fleet, and the next summer Charles W. Hawthorne began teaching painting en plein air. Two summers later he opened the Cape Cod School of Art. Within a decade, Provincetown became a mecca for painters, would-be painters, and other artists and bohemians. Some summers it seemed the whole population of Greenwich Village had arrived for the season. By World War I, the radicals John Reed and Louise Bryant were holed up on the Truro end of Commercial Street, while Marsden Hartley and Charles Demuth were redefining landscape painting and John Dos Passos was fragmenting the novel's narrative. In 1915, the Provincetown Players began to put on shows at Lewis Wharf (since burned); in 1916 they premiered Eugene O'Neill's first play, *Bound East for Cardiff*. After World War II, the painter and teacher Hans Hofmann became a magnet for abstract artists, luring such figures as Lee Krasner, Jackson Pollock, Franz Kline, Larry Rivers, and Mark Rothko into spending at least one season in the wild light of the Outer Cape. Many stayed longer. A founding member of the Fine Arts Work Center, Robert Motherwell spent forty summers painting and making prints in P'town in his journey to "peel away the inessential and present the necessary."

All this artistic activity helped reshape Provincetown as a bohemian village with a high tolerance for eccentricity and an open embrace of alternative lifestyles. In hindsight, it seems inevitable that P'town would become one of the country's leading gay resorts, a place where couples of whatever inclination could freely express their affection in public. Today, the town assessor estimates that half the P'town population is gay or lesbian, but such status is really of more interest to outsiders than to residents. If you live in P'town, you know who you are, and you're probably happy about it.

As Shore Road (Route 6A) enters Provincetown from Truro, it branches left and right into Commercial and Bradford Streets, respectively. These two thoroughfares "curve together around the bay like two spinsters on their promenade to church," as Norman Mailer once put it. Mailer lives in an anomalous brick house near the

A canine views the Provincetown Wharf.

split from Bradford, not far from where Kurt Vonnegut lived in 1951 when he wrote *Player Piano*. Although it's better marked on maps than on the road itself, two-way Bradford Street is designated as Route 6A and serves as the "quick" route back and forth across P'town. One-way Commercial Street follows the shore.

Until 1838, Provincetown didn't have streets—only foot-worn paths between the fishermen's houses and the wharves. When Front Street, later renamed Commercial, was laid out, the work crews went whole hog and put down a sidewalk some five planks wide, against the protests of some old-timers who thought it a waste of money. Writing in *Truro–Cape Cod* in 1883, Shebnah Rich reported, "Tradition says that some of the old people, particularly the ladies, who had strenuously opposed the project, declared that they would never walk on it, and were as good as their word, walking slip-shod through the sand as long as they lived." Those principled ladies would no doubt be amused at the current state of affairs, as the sidewalks are now so crowded in July and August that it's easier to walk in the street.

The three-mile stroll along Commercial Street, with its hollyhock-trimmed buildings and its sliver-like glimpses of the water, is half fun-house tour, half gauntlet of sensory assault. All of P'town's cultures, subcultures, cliques, and special interests are on parade here, with a cast of characters worthy of Fellini.

That's not to say that the whole street is an undifferentiated pepper pot of peculiarity. It moves in general from the decorous to the decadent and back again. Provincetown has been divided into East End and West End longer than anyone can remember, with MacMillan Wharf serving as the dividing line. During the town's halcyon days as a port, the whaling captains, ship owners, and merchants lived in the East End. When the summer people arrived from Boston and New York, they built or bought in the East End. And when the art colony began to coalesce, its centers of gravity—the Cape Cod School of Art and the Provincetown Art Association—stood well east of the wharf and its rail line. The East End developed as the genteel side of town, or at least what passes for genteel in Provincetown. Its shops display a bit more propriety than those of the West End, and it holds more of the eminent art galleries and the lion's share of expensive restaurants. The West End, meanwhile, has historically existed on the wrong side of the proverbial tracks—or, perhaps more accurately, the wrong side of the wharf.

If the East Enders get unruly, it's likely to be when they wrangle over questions of artistic merit or aesthetic theory. But the stable center in the artistic turmoil

Exploring cosmetic frontiers on Commercial Street.

HORNBLOWER ON CAPE COD

Conversation in general, which includes but is not limited to gossip, is both valued and widely practiced in Provincetown. Its citizens are a loquacious people, fond of stories of all kinds. It is common for a Provincetownian driving along Commercial Street to see a friend passing on foot or on a bicycle and stop to talk to that person at medium length. If you are in a car behind one of these impromptu klatsches, please do not honk your horn, unless the conversation goes on for a truly unconscionable period or you have mistakenly taken poison and are on your way to procure the antidote. It is impolite. Provincetown is an ecosystem, and these street sessions are among its inhabitants' innate characteristics. Displays of impatience or aggressiveness are not considered the badges of personal importance they are in some other places. Anyone in a great hurry is generally perceived not as a mover and shaker but simply as an intruder from a noisier, less interesting world and is likely to be ignored.

—Michael Cunningham, *Land's End,* 2002

remains the **Provincetown Art Association and Museum.** Founded in 1914 by artists and arts patrons with Impressionist sensibilities, the Art Association embraced what it still quaintly calls Modernism as early as 1927 and languished through the Depression and World War II, but survived to participate in the revival of artistic activity in the post-war years, when Provincetown became a center of Abstract Expressionism.

The Association owns nearly two thousand works by more than five hundred artists who work or have worked on the Outer Cape, and its museum mounts rotating exhibitions from the collection, juried annual exhibitions, and special shows focusing on single artists. The museum reflects a certain Provincetown sensibility—it doesn't open until noon, and membership categories define a "family" as two adults sharing the same address. *460 Commercial Street; 508-487-4372. Open daily Memorial Day–Sept., weekends Oct.–Apr.*

The best way to sample the current art scene in Provincetown is to gallery hop on Friday evenings, when most galleries schedule openings and often ply the viewing public with food and drink. After the galleries close, vigorous conversations continue into the wee hours at bars, cafés, and artists' studios. For listings, pick up a copy of the gallery guide at the Association or any of the participating galleries.

One of those establishments, the **Fine Arts Work Center,** was founded in the

A painting demonstration by Charles W. Hawthorne, circa 1915.

1970s to lure new generations of writers and visual artists to town with the incentive of a highly coveted paid residency from October through April. The Days family, then Provincetown's biggest contractors, created a group of studios over their offices shortly before World War I. Charles W. Hawthorne and Ross Moffett were among the first to take advantage of the bare-bones spaces, for which they paid $50 for the season, an affordable sum even for a penurious painter. The lumberyard evolved as a center of artistic activity, and as the Days family operations withdrew, the art scene grew. From 1961 to 1962, Robert Motherwell and Helen Frankenthaler rented the renovated barn on the property, because the small studios couldn't have accommodated the scale of their work. And in 1972, the Work Center purchased the historic studios for its residential program.

When P'town hibernates each winter, the Fine Arts Work Center is often the only place awake, hosting readings and exhibitions. During the summer, classes and workshops in creative writing and the visual arts dominate the calendar. The original aim of the enterprise has succeeded: former fellows constitute a core of accomplished writers and artists who continue to justify the community's claims as a leading art colony. *24 Pearl Street; 508-487-9960. Gallery open on weekdays.*

The Blue-water Fisherman *(circa 1916), by B.J.O. Nordfeldt.*

Farther up Pearl, the **Cape Cod School of Art** squats at a picturesque turn in the street. Some of the Outer Cape's larger deciduous trees surround the old red barn—like a sliver of Vermont set down on Cape Cod. Walk almost any leafy lane of the neighborhood and you'll practically trip over students at their easels, reconstructing the world in front of them through the color theory and compositional practices that Charles Hawthorne taught a century ago. Hawthorne was first drawn to

Provincetown by its similarity to French fishing villages, and in the early years of his teaching he often caused a stir by directing his students to set up their easels among the fishing boats on the main town wharf. *48 Pearl Street; 508-487-0101.*

Renamed in the mid-twentieth century for native son and Arctic explorer Donald MacMillan (1874–1970), **MacMillan Wharf** is the last stronghold of old Provincetown. It sits smack dab in the middle of town, tossing a briny bucket of cold seawater on modern affectations. Just when the smell of cocoa butter on tan skin begins to seem overbearing, the wharf offers the time-honored Cape Cod smelling salts of fresh fish, old bait, and aromatic diesel exhaust. Starting in the 1870s, railroad lines ran up the wharf to water's edge to load the catch for quick shipment to Boston and New York.

In those days, P'town's fishing fleet was extensive, and the opportunities offered by the sea drew hundreds of immigrants from Portugal, whose descendants now constitute a larger part of the local population than the old-time Yankees. One of the highlights of the late-June Provincetown Portuguese Festival is the Blessing of the Fleet, for which the thirty or so fishing boats are scrubbed down, freshly painted, and decked in pennants and banners.

Across the wharf from the fishing fleet, a handful of boats head out on whale-watching cruises to Stellwagen Bank, among them the **Dolphin Fleet of Provincetown.** Operated by the Avellar family, the Dolphin Fleet pioneered whale watching on the East Coast and works closely with research biologists. Every cruise has a naturalist from the Center for Coastal Studies aboard. *Chamber of Commerce Building, MacMillan Wharf; 508-349-1900.*

The **Expedition Whydah Sea Lab and Learning Center** fills a small wharf building just beyond the whale-watching fleet. Commanded by the pirate Black Sam Bellamy, the *Whydah* sank on April 26, 1717, off present-day Marconi Beach on the National Seashore side of Wellfleet. Many a salvager sought her treasure over the years, but in 1983 Barry Clifford found the ship—beneath twenty feet of water and ten feet of sand. When a bronze bell with the ship's name was brought to the surface two years later, it became official that the *Whydah* was the first pirate ship positively identified and salvaged.

In a slow, ongoing excavation, Clifford and his team have recovered thousands of gold and silver coins, as well as jewelry, cannons and cannon balls, and items as personal as a silk stocking. The exhibitions offer tantalizing examples of some of the historical riches, and they try to rehabilitate the poor image of pirate life, one of Clifford's personal fascinations. "Theirs was a democratic world in which they

TAKE IT TO THE BANK

In the 1850s, when Provincetown was second only to New Bedford as a whaling port, its ships sailed to the far reaches of the South Pacific and Indian Oceans to find whales. Nowadays, P'town's whalers reach their quarry in half an hour, for Provincetown is the closest port to Stellwagen Bank, the underwater ridge of glacial debris that arcs between Cape Cod and Cape Ann, north of Boston.

The drowned plateau of Stellwagen Bank is among the most nutrient-rich areas in the Gulf of Maine, and Cape fishermen were exploiting the schools of cod on what they called the Middle Bank long before Henry S. Stellwagen mapped it for the U.S. Navy Coast Survey in 1854. Fishermen still seek a living here, albeit under tight National Marine Sanctuary regulations. The giants of the sea have no such restraints. From April through November, endangered finback, minke, and humpback whales converge on Stellwagen for the rich stew of plankton and small fish it offers. Throughout the winter, many of the three hundred remaining northern right whales come to dine at the Stellwagen café.

Since Al Avellar led the first East Coast whale-watching expedition from Provincetown in April 1975, the modern whaling industry has exploded. Even the most callous cynic is likely to soften when a humpback breaches, slaps its flukes, and spins under the surface, demonstrating, as the poet Stanley Kunitz put it in "The Wellfleet Whale," "pure energy incarnate / as nobility of form."

selected their captain by vote and helped make the decisions that ran the ship," he has written. "They were not overworked or conscripted to a cruel captain, as were merchant and military sailors. In short, the pirate was a free man . . . ." *508-487-8899. Open May–Oct.*

Commercial Street and the wharf have shared paving for so many years that dry land has accreted beneath the piers, and wharf buildings have become part of the streetscape. Where the street and wharf intersect are two businesses that hark back to more innocent days. At **Provincetown Portuguese Bakery** (299 Commercial Street; 508-487-1803), a stalwart ethnic holdout against homogenization, someone is almost always standing in the window frying sweet doughnuts, called *malasadas,* in a large vat of oil. Across the street, **Cabot's Candies of Cape Cod** (276 Commercial Street; 508-487-3550) recalls the early days of Cape Cod tourism with more than thirty flavors of saltwater taffy pulled on the premises.

All strains of Provincetown history and culture converge at the **Pilgrim Monument and Provincetown Museum,** which stands on High Pole Hill—essentially the tallest sand dune on the Outer Cape. When Plymouth completed its grandiose National Monument to the Forefathers in 1889, Cape Codders set about creating their own tower, to remind the world that the Pilgrims landed here first. The tower, patterned on the Torre del Mangia in Siena, Italy, wasn't finished until 1910, but at 252 feet and 7.5 inches high, it was touted as the world's tallest all-granite monument. You can climb the 116 steps and 60 ramps for a sweeping view that puts Provincetown's tiny encrustation along the shore into perspective.

The museum at the base of the monument recaps P'town history with an eye for the colorful. The Arctic explorer Donald P. MacMillan is recalled not only by his dog whip and warm boots but also by the polar bear, the walrus, the white wolf, and the musk ox he brought back from the frozen north. A reproduction of the captain's quarters aboard a whaling ship is complemented by the beautiful handwritten journal of a Provincetown man aboard an 1865–66 whaling expedition that sailed to the Cape Verde Islands and the British West Indies, killing ten sperm whales and stowing twenty-five hundred gallons of whale oil. The Pilgrims get their due with dioramas telling how they explored the Outer Cape, made off with a corn cache,

A sunny afternoon on the Provincetown Wharf.

and had their first skirmish with the locals. Theatrical memorabilia recall the Provincetown Players and Eugene O'Neill's 1916–24 tenancy in P'town, and recount the 1940–70 glory days of the Provincetown Playhouse on Gosnold Street, which staged works by O'Neill, Edward Albee, and Tennessee Williams (who became a frequent summer visitor). *High Pole Hill; 508-487-1310. Open Apr.–Nov.*

Not too many years ago, the benches in front of **Town Hall** (260 Commercial Street; 508-487-7000) were known, especially late at night, as the Rack, or, sometimes, as the Meat Rack. It was the easiest place in town to find drugs, sex, or both. That scene has become less localized, however, and nowadays the benches are more likely to hold weary, shell-shocked tourists, most of whom haven't a clue that parts of Town Hall are air-conditioned, and that a fine collection of twentieth-century art lines its walls.

Ross Moffett painted the murals on the front staircases under the auspices of the Depression-era Federal Art Project of the Works Progress Administration, perfectly capturing the heroic-folklore ethos of the WPA. On one wall, fishermen spread their nets to dry, while on the other, townsfolk gather beach plums on the dunes. Two large canvases by Charles W. Hawthorne, *Crew of the Philomena Manta* and *Fish Cleaners,* dominate the rear hallway. Although Hawthorne was an exponent of outdoor light, both these masterly paintings are executed in muted, gloomy tones worthy of late Goya. *260 Commercial Street; 508-487-7000.*

It's worth peeking into the 1847 **Universalist Meeting House** (236 Commercial Street; 508-487-9137) to catch the sanctuary's trompe l'oeil decoration and the whalebone buttons on the ends of the pews before plunging into the more secular aspects of the **West End.** Astronomical inflation of the real-estate market has erased many East-West distinctions, but the West End was originally the home of common sailors, fishermen, mechanics—people who worked with their hands, earned little, and often owned less. When the Navy would send a thousand men on shore leave in P'town during World War I, they headed straight to the West End. And many a man in search of sport heads there still. The West End has a reputation as the party end of town, more gay than straight, more young than old. This is the part of town where P'town's vestigial propriety dissolves into whimsical shopping, casual food, and boisterous bars.

Travelers seeking to get in touch with their Inner Tourist need look no farther than **Marine Specialties,** as old-timers call the Army-Navy store. Here you pick up

Cabot's Candies of Cape Cod—a sugar lover's dream.

I LOVE A PARADE

The Fourth of July parade is a wildly eclectic community event, not so much a celebration of America's independence as the independence of Provincetown. American flags are hung alongside rainbow flags, middle-class families stand alongside shirtless muscle queens. It is a harmonious, almost surreal confluence of the gay and straight worlds.

The parade is led by the local contingent of the U.S. Coast Guard proudly marching with their rifles and the Stars and Stripes. Then comes the lone Provincetown fire truck, carrying the men of the volunteer fire department and a smiling baby, who sits with her father in the cab. Periodically, the truck's siren lets out a wail, and the crowd responds with enthusiastic whoops. Behind the fire truck comes the Ptown ambulance, with its simple sign: "Proud to be saving lives."

The next float tells you that you aren't in middle America anymore. There's a beaming geriatric drag queen dressed as a fairy standing atop this truck. She's wearing a great purple Afro wig and diaphanous wings. She uses her wand to bestow blessings on the crowd. Beneath her handlebar mustache she is beaming beatifically, and the crowd murmurs its appreciation.

—Peter Manso, *Ptown: Art, Sex, and Money on the Outer Cape*, 2002

shells, weathervanes, "genuine" ships' rum jugs, buoys, beginner's art sets, Greek fisherman caps, and surplus backpacks cast off from the Norwegian, French, Italian, and South African armies. *235 Commercial Street; 508-487-1730.*

Perhaps no single establishment so captures the evolution of Provincetown as the A-House, or **Atlantic House.** The core of the structure dates from 1798 and once served as a rooming house for fishermen and whalers. But the bar scene is the most legendary aspect of the A-House's history. Young Eugene O'Neill frequently got rip-roaring drunk here and even boarded upstairs. Tennessee Williams often stopped by for a drink, and no doubt some of the Abstract Expressionists threatened to beat him up. By the early 1950s, A-House was widely considered gay-friendly, and it now functions as the most dedicated of the gay male dance clubs. Although you might expect all-night bacchanalia at A-House, it faces the same 1 A.M. curfew as all other P'town drinking establishments. *6 Masonic Place; 508-487-3821.*

Frying malasadas *at the Provincetown Portuguese Bakery.*

The shops begin to peter out and the road takes a curve toward the water as Commercial Street continues through the West End. Propriety returns as the street becomes more residential. The architecture of the little houses has an improvised quality, as if the old shipwrights weren't quite sure how to build for dry land. Several West End houses sport blue plaques showing an icon of a house perched on a raft above wavy lines for water.

These were the homes of the hard-bitten nineteenth-century fishing community located outside the harbor at Long Point. "In lieu of lawns these people had patches of seaweed at their front doors, and children were cautioned against crossing the road at high tide," Josef Berger wrote with a trace of fancy in the WPA's 1937 *Massachusetts: A Guide to Its Places and People*. Before the Civil War, they saw the error of their ways (better to be inside the breakwater than outside when a storm comes) and simply floated their homes over to the mainland. The plaque on the two-story, clapboard-front private residence with a large barn at **76 Commercial Street** identifies it as the site of the European refugee Hans Hofmann's school of abstract painting.

Flying the flag on Commercial Street.

ART OF FISHING

My studio in the summer is on a hill. Beneath it are yellow dunes and beyond the dunes I can watch the community of fishermen at their ancient industry.

The fisherman who flings his nets can tell when they come up empty.

But when he has caught the fish, he knows by the sight and by the weight of the nets, he knows by the flash of the struggling forms in the sun, by the pull at his muscles in his shoulder and arm, by the rigid flexion of his throat and spine as he bends still anxiously but more and more triumphantly to draw his catch in further, to heave it aboard, to have it close and secure!

This is only a physical analogy.

It is not so easy to catch the fish in art. But when you have caught it, you know!

—That is my answer.

—Hans Hofmann, Summer 1944,
from the catalog *Hans Hofmann: Four Decades in Provincetown,* 2000

At the end of Commercial Street, cars sweep around a traffic-circle park, complete with American flag and a plaque identifying the "First Landing Place of the Pilgrims." It was a good spot to come ashore, as it lies nestled in the palm of Cape Cod's fist. From the park, it's possible to walk across the great stone jetty to Wood End Light and on to **Long Point Light,** every P'town sailor's beacon home at night. If you'd rather not leap small gaps between stones or climb up and down to bridge small chasms, you can also reach Wood End and Long Point from the marshy end of Herring Cove Beach, but it's a sloppy walk. In either case, it's best to make the trip at or shortly before dead low tide so that you don't have to contend with waves breaking high on the boulders. You'll walk past two hummocks of dirt remaining from hastily built Civil War forts and finally reach the tip of the tip of the Cape. It is a sobering and somehow liberating view. Provincetown is reduced to a rim of whitewash on the sweep of sand. Long Point is Provincetown taken to its absolute limit—the edge of the continent.

MARTHA'S VINEYARD

Martha's Vineyard is Cape Cod in miniature. The flounder-shaped island, just seven miles offshore from Woods Hole, reprises the Cape's geography in a mere hundred square miles of barrier beaches, sandy upland forests, seaside cliffs, and glacial kettle ponds. Amateur and professional historians bicker over who Martha might have been, but they can all see that grapes grow wild at the edges of the island's swamps; it hardly matters whether the explorer Bartholomew Gosnold noticed them or not during his whirlwind tour of the coast in 1602.

Archaeologists suggest that Martha's Vineyard was first settled around 2300 B.C. It has long been the home of the Aquinnah Wampanoag tribe—a technicality that didn't keep the British crown from issuing a pair of land grants that Thomas Mayhew Sr., of Massachusetts Bay Colony, bought for forty pounds sterling in 1641. Within a year, Mayhew was encouraging fellow English settlers to join him at what became Edgartown. During the colonial era, governance of the island switched between Massachusetts and New York, and in modern times it can still be difficult to determine, at least in summer, whether the island is principally Red Sox or Yankee territory. (The tilt is usually toward the Yankees—Vineyard folk like to back winners.)

The forty-five-minute passage from Woods Hole to Vineyard Haven aboard the Steamship Authority ferry is just long enough to for you size up your fellow travelers. The guys with toolboxes and lunch pails are probably carpenters headed Up Island to work on one of the new Chilmark mansions. The fashionable pair who drove aboard in a Land Rover are motoring to their cedar-shingled summer place on Cape Higgins. A young couple and their two children with four matching backpacks and bicycles are planning a day of cruising the wooded cycling trails in West Tisbury. The freckled young man standing at the rail in faded baseball cap and sockless topsiders is eager to return to his sloop in a deserted sandy cove on Chappaquiddick.

Once the ferry lands, they'll all turn left, leaving the terminal, and scatter at Five Corners toward their respective destinations. Main roads on Martha's Vineyard tend to be well-paved and straight. Minor roads often meander through the woods, and the pavement may suddenly end in a track of packed sand. Summer traffic also reprises conditions on Cape Cod—barely creeping, then slowing to a

The archetypal fishing village of Menemsha.

maddening halt in the congested Down Island towns. (For an explanation of Up Island and Down Island, see "Island Navigation," on page 218.) It can be faster to ride a bicycle than to drive, as bicycle trails abound in the towns and through the connecting woodlands. For all the development, much of Martha's Vineyard remains either agricultural or conservation land, and you can drive or ride seemingly great distances seeing only the occasional house. This chapter begins in Vineyard Haven and proceeds clockwise around the island.

■ **VINEYARD HAVEN** *map page 219, C-1*

Technically the village center of the Town of Tisbury, Vineyard Haven nestles in the cleavage between East and West Chop headlands on Martha's Vineyard's northern corner. As the landing point for the year-round auto ferry from Woods Hole, it has become the place where visitors eat and shop before moving on to the rest of the island. They would probably drink here, too, if they could, but Vineyard Haven is a dry town, despite the presence of the incongruously named **Black Dog Tavern** (Coastwise Beach Wharf, Beach Street Extension; 508-693-9223). The

WILD GRAPES

Where there are swamps there are generally grapes, and the rule has held from the beginning. Scent them from afar and follow your nose. Break through the barriers of wild rose thickets, green brier, sumach, poison ivy, and all the rest. Or better, insinuate yourself through with bag or basket, and in the center of the swampy place . . . . [T]he grape vines will be festooned around you, the leaves long since shriveled and subordinated, the fruit hanging in profusion. The grapes may be so purple as to seem black, with a bloom for perfection, or they may be rich red for the color of autumn, or palest green and bluish. Such is the miscellany of Martha's Vineyard, such the delight of her grapes which have come down through the centuries.

Berry picking is philosophical, but the picking of wild grapes is adventurous.

—Henry Beetle Hough, "Time of Wild Grapes," from *Singing in the Morning*, 1951

"tavern" serves food but no alcohol; its Labrador retriever logo plasters T-shirts and caps throughout the island.

Originally a fishing village named Holmes Hole, Vineyard Haven also supplied pilot skippers to steer ships across the treacherous shoals around Cape Cod. Bowing to newfound gentility, the town adopted its present name in 1871. The separation from its working-port past became complete in August 1883, when a fire burned the waterfront and most of Main Street. The blaze leveled the fine homes of many sea captains and merchants, but a pocket of elegant Greek Revival houses survives on William Street, parallel to Main Street.

Even though Vineyard Haven isn't the most traditionally religious of the island's communities, it does fairly bristle with spires. Over the years, the sturdy structure built on Church Street in 1833 as the Methodist Meeting House has served as a function hall, a church for varying denominations, and a Masonic hall. Since 1982, it's been the home of the **Vineyard Playhouse** (24 Church Street; 508-693-6450). This professional company produces theater all year, though summer is the big season. From Church Street, Main Street leads westward out of town past the **Liberty Pole,** a flagpole erected in 1898 by the "Sea-Coast Defence Chapter D.A.R." to memorialize the three Holmes Hole girls who destroyed a liberty pole in 1776 to keep British naval officers from confiscating it as a spar.

The East Chop Light (second from right), in the mid-1890s.

West Chop, about two miles from town, was one of the first summer communities on the island; at the end of the nineteenth century it was considered so remote from Vineyard Haven that it had its own ferry landing and post office. The post office still opens in the summer, but what draws most visitors to this headland of the harbor is **West Chop Light,** a stubby white lighthouse that echoes its partner on the opposing headland.

■ OAK BLUFFS   *map page 219, C-1*

The village of Oak Bluffs lies only three miles from the year-round ferry landing at Vineyard Haven. Beach Road, which heads east from Vineyard Haven's Five Corners, proceeds out over a peninsula in the harbor and crosses a small drawbridge as it enters the eastern headland. A brief detour north up Telegraph Hill takes you to **East Chop Light,** possibly even more picturesque than its West Chop counterpart. From late June through August, the lighthouse is open for sunset viewing on Sunday evenings. *508-627-4441.*

First-time visitors to Oak Bluffs can be excused for thinking they've stumbled into a Brothers Grimm theme park when they spy the three hundred or so remaining gingerbread cottages of the Martha's Vineyard Camp Meeting Association.

ISLAND NAVIGATION

Contrary to intuition, Up Island and Down Island on Martha's Vineyard have less to do with north and south than with west and east. They're terms of nautical origin, referring to longitude rather than latitude. One goes Up Island by heading southwest toward Aquinnah, where degrees of longitude rise, or Down Island to the bigger towns of Tisbury, Oak Bluffs, and Edgartown, where longitude declines. Even more than direction, the terms describe two different states of mind: the serene natural world of rustic Up Island, and the human bustle of Down Island.

Like domestic counterparts to saddle shoes, the cottages most often come in two-tone color schemes—lavender and royal purple, pink and white, lilac and jonquil, mint green and peppermint pink, blue and orange. Without much overstatement, it's possible to say that Martha's Vineyard was launched as a summer resort when its first open-air Methodist camp meeting convened on August 24, 1835. The weeklong revival session of sermons, joint prayer, shared confessions, and emotional public conversions was so successful that the Vineyard Methodists resolved to make the gathering—on the former sheep meadow they called Wesleyan Grove, after the founder of Methodism—an annual affair.

Over the ensuing years, attendance swelled; newspapers of the 1850s estimated that as many as twenty thousand people showed up for Big Sunday, the prayer-and-preaching climax of the week. The three thousand or so regulars slept in tents, some of them pitched on wooden platforms. In 1859, William Lawton of Providence, Rhode Island, erected the first cottage in order to save his family the misery of a leaky tent. Lawton's balloon-frame cottage—which was built in Rhode Island, brought over in pieces, and assembled on the spot—featured elaborate scrollwork along the eaves.

Cottages adorned with curlicues, spirals, scrolls, balconies, odd-shaped eaves, and other Carpenter Gothic fillips sprang up in Wesleyan Grove like mushrooms after a rain. The confluence of Christian fervor and architectural fancy soon produced a distinctive community of tiny gingerbread cottages that provided a base for more extensive summer visitation. If you already had a house, why come for just a week? If you couldn't come for the whole summer, why not rent out your house to someone who could? The conclave by the sea became known as Cottage

City; it managed to separate itself from Edgartown, to the southeast, in 1880, and took on the more "dignified" name of Oak Bluffs in 1907—by which time cottage builders had denuded the bluffs of oaks.

From mid-June until mid-October, volunteers staff the **Cottage Museum,** which offers the chance to pick up camp-meeting history and lore and to imagine living in one of the fanciful summer homes. The light yellow walls, aqua trim, and white scrollwork make the museum one of the more modestly decorated cottages. *Highland Avenue and Trinity Park; 508-693-0525.*

The name of Wesleyan Grove was changed to Trinity Park in deference to **Trinity Park Methodist Church,** a pea-green structure with a squared-off bell tower that was built in 1878. The **Tabernacle**—with its wooden roof, stained glass, and wrought-iron supports—was erected in 1879 to shelter camp-meeting attendees from rainstorms and other acts of God. The structure also serves the town as a venue for concerts, shows, and high school graduations. A plaque at the entrance to the park duly notes, "Surely God is in this place." *Trinity Park.*

Outside the camp-meeting grounds, the village of Oak Bluffs evolved as a Victorian summer resort. African-Americans had always been part of the camp-meeting scene, but in the early twentieth century, middle- and upper-middle-class

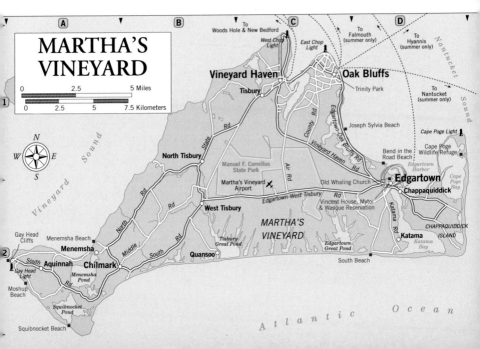

THE AFRICAN-AMERICAN VINEYARD

We were among the first blacks to vacation on Martha's Vineyard. It is not unlikely that the Island, in particular Oak Bluffs, had a larger number of vacationing blacks than any other section of the country.

There were probably twelve cottage owners. To us it was an agreeable number. There were enough of us to put down roots, to stake our claim to a summer place, so that the children who came after us would take for granted a style of living that we were learning in stages.

The early blacks were all Bostonians, which is to say they were neither arrogant nor obsequious, they neither overacted nor played ostrich. Though the word was unknown then, in today's connotation they were "cool." It was a common condition of black Bostonians. They were taught very young to take the white man in stride or drown in their own despair. Their survival was proved by their presence on the Island in pursuit of the same goal of happiness.

Every day, the young mothers took their children to a lovely stretch of beach and scattered along it in little pools. They made a point of not bunching together. They did not want the whites to think they knew their place.

—Dorothy West, *The Richer, The Poorer*, 1995

blacks started summer vacationing in Oak Bluffs. They congregated around the Reverend Oscar Denniston, a Jamaican-born pastor who began preaching in Oak Bluffs in 1900. The first wave of African-American summer people, such as the family of the novelist Dorothy West, came from Boston and other New England cities. They built their homes at first in the Oak Bluffs Highlands, although the African-American community later dispersed throughout the town. West, a notable figure in the Harlem Renaissance, lived on Martha's Vineyard full-time from 1943 until her death, in 1998.

The expansive green lawns of Ocean Park, with a white gazebo-cum-bandstand in the center, separate the village from the harbor. Mansard-roofed Victorian homes around the park feature large front porches for sitting out on summer evenings. It would no doubt disturb the revivalist preachers of yore, but one of the more successful commercial operations in town is the **Offshore Ale Company.** The brewery makes small-batch ales and sells them at its popular brewpub restaurant. *30 Kennebec Avenue; 508-693-2626.*

African-Americans pose in front of the Bradley Cottage in Oak Bluffs, circa 1880.

Situated amid the riot of gift and snack shops in tiny downtown Oak Bluffs, the **Flying Horses Carousel** has delighted generations of children. This fixed-platform carousel, one of the nation's oldest operating merry-go-rounds—constructed in 1876 at Coney Island, New York, and brought to Oak Bluffs in 1884—is lovingly maintained by the Martha's Vineyard Preservation Trust. *Oak Bluffs Avenue at Circuit Avenue; 508-693-9481. Open daily in summer.*

There are two routes to Edgartown from Oak Bluffs. The more scenic Beach Road (sometimes called Edgartown–Oak Bluffs Road) runs along a narrow strip between a two-mile-long barrier beach and Sengakontacket Pond, a salt pond linked to Nantucket Sound by two breaches in the barrier system. Locals call this sandy stretch State Beach; formally it's **Joseph Sylvia State Beach.** Parking spaces can be hard to find in the few small lots. The flat, open landscape has the distinction of enjoying sunrise over the water on one side and sunset over the water on the other—and simultaneous sunset and moonrise on full-moon days.

(above) Long-ago steamers and a train in Cottage City (Oak Bluffs), and (opposite) a summer garden in the present-day town.

Gothic Revival posts at the camp-meeting grounds in Oak Bluffs.

By following County Road inland to the Edgartown–Vineyard Haven Road, you can reach the **Felix Neck Wildlife Sanctuary,** a three-hundred-acre peninsula on the west side of Sengakontacket Pond. The land is named for Felix Kuttashamaquat, the Wampanoag sheep farmer who grazed his flock here in the seventeenth century. This Massachusetts Audubon Society sanctuary has three trails through four miles of varying habitats. Deer are abundant, as are painted turtles and the harmless garter, ribbon, black racer, and milk snakes. Nearly two hundred species of birds have been recorded at Felix Neck, and some, such as swallows, wild turkeys, and nuthatches, are plentiful. The refuge was a pioneer in establishing osprey nesting grounds on Martha's Vineyard, raising the number of nesting pairs from half a dozen to about seventy-five in the last quarter of the twentieth century. You can spot the brown-and-white speckled birds sitting in their messy nests atop artificial platforms or diving into Sengakontacket Pond for dinner. *Edgartown–Vineyard Haven Road; 508-627-4850. Visitors center open daily in summer; closed Mon. fall through spring.*

■ EDGARTOWN *map page 219, D-2*

The largest of the year-round communities on Martha's Vineyard, Edgartown exudes an air of Yankee permanence. The names of its four main through-streets have a practical ring—Summer, Winter, Water, and Main—and the few other lanes of the central village honor either their landmarks (School, Church, Dock) or one of the founding families (Mayhew, Daggett, Kelly, Cooke, Davis). First settled in 1642 as Great Harbour, the village took the name of Edgar, the son of King James II, when it incorporated in 1671. By the mid-eighteenth century, Edgartown was home port to much of the American Arctic whaling fleet, and the village prospered well into the nineteenth century, with its citizenry refining whale oil, making spermaceti candles, and producing great quantities of mittens, socks, wigs, and other woolens from the flocks of sheep that grazed all across the island. But greasy industry and cozy pastoralism lie in the distant past. Most of Edgartown's modern wealth comes from the mainland via summer people and retirees.

The village's Yankee ghosts assume a bit of corporeality in a three-property tour offered by the **Martha's Vineyard Preservation Trust** (508-627-8619), which

Edgartown street scene from the late nineteenth century.

Main Street, Edgartown, in the late 1800s, with the Old Whaling Church on the right.

rescues touchstones of island history and traditions. The tour, conducted from spring to fall by knowledgeable guides, begins at the **Vincent House,** the oldest standing residence on Martha's Vineyard. Built in 1672, this one-story full Cape (see "The Cape Cod House," on page 71) has a center chimney and two windows on each side of the central entrance. Cutaways in some of the walls reveal the way the house was framed in the island's native pine and oak and the exterior walls filled with a mixture of clay and straw—the "wattle and daub" of rustic English building practice. Amazingly enough, the House was inhabited until World War II, albeit at a different location. The five rooms are filled with artifacts that show the evolution of life on Martha's Vineyard over four centuries. *99 Main Street Rear.*

The Vincent house hints at Edgartown's humble origins, but the **Dr. Daniel Fisher House** represents an era of great prosperity. Fisher moved to Edgartown at age twenty-four and soon became the island's leading physician. But his business acumen may have eclipsed his medical talent. With the help of his wife's money (he married into the rich Coffin family of Edgartown), Fisher invested in virtually every whaling vessel of his time and invented a king-size sperm-whale-oil candle brighter than any other. His factory won a monopoly contract to supply all the Federal lighthouses with the beacons, and at its peak Fisher's enterprise was fashioning sixty tons of candles a year. Whaling ships needed hardtack for their provisions, so Fisher opened a hardtack bakery—and built a gristmill to grind the flour. The money came pouring in (a quarter of a million dollars a year at one point), so he cofounded the Martha's Vineyard Bank and served as its president. When he built his showpiece mansion in 1840, he spared no expense. Martha's Vineyard no longer had forests of big trees, so Fisher had timbers floated over from the mainland, and he sent to Italy for the marbles that encase his fireplaces. Restored in 1992, the Fisher House is a popular wedding venue, with brides making dramatic entrances down the grand staircase. *99 Main Street.*

Next door to the Vincent and Fisher houses, the **Old Whaling Church** was built in 1843 at the behest of Edgartown's Methodist whaling captains. Handhewn fifty-foot beams were felled in Maine and freighted down to the Vineyard on coasting schooners. The straightforward meetinghouse design of this final project of Frederic Baylies Jr., a local architect, echoes the capacious proportions and dignified curves of a whaling vessel's hull. The church's ninety-two-foot clock tower, visible miles out to sea, was the first sight of land for many home-bound sailors. The Preservation Trust purchased the building from its Methodist congregation in 1980 and has restored it, complete with a functioning 1869 Simmons-Fisher tracker organ. The eight-hundred-seat facility hosts the local Town Meeting and serves as a performance center. *89 Main Street.*

Simply walking around compact Edgartown is a pleasure. Showpiece houses along Water Street—a block removed from the docks, but close enough to keep an eye on the masts and spars—were built mostly for whaling captains in the first quarter of the nineteenth century. Restrictive aesthetic zoning and local custom conspire to maintain the Greek Revival style of the district. Each of these foursquare homes, it seems, is painted glaring white, blinkered by black shutters, and surrounded by a white picket fence. The sidewalks tend to be brick, and many of the houses feature a railed walkway between the twin chimneys (one for the kitchen, the other for the living room). These walkways are almost always called widow's walks—but however romantic the notion, they weren't constructed as rooftop aeries from which lonesome wives could watch for their husbands' return. Rather, they made it possible to extinguish chimney fires without having to scale the steeply pitched roofs.

Capt. Valentine Pease lived at the modest two-story white Federal dwelling at 80 South Water Street, where a whale silhouette graces the lintel above the door. He was master of the *Acushnet,* the whaling bark on which young Herman Melville gathered the experiences that give *Moby-Dick* the ring of authenticity. Pease apparently bore Melville no hard feelings about jumping ship halfway through the voyage, as the novelist visited the sea captain several times at his Edgartown home.

Two massive trees that hint at distant shores loom on South Water Street less than a block from the Pease house. The larger of the two is a **pagoda tree,** brought from China as a potted seedling by Capt. Thomas Milton in the mid-nineteenth century. The frequently repeated story is that Milton so liked the spot that he bought the adjacent lot and built the house now shaded by the tree. Nearby stands a massive **little-leaf linden,** a European shade tree that normally reaches less than half the size of the Edgartown specimen. Its history is less documented, but it appears to be roughly the same age as the pagoda tree—and it blossoms with sweet-scented flowers in June. Yet the pagoda and linden trees are perhaps upstaged by another botanical souvenir that sailors brought back to the Vineyard. Creeping honeysuckle spreads, kudzu-like, over every surface in Edgartown, even lading the boughs of evergreens. The heady scent it gives the summer night air has led residents to forgive its invasive ways.

As Water Street crosses Main Street, it becomes North Water—an impressive parade of fine shops, fine restaurants, and fine lodgings. At its tip are Edgartown Light and a small, stony beach. The lighthouse marks the channel between Edgartown harbor and the irregular land mass of Chappaquiddick, which forms the easternmost corner of Martha's Vineyard. In years when the barrier beach at Norton Point is breached, Chappaquiddick is an island. No bridge crosses the channel, but a small ferry, the *On Time II,* makes the run in about two minutes. Because it can hold only two or three vehicles at a time (with additional space for pedestrians), drivers sometimes have to wait up to an hour in the summer to make the crossing.

The best way to beat the auto bottleneck is to cycle Chappaquiddick. Whaling captains, fishing families, and a small cluster of Wampanoags lived here in the colonial era, and sheep once roamed the rolling, scrubby landscape. Today houses tend to be hidden up long, chained driveways to protect the privacy of their millionaire inhabitants. Yet many of the best parts of Chappaquiddick remain public, thanks to the stewardship of the Trustees of Reservations.

Full sail in Edgartown Harbor.

Following Chappaquiddick Road from the ferry landing, the small Japanese-style gardens of **Mytoi** come up just past the point where Chappaquiddick Road ends and Dike Road begins. Created in the late 1950s, the gardens were destroyed by Hurricane Bob in 1991, then painstakingly restored over the next nine years. While a formal garden set into fourteen acres of pine woods seems a bit like gilding the lily, Mytoi—with its tiny stream, arching bridge, stone garden, and rustic shelters—is a popular stop for contemplation. *Open year-round.*

Dike Road continues to the site of the infamous Dike Bridge, where Mary Jo Kopechne drowned on the night of July 18, 1969, when Senator Edward M. Kennedy's car went off the twelve-foot-wide, seventy-five-foot-long bridge, since replaced. Kennedy entered a plea of guilty to "leaving the scene of an accident involving personal injury" and received a two-month suspended sentence. The resulting scandal effectively doomed the senator's presidential ambitions.

The new bridge hardly looks daunting by daylight as it crosses the inlet to Poucha Pond and continues across to **Cape Poge Wildlife Refuge.** The barrier beach of Cape Poge, estimated to have been formed six thousand years ago, may be the oldest of the Cape Cod region. This is one of the rare barrier beaches where off-road vehicles are not only permitted but even somewhat encouraged on the sandy tracks above the beach's winter berm. Permits are required to drive here, but the tracks cover almost the entire seven-mile-long eastern rim of Martha's Vineyard. Sections of the beach below the berm are closed during breeding seasons for piping plovers and other endangered shorebirds. Swimming on Cape Poge beaches can be daunting, because waves are big, currents are swift, and riptides are common.

The long finger of the cape curls back on itself like a fiddlehead. Cape Poge Gut, the narrow channel between the tip of the cape and the main body of Chappaquiddick, has swift currents and rushing tides that oxygenate the water. Fishermen tend to keep mum, fearing an influx of competition, but the Gut is considered one of the best saltwater fly-fishing spots in the world for bonito, little tunny (also known as false albacore), striped bass, and bluefish. *Chappaquiddick Road and Dike Bridge Road; 508-693-7662.*

Wasque Reservation, at the southeast corner of Cape Poge, is an altogether different landscape. The sandy heath supports low-lying grasses and sedges, along with blueberry, black huckleberry, and bayberry thickets. The marshes surrounding Poucha and Swan ponds are particularly hospitable to wading birds, geese, and ducks, making the reservation a bird-watcher's delight. Swimming is prohibited. *Wasque Road; 508-693-7662.*

Naked Truth

Our beaches at Martha's Vineyard are full of half broken-down middle-aged men and women, folks of real solid accomplishment some of them, who put on the most outrageous personal exhibitions, in full and glaring sunlight. We've always had the sensible practice up there of swimming naked, but in the course of years, this has grown into a cult of nudity and most any time you go down on our shores, you are affronted with some of the most extraordinary sights in the world. Draped all over the rocks or standing up in prominent positions here and there, often strutting flamboyantly up and down the beach, aggregations of female skin and bone with old dried-out udders hanging off or oppositely, monumental collections of bulbous flesh, are matched with hairy, pot-bellied, fat-assed male caricatures of the human race. You never see any of the young and beautiful around. These all wear bathing suits and keep well off to themselves in the more distant reaches. Once or twice I've seen a young Venus come naked out of the Martha's Vineyard sea, but generally it's something to make you wish you hadn't lived so long.

—Thomas Hart Benton, *An Artist in America*, 1937

Chappaquiddick has the wildest and most pristine beaches on the Vineyard, but the best swimming beach is back in Edgartown proper. **South Beach** is five miles from the village center via South Water Street, but in the summer it's best to use the beach shuttle bus rather than to hope for one of the rare legal parking spaces. Three miles of soft, tan sand stretch along the ocean. Sandy islands break the waves lapping one end of the beach, making for excellent swimming. The other end of the beach is exposed to the ocean and often enjoys powerful surf. Unfortunately, it also suffers from riptides that can whisk even the strongest swimmer out to sea. Riptides are usually visible as a rift in the waves; when the rips are running, stay out of the water.

South Beach is part of a series of barrier beaches that stretch along the south side of Martha's Vineyard. They are broken up by long salt-pond inlets with famously rich oyster beds. West Tisbury–Edgartown Road lies inland, and most of the roads dribbling south from it, following the shores of the salt ponds, are little more than sandy tracks through pitch-pine forest to private land.

(following pages) Dunes at Chappaquiddick.

■ WEST TISBURY *map page 219, B-2*

The village of West Tisbury is neither Up nor Down Island, but serves rather as an agricultural buffer between the two. First called Newtown to differentiate it from Great Harbour (later Edgartown), the central plain of West Tisbury has always had the island's most fertile land. The geologist Nathaniel S. Shaler, on visiting the area in 1874, commented, "I have never seen better ground for the gardener. Strawberries grow as in southern France; roses have a glory unattainable anywhere in New England."

The heart of West Tisbury village is **Alley's General Store** (State Road; 508-693-0088), where a sign aptly advises, "If you don't see it, ask for it." Established in 1858, the store is widely thought to be the oldest operating retail business on Martha's Vineyard, and it certainly has the broadest range of merchandise, from food to clothing to plumbing supplies. Alley's was renovated in 1993 by the Martha's Vineyard Preservation Trust and now belongs to the Aquinnah Wampanoag tribe. The deli section, Back Alley's, is a good source for picnic fixings.

The shingled barn sitting back from the road on the west side of the village is the **Grange,** the former Agricultural Hall where the Martha's Vineyard Agricultural Fair was held from 1859 until 1994, when it moved to more spacious grounds on Panhandle Road. Also restored by the Martha's Vineyard Preservation Trust, the post-and-beam landmark often serves as the venue for cultural, political, and social events. But the biggest doings occur on Wednesday and Saturday mornings from summer through early fall, when year-round and summer residents mingle and even talk to one another at the lively farmers' market as they peruse the Swiss chard, the raspberries, and the plump tomatoes.

At the center of West Tisbury, drivers must choose between plunging into the rural countryside of Up Island or returning toward Vineyard Haven. State Road, which leads north back toward relative civilization, passes **Eileen Blake's Pies & Otherwise** (515 State Road; 508-693-0528), a front-yard gazebo where Blake has been selling homemade pies for three decades. One of her specialties is burgundy pie, filled with a mix of blueberries and cranberries. For a different kind of artisanry, watch for **Martha's Vineyard Glass Works** (State Road, West Tisbury; 508-693-6026), where the master glass artists Andrew Magdanz, Susan Shapiro, and Mark Weiner spend their summers. The small shop adjacent to the studio also carries the work of up-and-coming glass artists, including some who have been students or apprentices at the Glass Works.

Head of the Pond Way leads east from State Road along a network of dirt roads to **Chicama Vineyards** winery, the island's most successful winery and one of the first in New England to grow vinifera grapes; its first plantings were in 1971. In addition to a wide range of still wines, Chicama also makes a sparkling chardonnay using the traditional champagne method. The winery shop, open in the afternoon, is something of a boon on an island with so many dry towns. *Stoney Hill Road; 508-693-0309.*

The other fork at West Tisbury village center, South Road, heads Up Island. Drivers usually whiz right past the small, shingled **Joshua Slocum House,** a private dwelling across from West Tisbury Fire Station #1. Lone sailors everywhere celebrate Slocum for his solo circumnavigation of the globe in his thirty-seven-foot sloop *Spray.* He left from Boston on April 21, 1895, and returned to Newport, Rhode Island, on June 27, 1898. When his account of the journey, *Sailing Alone Around the World,* was published in 1900, it became an immediate bestseller and enabled Slocum to build this small West Tisbury house, the first home he ever owned on dry land. He continued long-distance sailing until 1909. That year, he set out alone from Vineyard Haven on November 14 bound for South America, and vanished at sea at the age of 65.

■ **UP ISLAND** *map page 219, A-2*

Summer people treat the Up Island towns as a kind of Zen nirvana, and even locals have been known to head to rural Chilmark and Aquinnah to get away from it all. James Thurber, an occasional summer visitor to Chilmark, quipped to a *Vineyard Gazette* reporter in 1941, "I love the Vineyard. There are so many nice quiet little roads that take you away from all the water." Affecting the point of view of the quintessential urbanite (he drew cartoons and wrote essays for *The New Yorker,* the signature publication of his breed), Thurber allowed that "sometimes I like to just sit on the beach and watch the water, but I don't believe in getting wet. I think it's just a notion people get . . . . Salt water always gives me a headache."

By contrast, the painter Thomas Hart Benton summered in Chilmark from the early 1920s through the summer before his death, in 1975, and found the whole experience of Up Island bracing, beaches and all. Benton wrote in his autobiography, *An Artist in America,* "It was in Martha's Vineyard that I really began to mature my painting—to get a grip on my emerging style and way of doing things. I painted the landscape there and the old people. About the old Yankees of the

island there was something deeply appealing. Many of them, for all their crotchety ways, had the nobility of medieval saints."

Coming into Chilmark from West Tisbury on South Road, drivers are nearly in hailing distance of the ocean beaches that Benton and his wife, Rita, frequented, often in a state of undress. A scrub-pine forest hides the shore from the road, but dirt paths lead south to a long barrier beach system punctuated by eruptions of high cliffs. **Lucy Vincent Beach** makes the news every so often when the powers that be on Martha's Vineyard clamp down on the long tradition of nude sunbathing.

The Chilmark Library marks Beetlebung Corner, the center of Chilmark Village and the pivot point of all Up Island travel. Northbound Menemsha Road continues straight ahead toward the archetypal fishing village of **Menemsha,** which was established in 1671 as a feudal manorial estate belonging to the redoubtable Thomas Mayhew Sr. Menemsha settlers had to pay annual quit-rents to the lord of the manor until the village incorporated under colonial law in 1714. These days, lobster boats, draggers, gill netters, and harpoon boats all tie up and bring their catch to **Dutcher Dock.** A couple of fish markets cater to both retail and wholesale trade, chief among them **Larsen's** (508-645-2680). Impatient hungry travelers can avail themselves of the raw bar (oysters, cherrystones, and littlenecks); the market also steams lobster, clams, and mussels while customers wait. **Home Port Restaurant** (512 North Road; 508-645-2679), between the Coast Guard Station and the harbor, has been serving shore dinners of corn, lobster, steamed clams, mussels, and dessert since 1931, but you may have to settle for the take-out window if you haven't made a reservation.

Menemsha and **Aquinnah** are separated by a fifty-yard channel at the mouth of Menemsha Pond, dug by the state in the late nineteenth century to improve the Menemsha harbor for fishermen. There is no bridge across the strait, but bicyclists and pedestrians can avail themselves of a small ferry. Otherwise, it's back to Beetlebung Corner to follow Middle Road across a series of isthmuses to Aquinnah. Alternately known as Gay Head, Aquinnah is a thirty-four-hundred-acre peninsula that has been an island at times, and it threatens to become one again if sea levels continue to rise. Its geology is so peculiar that its nearest counterparts lie in upstate Vermont and at the tip of the Gaspé Peninsula in Québec. While Cape Cod and its associated islands are almost entirely glacial in origin, the

Self-Portrait with Rita (1922), by Thomas Hart Benton.

foundation of Aquinnah is a portion of ancient sea floor upthrust by a cataclysmic event many eons ago. Viewed from the air, it resembles a wedge of cheese—high on the northwest point and sloping nearly to sea level where it joins the rest of Martha's Vineyard. At the foot of the slope are two huge ponds. When the winter is cold enough, the fresh-water pond of Squibnocket freezes into a vast skating rink—all the more remarkable because skaters can hear the Atlantic surf pounding on Squibnocket beach only a hundred yards away.

This primal landscape, literally a land apart from Martha's Vineyard, has harbored the Aquinnah band of Wampanoags from the near-extinction suffered by their mainland brethren. The Aquinnah, who received Federal tribal recognition in 1987, own about half the land on the peninsula, including the geological marvel known as the **Gay Head Cliffs.** The highest point on the peninsula, the cliffs expose stratified layers of sand, gravel, and clay sediment that accumulated on the ocean floor over a hundred-million-year period. Fossils in the eroded face of the brightly colored bands reveal everything from extinct species of giant sharks and whales to clams and crabs. One layer is lignite coal from the Cretaceous period (from 144 million to 65 million years ago). The Wampanoag hold these cliffs sacred, as well they might. They relate the history of the planet almost since complex forms of life first arose.

Direct access to the cliffs is granted only by the tribe. Visitors can park in the nearby pay lot and walk a quarter mile back on Moshup Trail to gain access to the beach, and follow the shore around the point to look up at the cliffs. The easier, if more distant, view is from a bluff near **Gay Head Light** (508-627-4441). There has been a lighthouse on this point since 1799 to warn ships away from the Devil's Ridge, a dangerous reef of glacial rocks that lies just offshore. The view from the light (open an hour before and after sunset during summer weekends) encompasses Vineyard Sound, the Elizabeth Islands, and, on a clear day, Buzzards Bay, where Cape Cod begins.

A child frolics beside the sea in Menemsha.

N A N T U C K E T

Nantucket is as much an idea as a place. Its original inhabitants called their sandy hummock Nanticut, which the tin-eared English settlers altered to Nantucket. It's one of the few places in New England where the Algonquian is exactly right. "Nanticut" means "faraway island," and Nantucket is every bit of that. Poking above the shoals twenty-six miles off Cape Cod, Nantucket is, as Jan Morris has written, "islandness epitomized." It is the Australia of Cape Cod, where isolation has bred a race of creatures similar to, but strangely unlike, those on the mainland.

The inhabitants of Nantucket take three forms. The first are those born into the clans of Coffin, Starbuck, Folger, Macy, Swain, and the other families who populate the graveyards and the unrecorded Nantucket social register. Then there are the wash-ashores, who arrived like grass seeds on the tide, took root on the dunes, and progressed to become the tradesmen and artisans who keep the economy humming. Finally, there are the summer people, for whom a seasonal retreat on Nantucket is the attainment of desire—conspicuous consumption cloaked in modest gray shingles.

Spend five minutes with a Nantucketer and the talk will turn to real estate, for nothing is so absorbing as a commodity in short supply on an island only fourteen miles long and three and a half miles wide. Living in Nantucket town represents the pinnacle of social achievement. The sagging, weathered antique of a house on Centre Street will always trump the finest trophy house on a rise out on the moors. Second best is a rose-covered fisherman's cottage in Siasconset, or 'Sconset, as every self-respecting Nantucketer calls it. Anywhere else, and you might as well live on Martha's Vineyard.

European settlement began in 1659, when the "nine original purchasers" bought out Thomas Mayhew's interest in the island for thirty pounds sterling and beaver hats for Mayhew and his wife. Many of the early settlers were fleeing religious persecution on the mainland, and the island of heretics and dissenters soon became a Quaker stronghold. Lacking any significant natural resources, the settlers fell back on their own. They followed the lead of their Wampanoag neighbors and began inshore whaling around 1690; in 1715, they led the American fleets into deep water. Nantucket grew fat on whaling—until the sandbar across

Beachfront blossoms at Siasconset.

the harbor made it impossible for the ever-larger whale ships to reach its wharves. By 1840, New Bedford had surpassed Nantucket as a whaling port. Seeking new opportunities, some Nantucketers sailed for California to pan for gold. Others enlisted in the Union Army in the Civil War, and the island's population plummeted. In 1869, the last whaling vessel, the *Oak*, sailed from Nantucket, and never returned. In *Nantucket, A History*, Robert A. Douglas-Lithgow wrote, "In this year, 1870, the town has reached the nadir of her misfortunes. Not a ship remains to the island; scarcely a sound is heard where erstwhile the busy hum of a mighty industry echoed and re-echoed . . .: all is silent save the lapping of the waves on her sandy shores."

A year later, the first steamship arrived, and Nantucket turned to tourism. Cottage communities began to rise on Surfside and Brant Point and among the fishermen's homes at 'Sconset. In 1881, the Nantucket Railroad opened to provide on-island transportation, and when it failed, in 1918, Nantucketers first permitted automobiles, a decision that many rue to this day. (Casual travelers should plan on walking, bicycling, or riding the cheap local transit. Ferrying over an auto is expensive, and reservations must often be made months in advance.) In making the switch from the whaling industry, Nantucket transformed its greatest

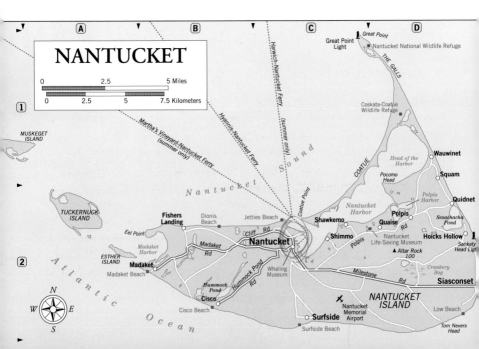

No Illinois

Nantucket! Take out your map and look at it. See what a real corner of the world it occupies; how it stands there, away off shore, more lonely than the Eddystone light-house. Look at it—a mere hillock, an elbow of sand; all beach, without a background. There is more sand there than you would use in twenty years as a substitute for blotting paper. Some gamesome wights will tell you that they have to plant weeds there, they don't grow naturally; that they import Canada thistles; that they have to send beyond seas for a spile to stop a leak in an oil cask; that pieces of wood in Nantucket are carried about like bits of the true cross in Rome; that people there plant toadstools before their houses, to get under the shade in summer time; that one blade of grass makes an oasis, three blades in a day's walk a prairie; that they wear quicksand shoes, something like Laplander snow-shoes; that they are so shut up, belted about, every way inclosed, surrounded, and made an utter island of by the ocean, that to their very chairs and tables small clams will sometimes be found adhering, as to the backs of sea turtles. But these extravaganzas only show that Nantucket is no Illinois.

—Herman Melville, *Moby-Dick; or, The Whale*, 1851

liability—its isolation—into an asset. It was close enough to reach in a half-day ferry trip, far enough out to sea to float in the realms of the imagination.

■ **NANTUCKET TOWN**   *map page 242, C-2*

During the summer, Nantucket Memorial Airport is one of the busiest airstrips in the country, but it's more satisfying to approach the island by ferry, watching the small bump in the water grow ever larger on the horizon until—suddenly—the behemoth ferry is sliding between the stone jetties, slipping through the channel at Brant Point Light, and gliding to a halt at Steamboat Wharf. The voyage may lack the sense of occasion that old-time whalers felt when their barks scraped over Nantucket Bar and entered safe harbor, but the little gray lady in the sea, as sailors called her, is still a welcome sight.

Nantucket town is mistress of the art of illusion. Patina is everything. Her weathered face still fronts the sea as if it were 1850, and at a distant glance she seems a perfectly preserved ancient Quaker beauty, spare and austere, bright eyes

Illustration from the log of the ship Washington, *kept by its captain during a voyage from 1842 to 1844. (opposite) Whaling Museum custodian and a sperm whale jaw in the 1930s.*

gleaming in a face of strong bones. But instead of whale-oil warehouses and a sper-maceti-candle factory, the docks are lined with gift shops and galleries that entice tourists the way painted ladies meet the fleet in less inhibited ports.

Plaques on almost every building announce their date of construction. None of the pre-1846 harborfront survives—the Great Fire burned all the wharves and a third of the village. Casks of whale oil ruptured and burned so hot and bright that not even cinders were left at dockside. Ostentation actually saved the town. Though rejected by the Quakers as too immodest, the town's handful of brick buildings ultimately contained the blaze. Nantucket rebuilt immediately.

The spermaceti-candle factory constructed on Broad Street after the Great Fire fittingly houses the Nantucket Historical Association's **Whaling Museum,** which owns one of the world's most extensive collections of whaling gear and memora-bilia. The island seems fated to have turned to whaling. Writing in 1880 with the advantage of considerable hindsight, Obed Macy noted in his *History of Nantucket,* "In the year 1690 some persons were on a high hill observing the whales spouting and sporting with each other, when one observed: 'there'—pointing to the sea—'is a green pasture where our children's grandchildren will go for bread.'"

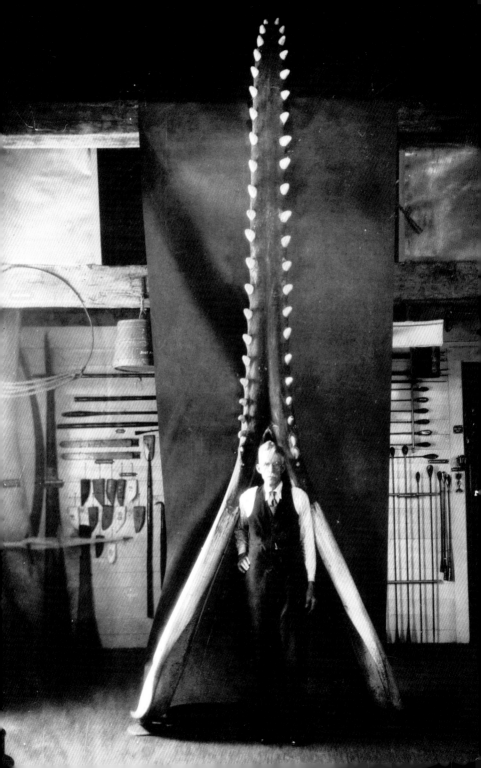

By 1730, the little island was home port to more whaling vessels than the rest of the American colonies combined, and on the eve of the American Revolution, in 1768, 125 whaling barks hailed from Nantucket. The islanders specialized in hunting sperm whales, sailing to the far reaches of the globe in search of their quarry and literally redrawing the maps of the world's oceans in the process. They were the first whalers to sail the Pacific (1791), the first to land in Hawaii (1819), and the first to reach the coast of Japan (1820). In 1821, Nantucket whalers were the first to report sighting Antarctica and the first to hunt in the iceberg-studded waters of the Arctic Ocean. Histories of the American whaling industry claim that more than thirty reefs and islands in the Pacific are named after Nantucket merchants and whaling captains.

Within the collection of the Whaling Museum, scrimshaw and whalebone carvings speak of the tedious hours spent at sea, while war clubs, shark's-teeth spears, and even a miniature Maori canoe attest to the exotic adventure of South Seas exploration. But the museum focuses primarily on the greasy and dangerous work of hunting, killing, and processing whales. You don't need to linger long over the various harpoon tips and their particular effects on the quarry before the bloody horror of the enterprise becomes palpable. Study instead the lines of a whaleboat and the elegant skeleton of a whale. Their similarities are instructive—a confluence

---

LETTER FROM NANTUCKET

Those children born at the sea-side, hear the roaring of its waves as soon as they are able to listen; it is the first noise with which they become acquainted, and by early plunging in it they acquire that boldness, that presence of mind, and dexterity, which makes them ever after such expert seamen. They often hear their fathers recount the adventures of their youth, their combats with the whales; and these recitals imprint on their opening minds an early curiosity and taste for the same life. They often cross the sea to go to the main, and learn even in those short voyages how to qualify themselves for longer and more dangerous ones; they are therefore deservedly conspicuous for their maritime knowledge and experience, all over the continent. A man born here is distinguishable by his gait from among a hundred other men, so remarkable are they for a pliability of sinews, and a peculiar agility, which attends them even to old age.

— J. Hector St. John de Crèvecoeur, *Letters from an American Farmer*, 1782

Painters at Brant Point are themselves a painterly picture.

of cetacean evolution and human ingenuity. When the museum reopens in 2005 after a year of renovations, a new centerpiece will be the skeleton of an adult sperm whale that perished on a Nantucket beach at the end of 1997—likely the victim of a boat collision rather than of a harpoon. *13 Broad Street; 508-228-1894. Open daily Memorial Day–Columbus Day; call for off-season hours.*

Founded in 1894, the **Nantucket Historical Association** maintains an extraordinary historical library and also opens several other buildings to the public during the summer season—including the 1746 **Old Mill** at the top of West York Street, where corn is ground daily, and the 1686 **Oldest House** on Sunset Lane, a set piece of early Nantucket life. The most telling structure, however, is the handsome **Hadwen House.** Born in Newport, Rhode Island, in 1791, William Hadwen moved to Nantucket in 1829 and went into partnership with his cousin Nathaniel Barney. Their whale-oil and candle factory, on outer Main Street, did well. In 1845, Hadwen followed the model of fellow merchants and had this mansion constructed in a prominent spot on Main Street. Quaker asceticism was on the wand. Wealth had become something to celebrate, and Hadwen did. The house's

elaborate lighting fixtures, marble fireplace, and fine furnishings rival the sumptuous appointments of Boston, Providence, and New York town houses of the era.
Fortune continued to smile on Hadwen. Both his house and his factory survived
the Great Fire, and, in 1849, he and Barney took over the brick spermaceti-candle
factory that now houses the whaling museum. *96 Main Street; 508-228-1894.*

Although it may seem otherwise, the bumpy cobblestones on Main Street
weren't put there to trip up tourists. In 1839, the merchants cobbled the lower
reaches of the street so that wagons laden with barrels of whale oil would no longer
founder in the ruts. In a burst of building, mansions like Hadwen's suddenly rose
along the outer reaches, their bright facades casting long shadows on the older,
bare-bones gray-shingled homes. The captains of the whaling industry poured
their riches into the **Pacific National Bank** (61 Main Street), still the town's most
active repository and lender. Strict regulation prohibits external alterations to the
old houses, and new construction must use historically appropriate materials. As a
result, Nantucket town looks much as it did a century ago. One laudable twentieth-
century innovation, however, was the soda fountain, two of which can be found
next door to each other at **Congdon's Pharmacy** (47 Main Street; 508-228-0020)
and **Nantucket Pharmacy** (45 Main Street; 508-228-0180). The Nantucketers'
idea of their place in the world is amply illustrated by the compass rose on the side
of the building at the corner of Main and Washington Streets, which **Nantucket
Looms** (16 Main Street; 508-228-1908) now occupies. First painted in 1922, the
sign shows direction and mileage to such diverse locations as Wauwinet, Cape
Verde, and New Zealand.

The most recent alteration to the town skyline came in 1968, when a heli-
copter lowered a bell tower and steeple onto the **First Congregational Church.**
The bell tower is open for visits from mid-June through mid-October. On a clear
day, most of the island is visible, but even in a light fog the town spreads out
below like a garden of low-lying plants creeping along the hollows and rises.
62 Centre Street; 508-228-0950.

Beaches border the shoreline edges of the town, both within the harbor and
outside it. As the name suggests, **Children's Beach,** on the harbor north of
Steamboat Wharf, is ideal for families with toddlers; it's also the site of free concerts and outdoor movies. South of the in-town wharves off Washington Street,

*The First Congregational Church towers majestically over Nantucket town.
(following pages) A glint of dawn illuminates a lonely Nantucket Harbor.*

STARRY EYED

On a clear night, far from the light pollution of the mainland, it's easy to understand how a Nantucket woman could become one of America's preeminent nineteenth-century astronomers. Maria Mitchell (1818–1897) studied with her father and then from the books at the Nantucket Athenaeum, where she was the first librarian. In 1847, using a telescope mounted atop the Pacific National Bank, she won renown by discovering a comet. A year later, she became the first woman elected a fellow of the American Academy of Arts and Sciences, and in 1865 became a professor of astronomy at Vassar College. Raised in a Quaker milieu where intellectual equality was taken for granted, Mitchell once wrote, "The eye that directs the needle in the delicate meshes of embroidery will equally well bisect a star with the spider web of the micrometer."

The **Maria Mitchell Association** maintains her birthplace (1 Vestal Street; 508-228-2896; www.mmo.org) as a historical museum, open from June through Columbus Day. The adjacent **Vestal Street Observatory** (3 Vestal Street; 228-9273) is open year-round for children's astronomy activities. The more powerful **Loines Observatory** (59 Milk Street Extension; 508-228-9273) holds open nights for lectures and telescope viewing year-round. The association, devoted to educating adults and children about astronomy, environmental science, and Nantucket history, also operates an **Aquarium** (28 Washington Street; 508-228-5387, open from June through Columbus Day) on the harbor to showcase Nantucket marine life.

Francis Street Beach is the adults' alternative—a good swimming beach on the calm harbor waters, with kayak rentals available. **Brant Point Beach,** on the other hand, sits just outside the harbor, where the stone jetties induce strong currents. Only experienced swimmers should go in the water here, but the beach is great for sunning or enjoying a picnic with the backdrop of the almost toylike Brant Point Light. Just west of Brant Point, **Jetties Beach** is the near-town sandy playground in the summer, with changing rooms, tennis courts, volleyball nets, food concessions, and a boardwalk to the beach. Windsurfing, sailing, and kayaking rentals and lessons are available. And the island's most extensive beach lies two miles south of town at **Surfside,** renowned not only for its sand and surf but also for its excellent kite-flying winds.

Nantucket youngsters bike down a rose-laden lane in 'Sconset.

■ POLPIS & SIASCONSET   *map page 242, D-2*

The town of Nantucket seems almost urban compared to the outlying reaches. About thirty-five percent of the island—more than thirteen thousand acres—has been set aside as conservation land. Nantucket's six dedicated bike paths make the circuit of most points of interest. Mopeds, available for rental but deeply detested by island residents, are banned from the bike paths.

You can explore the eastern end of the island by following the eight-mile Polpis Bike Path from town to 'Sconset and returning through conservation land on the six-mile Milestone Bike Path. The Polpis path has some moderate inclines, but since the highest point on Nantucket is only about a hundred feet above sea level, there are no real hills on the ride. The upland heath has a barren beauty all its own. Created by centuries of overgrazing and deliberate burning, it has become a self-perpetuating ecosystem of low-lying vegetation and low-profile animals, home to such rare species as the bushy rock rose, the short-eared owl, and the regal fritillary butterfly. The highland heath also provides a broad overview of the island, revealing it as a rise of sand above the water. Geologists estimate that Nantucket accreted about thirty-five hundred years ago from sand trapped around glacial debris, and that in another eight hundred to fourteen hundred years it will sink into the sea again. Smaller would-be islands lurk just beneath the surface of the ocean—the dreaded Nantucket shoals.

Along the path less than two and a half miles east of town, the **Nantucket Life-Saving Museum** squats on the hoop-shaped inlet of Polpis Harbor at Folger Marsh. Until the Cape Cod Canal opened in 1914, nearly all Atlantic ship traffic from New York to Boston and Europe had to navigate the shallow waters south and east of Nantucket, the so-called graveyard of the Atlantic. Beginning in an organized fashion in 1785, Nantucket lifesavers participated in an untold number of rescues and helped out in many disasters, including the July 1956 sinking of the ocean liner *Andrea Doria* after her collision with the *Stockholm*. Thanks to massive rescue efforts, only fifty-one of more than seventeen hundred passengers on the two ships perished. This small museum is a replica of the 1874 U.S. Life Saving Service Station on Surfside, one of four stations built on Nantucket, and the grim motto of the lifesavers—"You have to go out, but you don't have to come back"—is prominently displayed. Photographs, surfboats, and lifesaving gear bring the heroics to life. *158 Polpis Road; 508-228-1885. Open mid-June–Columbus Day.*

Cottage shop on Shell Street in Siasconset in the 1890s—the store still exists.

The Polpis Bike Path makes a dogleg southeast about a quarter of a mile after Polpis Harbor. Instead of following the path, though, continue northeast a short distance on Wauwinet Road to visit the Nantucket Conservation Foundation's **Squam Swamp** reservation. With modest stands of white oak, black oak, scrub oak, and tupelo, it's among the last places on the island where you can still see the landscape that greeted the first English settlers. One of the pools within the preserve is home to spotted turtles, which have yellow polka-dotted shells from eight to ten inches long. While not officially endangered, the uncommon reptiles are listed by the state as a "species of special concern."

The Polpis Bike Path continues around the eastern end of the island. The optical illusion of looking over the fairways to red-and-white-striped Sankaty Light makes the private Sankaty Golf Course look a bit like mini-golf—you almost wonder where the giant pirate is. The path concludes on the outskirts of the village of **Siasconset**. Originally established around 1700 as a lookout post for whales foolish enough to swim close to shore, 'Sconset developed over the next few centuries as one of Nantucket's premier fishing villages. The cottages that line the beach were originally the homes of fishermen. Fewer and fewer of the homes survive, for the Atlantic is gnawing away at the 'Sconset headland, chewing away the beach below. The cottages atop the bluff, however, are safe for the nonce.

Knee-deep in a berry bog at harvesttime.

In 1873, *Scribner's Magazine* called 'Sconset "the Newport of the Nantucketois." The Manhattan theater crowd discovered the village in the years before World War I, and it blossomed as a chic getaway. The quaintness has calcified over the years, and 'Sconset now wears its idiosyncrasies with considerable self-consciousness. Trellised roses climb the walls and cascade across the roofs of the little cottages—and of the sleek new homes built on the old cottage footprints. Beneath the hill, narrow **Siasconset Beach** is good for sunbathing but less well suited to swimming; currents can be strong and riptides are common.

The direct route back to Nantucket town along Milestone Bike Path passes along the **Milestone Cranberry Bog,** protected by the Nantucket Conservation Foundation. Nantucket began growing cranberries in 1857, and the crop remained a significant part of the island economy until the late 1930s. The cranberry-growing area encompassed the entire 234-acre bog, the largest contiguous cranberry bog in the world, until 1959, when it was broken down into more manageable tracts. During the harvest, from late September into early November, the flooded bogs are "paddled" to make the berries float. One of the more colorful sights of fall is the crew corralling the berries on the surface of the water so that they can be vacuumed into waiting trucks.

A Tisket, a Tasket

The Nantucket Lightship Basket is the island's quintessential fashion accessory, a badge of taste (and usually wealth) that becomes ever more desirable with the patina of age. The rattan basket was already an established form when the *New South Shoal Lightship* was placed in service in 1856 as a floating lighthouse. The first crew made baskets to pass the time, and the Nantucket Lightship Basket began its evolution toward a piece of polished folk art. No baskets were woven on lightships after 1892, but the name stuck.

In the late 1940s, master weaver José Formoso Reyes popularized the basket as a lidded purse. Reyes' baskets are so highly prized that they now bring thousands of dollars. The authentic Nantucket Lightship Basket is woven on a mold, with a wooden bottom, and must be made on Nantucket, where a number of artisans continue the craft and give demonstrations throughout the summer at the **Nantucket Lightship Basket Museum**. The museum's historic exhibits are a good way to cultivate lightship-basket connoisseurship, should you decide to invest in one. *49 Union Street; 508-228-1177. Open Memorial Day–Columbus Day.*

Mitch Ray splits staves for lightship baskets, circa 1940.

■ WAUWINET, GREAT POINT, & COATUE
map page 242, C/D-1/2

After three and a half centuries of European settlement, Nantucket should be a well-tamed world, yet one large slice of the island still feels primal and untouched, hardly altered since the "nine original purchasers" arrived. The barrier beach system that wraps around Nantucket harbor like a comforting arm, shielding the anchorage from the raging sea, retains the mystery of unexplored, unexploited territory. It nestles close to the town, yet it couldn't be further away in spirit were it on the other side of the globe. Quite simply, the shifting sands and marshes of Coatue Point, Great Point, and Coskata peninsula have been too unstable and inhospitable to settle. And for that reason, this entire northeastern shoreline of Nantucket island has been virtually left alone.

Despite the physical complexity of the barrier beaches of the **Coskata-Coatue Wildlife Refuge,** it's not hard to understand how the system formed. The area now called Wauwinet was the original northeastern corner of the island. To the north was the large island of Coskata and, farther north, the small island that has become Great Point. Near what is now the harbor entrance was the small island of Coatue. Over the millennia, drifting sand caught hold and barrier beaches grew across the gaps, connecting Wauwinet north to Coskata, and Coskata north to Great Point and west to Coatue.

Fishermen were well aware of the weak points in the beach system, hauling their boats across the dunes at Wauwinet to enter and leave the harbor without having to go around the long barrier of Coatue Point. Although there was no road from town to Wauwinet until the twentieth century, the Wauwinet House opened here in the mid-nineteenth century as a restaurant serving shore dinners to patrons who arrived by boat. Later in the century, the restaurant began building rooms for guests to stay the night, and by the mid-twentieth century the property had become a full-fledged resort. Its current incarnation, the **Wauwinet Inn,** is an upscale lodging providing every imaginable creature comfort in a luxurious beach-house atmosphere.

There are two ways to explore this Nantucket wilderness—by road from Wauwinet, roughly five miles east of Nantucket town, or by boat (preferably kayak) from within Nantucket harbor.

(opposite) Daffodils, tulips, lobsters, and corn at a Nantucket picnic. (following pages) Great Point Light, at the tip of Coskata peninsula.

The road into the wildlife refuge begins at a gatehouse by the Wauwinet Inn. Four-wheel drive vehicles are permitted on the path north to Great Point and west about halfway down the Coatue peninsula. Drivers must first let most of the air out of their balloon tires at the gatehouse, where there is also an air pump for re-inflation. Unless you have your own suitable vehicle, the best way to venture onto the barrier beaches is with one of the guided **Great Point Natural History Tours** (508-228-6799), which from mid-June through September depart from the Wauwinet Inn parking lot.

The rutted sand road is full of dips and holes, and even an off-road suspension can't dampen the sensation of being at sea in a rocking boat. The road passes along the back side of high dunes, where it's not uncommon to see greyhound-sized white-tailed deer bounding across the sand. The guided tour usually heads straight across Coskata onto the narrow isthmus called the Galls, which connects

A haul of Nantucket scallops.

to Great Point. The Atlantic laps the Galls on both sides and litters it with drift-wood and flotsam. From May into October, surfcasters fishing for bluefish usually line both beaches.

Great Point, a knob of land at the end of the peninsula, wraps back on itself to contain a small saltwater cove. Great Point Pond is a popular spot for family scal-lopers, who have the bay-scallop season to themselves during the month of September. At the tip, **Great Point Light** still warns mariners of the dangerous currents and riptides. The first lighthouse erected here, in 1780, was built of wood and fitted with a whale-oil candle that produced a nine-inch flame. Its light, mag-nified through a Fresnel lens, was said to be visible from eighteen to twenty miles at sea. Although that lighthouse burned in 1816, it was replaced two years later with a stone tower that stood until 1984, when a powerful spring storm toppled it into the sea. The Coast Guard was ready to erect a mundane steel tower, but Nantucketers were adamant about having a proper lighthouse. Their lawyers dug into the old papers and found a provision that required the federal government to replace the light with one just like it. The current Great Point Light, erected in 1986, nearly replicates the 1818 tower but stands on dry ground a hundred yards west of its predecessor. The vista from the top of the lighthouse is sweeping; the dangerous rips are clearly visible less than a mile from shore.

The perspective from above the ocean, though, can't rival the view from the sur-face. Good spots to put in a kayak to explore **Coskata** and **Coatue** include Wauwinet and Pocomo Head, making a vigorous one-mile paddle across the head of Nantucket Harbor to the refuge. Sitting low in the water, even behind the pro-tection of the barrier beach, Nantucket seems but an interruption in the ocean, a mere oasis of semisolid shore.

A kayak provides access to the back shore of the barrier beaches, a network of rivulets among the salt marshes, where blue herons suddenly startle as you round a bend in the grasses. American oystercatchers warn you away with their clarion *kleep!* and loons suddenly lift from the water to fly off in a hooting cackle. No whales spout and frolic on the horizon—they've been hunted to near extinction—but there are riches in the sea nonetheless. Creep up in the shallows, where the tide runs so thin you nearly scrape the mud, and you can reach your hand over the side and haul the bounty from water: quahog, mussel, bluepoint oyster. Striped bass minnows glimmer past, their prickly dorsals rubbing against the kayak's skin. Faraway island is no mystery at all. There is bread upon the waters.

PRACTICAL INFORMATION

■ AREA CODES

The chief area code for Cape Cod and southeastern Massachusetts is 508. The 774 area code is also reserved for the region, and some cellular telephones may use it.

■ METRIC CONVERSIONS

1 foot = .305 meters   1 mile = 1.6 kilometers   1 pound = .45 kilograms
Centigrade = Fahrenheit temperature minus 32, divided by 1.8

■ CLIMATE

The proximity of the ocean moderates all of Cape Cod's seasons. During the summer, daytime highs are usually in the upper 70s Fahrenheit, evening lows in the low 60s. Rain is moderate. Fall is resplendent, temperate, and typically the driest season. Winter is less fierce than elsewhere in New England, but many attractions, lodgings, and restaurants are closed. Spring tends to be moist and often foggy.

■ GETTING THERE AND AROUND

By Air
Logan International Airport (BOS) in Boston receives flights from many domestic and international carriers. *I-93 North, Exit 20; 617-561-1800 or 800-235-6426; www.massport.com/logan.*

 T. F. Green State Airport (PVD), ten miles south of Providence, Rhode Island, is convenient to New Bedford and Cape Cod. *U.S. 1, Warwick, RI; 401-737-4000; www.pvdairport.com.*

 Nantucket Memorial Airport (ACK) has the best air service on Cape Cod and the islands, with direct flights from Portsmouth and Manchester, New Hampshire; Bedford, Boston, and New Bedford, Massachusetts; Providence, Rhode Island; White Plains and New York, New York; Philadelphia; Baltimore; and Washington, D.C. *30 Macy Lane, Nantucket; 508-325-5300; www.nantucketairport.com.*

Cape Cod, Martha's Vineyard, Nantucket, and the Massachusetts mainland, as seen from the Space Shuttle.

Martha's Vineyard Airport (MVY), in West Tisbury, receives flights from Boston, New Bedford, Hyannis, and Nantucket. *Airport Road; 508-693-7022; www.mvyairport.com.*

Barnstable Municipal Airport (HYA) has direct service from Boston, New York, Martha's Vineyard, and Nantucket. *Barnstable Road, Hyannis; 508-775-2020; www.town.barnstable.ma.us/Departments/Airport.*

Provincetown Municipal Airport (PVC) has service from Boston. *Airport Road, Provincetown; 508-487-0240; www.massairports.com/Provincetown%20Frame.htm.*

By Car

From Boston, follow Route 3 south to Route 6. From points west and south, follow I-495 to Route 25 to the Buzzards Bay traffic circle, where you can choose between Route 6A or Route 28.

Route 28 follows the western and southern shores of Cape Cod, with parking for the Martha's Vineyard ferry in Falmouth or the Nantucket Ferry in Hyannis. Route 6A follows Cape Cod Bay. Route 6 cuts through the middle of the Cape, with turnoffs to most Cape towns; it's the only route that continues to the tip of the Outer Cape.

By Bus

Bonanza Bus Lines (888-556-3815; www.bonanzabus.com) serves New Bedford and Cape Cod. **Plymouth & Brockton** (P&B) **Street Railway Company** (508-746-0378; www.p-b.com) serves Plymouth and Cape Cod. Connecting buses from other East Coast cities are provided by **Peter Pan Bus Lines** (800-237-8747, www.peterpanbus.com).

By Ferry

Bay State Cruise Company (617-748-1428 or 508-487-9284; www.baystatecruises.com) and **Boston Harbor Cruises** (617-227-4321 or 877-733-9425; www.bostonharborcruises.com) offer summer service between Boston and Provincetown.

Capt. John Boat Lines (508-747-2400; provincetownferry.com) offers small-boat summer service between Plymouth and Provincetown.

Falmouth-Edgartown Ferry (508-992-1432; www.falmouthferry.com) offers small-boat summer service between Falmouth and Edgartown.

Freedom Cruise Lines (508-432-8999; www.nantucketislandferry.com) offers small-boat summer service between Harwichport and Nantucket.

Hy-Line Cruises (888-778-1132; www.hy-linecruises.com) offers summer service between Hyannis and Martha's Vineyard and Nantucket.

Island Queen (508-548-4800; www.islandqueen.com) offers small-boat summer service between Falmouth and Martha's Vineyard.

Martha's Vineyard & Nantucket Steamship Authority (508-477-8600; www.steamshipauthority.com) offers year-round service between Woods Hole and Martha's Vineyard, and between Hyannis and Nantucket; plus summer service between Oak Bluffs and Nantucket. Most ferries accept automobiles; reservations are advised.

Schamonchi Ferry (508-997-1688) offers summer service between New Bedford and Martha's Vineyard.

■ LOCAL PERMITS

■ SHELLFISHING

Permits to dig your own shellfish are managed by each town and can be obtained from town halls. Wellfleet and Harwich actively encourage shellfishing by setting aside special areas and offering reasonably priced short-term permits. No license is required for saltwater angling. Freshwater angling requires a Massachusetts license, available from town halls and sporting-goods stores.

■ PARKING

Some beaches charge for parking when you arrive; others require a permit, which can be obtained from the town hall. Resident parking permits are available with proof that you are renting a cottage or a hotel, motel, or inn room.

■ FOOD

Dining on Cape Cod usually comes down to whether you'd like your fish broiled, steamed, or fried. New Bedford, Provincetown, and Chatham are busy fishing ports. While the cod are no longer so thick in the surrounding waters that, as the early explorers liked to claim, a person could walk from boat to boat on their backs, the halibut and tuna fisheries show amazing resilience, and swordfish boats regularly return from the offshore banks with full holds. Shellfish make up an even bigger part of Cape and island dining. Aficionados of oysters rank Wellfleet bluepoints as some of world's finest, and the mussels farmed on ropes on the sandy shoals off Chatham could send a Belgian into paroxysms of delight. Cherrystone clams fill out the raw bars, while the larger quahogs appear baked with a bread stuffing or chopped in creamy clam chowder. Cape Cod crabs are small, sweet, and plentiful, and lobster is as much a fixture on Cape tables as it is farther north in Maine. The Cape shrimp season is extremely brief—usually just a few weeks in late winter—so most shrimp on restaurant menus comes from the Gulf of Mexico.

Pockets of Cape Cod and even the islands remain agricultural, and the summer harvest of sweet corn and tomatoes graces most restaurant tables. Berry crops begin in June with strawberries (Falmouth once claimed to be the strawberry capital of the world), and continue through the summer and into the fall with cultivated raspberries in July, blueberries and wild blackberries in August, and cranberries in September and October.

While the basic ingredients remain remarkably consistent, the dining experience is richly varied. You can walk up to a dockside or beachside hut and order spectacular fish dinners to eat on outdoor picnic tables—or get dressed up for a five-course meal at a candlelit table set with fine china and crystal. One night you might sup on a Mediterranean bouillabaisse, then turn around the next day and enjoy garlicky plank-grilled mackerel in the Portuguese style—or just go for bluefin sushi fresh off a day boat. Some restaurants barely bother with menus, relying primarily on a blackboard that lists the catch of the day.

■ **FAVORITE RESTAURANTS**

Cape Sea Grille. Chef Douglas Ramler brings French Riviera inspiration to Cape seafood. *Sea Street, Harwichport; 508-432-4745. Closed Dec.–Mar. 31.*

Chillingsworth. The formal dining rooms at this Cape institution offer haute style and a prix-fixe menu; the bistro has imaginative but simpler New American dishes. *2449 Route 6A, Brewster; 508-896-3640. Closed late-Nov.–mid-May.*

Clem & Ursie's Restaurant and Market. Portuguese specialties like sea clams with linguiça are the draw at this ultracasual spot outside Provincetown. *85 Shankpainter Road, Provincetown; 508-487-2333. Closed mid-Oct.–Mar.*

Dancing Lobster Café Trattoria. Chef-owner Pepe Berg cut his teeth cooking in Lyon and at Harry's Bar in Venice. Now he serves superb lobster dishes, sumptuous veal, and snappy thin-crust pizza. *371–373 Commercial Street, Provincetown; 508-487-0900. Closed mid-Oct.–Memorial Day.*

Dunbar Tea Shop. A throwback to early days of Cape tourism, this small, terribly British shop serves comforting pots of tea, tiny sandwiches, pies, cakes, shortbreads, and scones. *1 Water Street (Route 130), Sandwich; 508-833-2485. Afternoons only.*

The Flume Restaurant. Homey comfort food rules at this Wampanoag restaurant, where spring shad roe is a specialty and regulars swear by the gigantic desserts. *Lake Avenue (off Route 130), Mashpee; 508-477-1456. Closed Dec.–Easter.*

Home Port Restaurant. Since 1931, Home Port has been *the* place to eat fish in a fishing village. Reserve weeks ahead for a sunset table, or be ready to order from the takeout window. *512 North Road, Menemsha, Martha's Vineyard; 508-645-2679. Closed mid-Oct.–May.*

Mill Way Fish & Lobster Market. Ralph Binder, a brilliant chef, has reconceived the lowly clam shack as a haute destination. Don't miss his seafood sausages packed with shrimp, scallop, and lobster meat. *275 Mill Way, Barnstable; 508-362-2760. Closed late Dec.–Good Friday.*

OceAnna. This elegant but affordable restaurant is a showcase and training ground for a local culinary-arts school. The emphasis is on fine seafood, such as lobster fritters with citrus aïoli. *95 William Street, New Bedford; 508-997-8465.*

Oystermen's Grill and Fish Market. Local fish is perfectly prepared any way you want it—except fried. There's excellent sushi and a raw bar. *975 Route 6, Wellfleet; 508-349-3825. Closed mid-Oct.–Memorial Day.*

The Regatta. A circa-1790 mansion provides the exquisite setting for excellent meals with contemporary twists on classic haute cuisine. The wine list is legendary. *Route 28, Cotuit; 508-428-5715.*

Straight Wharf Restaurant. Local fish and shellfish are prepared here Mediterranean-style. The waterfront setting (literally steps from the Boat Basin) makes this place a scenic favorite. *6 Harbor Square, Nantucket; 508-228-4499.*

Swan River Seafoods Restaurant. It doesn't get much simpler. The fishermen unload their catch here, and the kitchen broils, steams, or fries it to order. There's a fabulous view over the marshy mouth of Swan River. *5 Lower County Road, Dennisport; 508-394-4466. Closed mid-Sept.–late May.*

■ LODGING

Tourism has been the leading industry in most portions of Cape Cod and the islands for the better part of the past century—an economic fact that translates into plentiful choices for lodging. While most of the destination grand hotels of the late nineteenth century closed long ago, they have been replaced by hundreds of motels and cottage communities and an increasing number of small inns and bed-and-breakfast operations crafted from older residences. Chain lodgings don't dominate Cape accommodations. Most properties are independently owned and operated, and depend on Web sites and local advertising to fill their rooms. While chambers of commerce (see Official Tourism Information, below) generally do not offer booking services, they'll usually supply extensive information about their member properties.

Many lodgings open for the season on weekends in late April or early May, and daily around Memorial Day. Some beachfront motels close after the Labor Day weekend, and the majority close for the season after the Columbus Day weekend. But a number of fine lodgings on the Cape stay open at least until Christmas, and a few remain open all year, to capitalize on the region's off-season appeal. Prices tend to peak in July and August, often doubling the spring and autumn rates. It's wise to reserve rooms (or camp sites) as far in advance as possible for the busy months of July through September.

■ FAVORITE LODGINGS

Chatham Wayside Inn. This classically restored 1860 inn, with a tasteful addition, makes a perfect base for exploring. It's in the center of Chatham, next to the band-concert gazebo. *512 Main Street, Chatham; 508-945-5550 or 800-391-5734; waysideinn.com.*

Colonial Inn. The location, on Edgartown's toniest street and just steps from the waterfront and shopping, couldn't be more central. The rooms, all on upper levels, are simply decorated. *38 North Water Street, Edgartown, Martha's Vineyard; 508-627-4711; www.colonialinnmvy.com.*

Crowne Pointe Historic Inn. A cluster of older buildings has been perfectly modernized along *Architectural Digest* lines. The draws include sybaritic spa treatments, quiet grounds, and poolside schmoozing. *82 Bradford Street, Provincetown; 508-487-6767; www.crownepointe.com.*

The Inn on Onset Bay. The rooms and guest cottages at this restored Victorian inn overlook Onset Harbor and a long sandy beach. Several rooms share baths. *181 Onset Avenue, Onset (Wareham); 508-295-4800; www.innononsetbay.com.*

Palmer House Inn. At this restored Queen Anne, the rooms are classics of the Victorian B&B style. A freestanding private suite with a Jacuzzi makes a romantic getaway. *81 Palmer Avenue, Falmouth; 508-548-1230 or 800-472-2632; www.palmerhouseinn.com.*

Sandpiper Beach Inn. A mix of former beach houses and motel units offers a laid-back beach-bum atmosphere and a private Nantucket Sound beach. *16 Bank Street, Harwichport; 508-432-0485 or 800-433-2234; www.sandpiperbeachinn.com.*

Ship's Knees Inn. The rooms in this circa-1820 sea captain's home and in a newer addition are decorated in a nautical style. Nauset Beach is a short walk away. *186 Beach Road, East Orleans; 508-255-1312; www.shipskneesinn.com.*

Wauwinet Inn. The epitome of Nantucket style, the Wauwinet Inn boasts every imaginable creature comfort in a beach-house ambience—and a superb restaurant to boot. *120 Wauwinet Road, Nantucket; 508-228-0145 or 800-426-8718; www.wauwinet.com.*

Wedgewood Inn. Some of the nine guest rooms of this circa-1812 sea captain's home turned B&B have fireplaces, screen porches, and/or decks. *83 Main Street, Yarmouthport; 508-362-5157; www.wedgewood-inn.com.*

Wingscorton Farm Inn. The rooms here are in a 1758 farmhouse on a working farm. Guests have the run of the spread, where they can check out chickens, goats, sheep, pigs, and even a llama. The farm breakfasts (included) are the stuff of legend. *11 Wing Boulevard, East Sandwich; 508-888-0534.*

■ **RESERVATION SERVICES**
Cape Cod. *508-255-3824; www.bedandbreakfastcapecod.com.*
Martha's Vineyard & Nantucket. *508-693-7200; www.mvreservations.com.*
Nantucket. *508-257-9559; www.nantucketaccommodation.com.*

■ Hotel and Motel Chains

Best Western. *800-528-1234; www.bestwestern.com.*
Comfort Inn. *800-228-5150; www.comfortinn.com.*
Days Inn. *800-325-2525; www.daysinn.com.*
Econolodge. *877-424-6423; www.econolodge.com.*
Holiday Inn. *800-465-4329; www.6c.com.*
Marriott Hotels. *800-228-9290; www.marriott.com.*
Motel 6. *800-341-5700; www.motel6.com.*
Radisson. *800-333-3333; www.radisson.com.*
Ramada Inns. *800-272-6232; www.ramada.com.*
Sheraton. *800-325-3535; www.sheraton.com.*
Travelodge. *800-578-7878; www.travelodge.com.*

■ Camping

Bourne Scenic Park. This town-run campground, directly on Cape Cod Canal, has a saltwater swimming pool, a picnic area, and playgrounds. *370 U.S. 6 Scenic Highway, Bourne; 508-759-7873; www.bournerecauth.com/bsp.*

Nickerson State Park. More than 420 wooded campsites are scattered over 1,900 acres that are replete with ponds, biking and hiking trails, and other opportunities for recreation. *Route 6A, Brewster; 508-896-3491; www.state.ma.us/dem/parks/nick.htm. Reservations: 877-422-6762 or visit www.reserveamerica.com.*

Scusset Beach State Reservation. The 98 campsites, with electric and water hookups, are practically on the beach at Cape Cod Canal. *140 Scusset Beach Road, Sandwich; 508-888-0859; www.state.ma.us/dem/parks/scus.htm. Reservations: 877-422-6762 or visit www.reserveamerica.com.*

■ Official Tourism Information

Cape Cod Chamber of Commerce. *888-332-2732; www.capecodchamber.org.*
Destination Plymouth. *508-747-7535; www.visit-plymouth.com.*
Martha's Vineyard Chamber of Commerce. *508-693-0085; www.mvy.com.*
Nantucket Island Chamber of Commerce. *508-228-1700; www.nantucketchamber.org.*
New Bedford Office of Tourism. *800-508-5353; www.ci.new-bedford.ma.us.*

■ USEFUL WEB SITES

Cape Cod Baseball League. Full summer schedule and individual team information. *www.capecodbaseball.org.*
Cape Cod Antiques Dealers Association. Antiques all over the Cape. *www.ccada.com.*
Cape Cod Disability Access Directory. A resource guide. *www.capecoddisability.org.*
Cape Cod Potters. Map, hours, and specialties of art potters on Cape Cod. *www.capecodpotters.com.*
Cape Cod Times. Daily newspaper, including tide charts. *www.capecodonline.com.*
Cape Week. Events and entertainment listings for the Cape and islands. *www.capeweek.com.*
Heritage Discovery Network. Historic and cultural sites and events. *www.capecodcommission.org/hdn.*
The Inquirer and Mirror. Resources for Nantucket. *www.ack.net.*
National Park Service. Cape Cod National Seashore and New Bedford Whaling National Historical Park. *www.nps.gov.*
SMART Guide. Car-free travel to the Cape and islands. *www.smartguide.org.*
Vineyard Gazette. Resources for Martha's Vineyard. *www.mvgazette.com.*
Weather. *www.accuweather.com.*

■ FESTIVALS AND EVENTS

■ APRIL
Daffodil Festival, Nantucket. An antique-car parade highlights the social event of the spring. *508-228-1700.*

■ MAY
Cape Cod Canal Striped Bass Fishing Tournament. Anglers converge for fishing frenzy. *508-759-6000.*
Maritime Days. Lighthouse tours and other events throughout the Cape. *508-362-3828.*

■ JUNE

Annual Portuguese Festival, Provincetown. Food holds center stage—until the Blessing of the Fleet. *508-487-2576.*

Cape Cod Baseball League. The season begins. *www.capecodbaseball.org.*

Nantucket Film Festival, Nantucket. More than thirty film showings spotlight screenwriters. *www.nantucketfilmfestival.org.*

■ JULY

Barnstable County Fair. A nine-day agricultural fair. *508-563-3200.*

Edgartown Regatta. Martha's Vineyard's biggest boat-racing event has been an annual spectacle since 1924. *508-627-4364.*

July 4 Parades. The Cape and islands show their colors on Independence Day, from the earnest (the American History Costume Parade in Fairhaven—508-979-4085) to the outrageous (in Provincetown—508-487-3424). More conventional celebrations take place in Orleans (508-255-1386) and Edgartown (508-627-6180). The festivities in Nantucket (508-228-1700) include a water fight between fire-brigade teams on Lower Main Street, at site of the Great Fire.

Mashpee Wampanoag Indian Pow Wow. Traditional dances and food celebrate Native American culture. *508-477-0208.*

■ AUGUST

Cape and Islands Chamber Music Festival. A three-week series, in venues throughout the Cape. *800-229-5739; www.capecodchambermusic.org.*

Feast of the Blessed Sacrament, New Bedford. This Azorean festival is said to be New England's largest ethnic celebration. *508-992-6911.*

Martha's Vineyard Agricultural Society Livestock Show and Fair, West Tisbury. Island farmers have displayed their prize livestock and crops here since 1859. *508-693-4343.*

Possible Dreams Auction, Edgartown, Martha's Vineyard. Bidders vie for the chance to rub shoulders with celebrity summer people. *508-693-7900, ext. 374; www.possibledreamsauction.org.*

Sandcastle and Sculpture Day, Jetties Beach, Nantucket. A competition to create the most fanciful, creative figures in sand—only to see them washed away by the tide. *508-228-1700.*

■ SEPTEMBER

Bourne Scallop Festival, Buzzards Bay. Breaded scallops, crafts, and entertainment. *508-759-6000.*

Glass Show and Sale, Sandwich. More than fifty dealers in antique and collectible glass. *508-888-0251.*

Harwich Cranberry Festival. A ten-day event, with food, crafts, and fireworks. *508-430-1165.*

Martha's Vineyard Striped Bass and Bluefish Derby. Serious anglers compete for serious prizes. *www.mvderby.com.*

■ OCTOBER

Cape Cod Pathway Walking Weekend. Guided walks throughout the Cape. *508-362-3828.*

Cranberry Harvest Festival, Edaville USA, Carver. Crafts, food, and cranberry harvesting and displays. *508-295-5799.*

Wellfleet Oysterfest. Champion shuckers compete, and restaurants show off their oyster dishes. *508-349-0330, ext. 116.*

■ NOVEMBER

Pilgrims' Progress, Plymouth. A parade from the harbor to the Burial Hill reenacts the first Thanksgiving. *508-747-7535.*

■ DECEMBER

Christmas Strolls and Events. Holiday celebrations lure shoppers to Falmouth (508-548-8500), Hyannis (508-362-5230), Dennis (508-385-9928), Sandwich (508-759-6000), Edgartown (508-627-9510), and Nantucket (508-228-1700).

RECOMMENDED READING

Baseball by the Beach (1998), by Christopher Price. An enthusiastic fan chronicles the history and evolution of the Cape Cod Baseball League.

Becoming Cape Cod (2003), by James O'Connell. A scholarly study, illustrated with vintage postcards, dissects the transformation of Cape Cod from a rural backwater into a premiere tourist destination.

Cape Cod (1865), by Henry David Thoreau. The Concord curmudgeon wrote about his journeys on Cape Cod with considerable humor. This posthumous compilation from three trips portrays Cape life before the amenities arrived.

Cape Cod: Its History and Its People (1930), by Henry C. Kittredge. A proud account by a native son remains the definitive history of Cape Cod.

Cape Cod Pilot (1937), by Josef Berger (Jeremiah Digges). Berger worked days on the Federal Writers Project guide to Massachusetts, but saved his most colorful tales for this slender volume of local lore.

Death of a Hornet (2000), by Robert Finch. These meditative essays on the nature of nature on Cape Cod are rooted in a keen awareness of place.

The Enduring Shore (2000), by Paul Schneider. History and geology interweave with environmental observation, mostly from the seat of a kayak.

Expedition Whydah (1999), by Barry Clifford with Paul Perry. This history of Cape Cod piracy recounts the exploits of Black Sam Bellamy, and chronicles Clifford's own saga—how he found and excavated Bellamy's ship, the *Whydah*.

The Great Beach (1963), by John Hay. The dean of Cape Cod nature writers finds a universe in the beach that became the Cape Cod National Seashore.

In the Heart of the Sea: Journal of the Whaleship Essex (2000), by Nathaniel Philbrick. A sperm whale sank the *Essex* in 1820. Philbrick brings to life the entire whaling enterprise, including the horrifying ordeal of the few men who lived to tell the tale.

Land's End (2002), by Michael Cunningham. The best-selling author and former fellow at the Fine Arts Work Center has penned an insider's love letter to Cape Cod's most idiosyncratic town.

Moby-Dick; or, The Whale (1851), by Herman Melville. Windy as a proper nor'easter, the American classic charts the dank streets of New Bedford and the depths of the human soul—and it brims with information about whaling.

The Outermost House (1928), by Henry Beston. What happens when a summer person decides to stay for the winter? Beston did, carving out this classic account of the lonely beach in all seasons.

The Salt House: A Summer on the Dunes of Cape Cod (1999), by Cynthia Harrington. Another former fellow of the Fine Arts Work Center, Harrington charts the aesthete's life as she and her artist husband spend summers in one of the few remaining dune shacks.

Singing in the Morning (1951), by Henry Beetle Hough. Essays by the longtime editor of the *Vineyard Gazette* celebrate the seasons in an era when the Vineyard enjoyed a simpler way of life.

Swimming at Suppertime (2002), by Carol Wasserman. Droll essays chronicle the down-to-earth lifestyle of year-round Cape residents, also revealing what they really think about summer people.

The Times of Their Lives: Life, Love, and Death in Plymouth Colony (2000), by James Deetz and Patricia Scott Deetz. The authors have drawn on extensive historical records in an engaging chronicle that reveals the human side of figures who have become historical icons.

Tough Guys Don't Dance (1984), by Norman Mailer. America's most pugnacious novelist writes engagingly (if long-windedly) about murder, mayhem, and marijuana on the Outer Cape.

The Wedding (1995), by Dorothy West. An Oak Bluffs wedding serves as the occasion for Harlem Renaissance author West to examine social class and racial identity in the Martha's Vineyard African-American community.

INDEX

ACKNOWLEDGMENTS

■ FROM THE AUTHORS

The authors wish to thank Daniel Mangin, who originated this project at Compass American Guides, for his enthusiastic encouragement and unstinting belief in the book. Thanks too to Fabrizio La Rocca for his faith in us, and to legions of town librarians, historical society volunteers, museum staffers, National Park Service rangers, and not a few bartenders and innkeepers, for their sage advice and illuminating lore. We'd also like to thank Kindra Clineff for her evocative images, which show what we could only tell.

■ FROM THE PUBLISHER

Compass American Guides would like to thank Rachel Elson for copyediting the manuscript and Lisa Goldstein for proofreading it. All photographs in this book are by Kindra Clineff unless noted below. Compass American Guides would also like to thank the following individuals and institutions for the use of their illustrations or photographs:

New Bedford & Environs
Page 48, New Bedford Whaling Museum

Cape Cod Canal Region
Pages 78–79, Heritage Museums and Gardens, Sandwich, Massachusetts

Upper Cape
Page 130, Marine Biological Laboratory

Nantucket Sound
Page 133, Hyannis Chamber of Commerce (photo by Jay Elliott)

Page 138, Hyannis Chamber of Commerce (Jay Elliott)
Page 156, Rogers Family/Bruce M. Clark

Outer Cape
Page 196, Provincetown Art Association and Museum
Page 203, Provincetown Art Association and Museum
Page 204, Provincetown Art Association and Museum

Martha's Vineyard
Page 217, Society for the Preservation of New England Antiquities Collection
Page 221, Martha's Vineyard Historical Society Collection
Page 222, Martha's Vineyard Historical Society Collection
Page 225, Society for the Preservation of New England Antiquities Collection
Page 226, Society for the Preservation of New England Antiquities Collection
Page 236, National Portrait Gallery, Smithsonian Institution/Art Resource, NY

Nantucket
Page 244, Nantucket Historical Association (1973.40.1)
Page 245, Nantucket Historical Association (P1917)
Page 255, Nantucket Historical Association (GPN4351)
Page 257, Nantucket Historical Association (P751)

Practical Information
Page 264, Spaceshots

■ ABOUT THE AUTHORS

A writing team for more than two decades, Patricia Harris and David Lyon have published extensively on travel, food, the arts, and popular culture in magazines and newspapers and on the Web. They are the authors of more than a dozen books, including *Escape to Northern New England* and the *Boston* and *Montréal* volumes of the Compass American Guide series. When not on assignment, they can usually be found in a third-floor walkup in Cambridge, Massachusetts.

■ ABOUT THE PHOTOGRAPHER

Kindra Clineff travels throughout the United States and abroad, specializing in editorial, lifestyle, and travel photography. She is the principal photographer for the Massachusetts Office of Travel and Tourism and has shot advertising campaigns for the tourism offices of Connecticut and Rhode Island. She regularly produces feature assignments for *This Old House, Country Home, Coastal Living, Cooking Light,* and *Yankee Magazine,* and images from her extensive library of New England have been published in numerous books and calendars.